Banishing the Cross

The Emergence of a Mormon Taboo

by Michael G. Reed

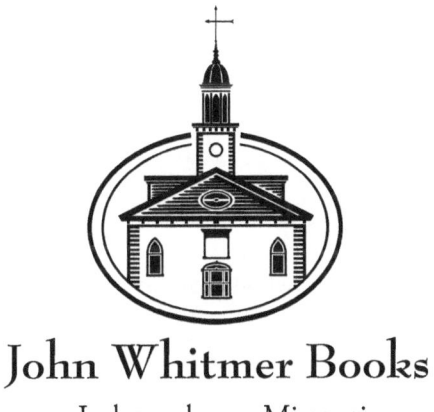

John Whitmer Books
Independence, Missouri
2012

© 2012 by Michael G. Reed

Published by John Whitmer Books
John Whitmer Books is a trademark of the John Whitmer Historical Association

ISBN-13 978-1-934901-35-9

View our complete catalog online at www.JohnWhitmerBooks.com
Learn more about the John Whitmer Historical Association at www.JWHA.info

Cover and interior design and typesetting by John Hamer

PRINTED IN THE UNITED STATES OF AMERICA

Banishing the Cross

The Emergence of a Mormon Taboo

To my sons Benjamin and Samuel

Acknowledgments

I am indebted to Philip C. DiMare, Jeffrey Brodd, Robert A. Rees, John Hamer, and Newell Bringhurst, who spent countless hours as readers and mentors. Their guidance and hospitality has been beyond measure, as they have helped me in various stages of production to see this book through to completion. Generous help was additionally provided by other readers for which I have much gratitude: Matthew T. Wirthlin, Edward Jones, John McFadyen, Peter K. Bellville, Craig L. Foster, Biloine W. Young, William D. Russell, and my father Kenneth A. Reed. Thanks are also due to several others—including Ryan K. Smith, Nicholas Literski, Clinton Bartholomew, D. Michael Quinn, Seth Bryant, Ronald E. Romig, Joseph Antley, Clair Barrus, Rick Grunder, Hugo Olaiz, Matthew Grow, Paul L. Anderson, Vickie Speek, and Lachlan McKay—who were so kind in answering questions over the past few years.

Many more people have been helpful throughout cyberspace (on blogs and message board forums) by engaging me in debates to help test my arguments, as well as those who have kindly shared feedback and words of encouragement. Special thanks also to Gregory Prince, the staff from the LDS Church History Library, BYU Special Collections Library, Community of Christ Library, and USU Folklore Archives for providing needed documents, and to the staff at the Pioneer Memorial Museum (Salt Lake City), who were very accommodating during my visits. Above all, I express overwhelming gratitude to my dear friend Michelle Kahler, not only for her continuous assistance—helping me plan research trips, recall random words at a moments notice, etc.—but most importantly for her encouragement and patience as I worked to complete this daunting project. Undoubtedly, her support made the completion of this book possible.

TABLE OF CONTENTS

List of Illustrations x

Introduction 1

1. Early Mormonism in Context 8
2. The Cross in Early Nineteenth Century Catholic and Protestant America 27
3. Mormon Magic, Freemasonry, and the Cross 37
4. Pre-Columbian Crosses 61
5. Mormon Crosses before the Institutionalized Taboo 67
6. The Ensign Peak Proposal 86
7. The Emergence of the Mormon Cross Taboo 102
8. Opposition to the Cross Institutionalized 110
9. The Taboo Reinforced 117
10. Comparative Perceptions of the Cross 123
11. Conclusion 145

Appendix: Early Christians and the Cross 149

Bibliography 159

Index 169

About the Author 172

List of Illustrations

Figure 1.1: Ancestors of Joseph Smith Jr. and the immediate family of Joseph Sr. and Lucy Mack Smith. Courtesy of John Hamer. 15

Figure 1.2: Vermont, New York and vicinity (boundaries as of 1816). Courtesy of John Hamer. 19

Figure 1.3: Competing Mormon leaders and factions (boundaries as of 1844). Courtesy of John Hamer. 25

Figure 3.1: Image from Heinrich Cornelius Agrippa's Occult Philosophy (London 1655), book 4. 40

Figure 3.2: Image from Francis Barrett's The Magus (London 1801), 2:128. 40

Figure 3.3: Image from Reginald Scot's Discovery of Witchcraft (London 1584), 231. 41

Figure 3.4: Image from Ebenezer Sibl[e]y's New and Complete Illustration of the Occult Sciences (London, ca. 1795), 4: 1102. 41

Figure 3.5: Smith family "Saint Peter Bind Them" parchment. Courtesy D. Michael Quinn and Signature Books. 42

Figure 3.6: The Smith family's "Holiness to the Lord" parchment contains a number of symbols believed to have magic power, including three crosses. Courtesy D. Michael Quinn and Signature Books. 42

Figure 3.7: The Smith family's "Jehovah Jehovah Jehovah" parchment contains several crosses amid other symbols. Courtesy D. Michael Quinn and Signature Books. 43

Figure 3.8: Pentagram windows on the replica Nauvoo Temple, surrounded by cruciform stonework, photo by Jim Hill. 50

Figure 3.9: Five Wounds of Christ, George Oliver, "The Theocratic Philosophy of Freemasonry, in Twelve Lectures" (London 1856; also published in London 1840 and New York 1855), lecture vii. 51

Figure 3.10: Joseph Smith's Masonic Apron. Photo by Val Brinkerhoff, courtesy Community of Christ Archives. 54

Figure 3.11: Joseph Smith's serpent walking cane is decorated with a shield emblazoned with a cross on display in the LDS Museum of Church History and Art. Photos by author. 55

Figure 4.1: A facsimile of the "Tablet of the Cross," a Mayan carving in Palenque. 64

Figure 5.1: The cross marking the first of the twenty-four temples to be built at the centerplace of the City of Zion (detail from the first Plat of Zion). 68

Figure 5.2: Hair Art from the officer ladies of the 20th Ward Relief Society,

LIST OF ILLUSTRATIONS　　xi

E.R. Snow, M.B. Cook, M.T. Smoot, M.E. Dorne, Whitney, E. Howard, H. Kimball, B.W. Smith, Z.D. Young, Annie Adkins Savage; on display in the Pioneer Memorial Museum (Salt Lake). Photo taken by author. 70

FIGURE 5.3: Marriage certificate of Matthew Urie Bailey and Mary Isabella Hales (22 June 1884; Heber City, Utah), in the "Life's Cycle" display at the Pioneer Memorial Museum (Salt Lake). Photo taken by author. 70

FIGURE 5.4: Framed cross hanging in Manti Temple. "A display at a bazaar" (c. 1886–1888). Used by permission, L. Tom Perry Special Collections, Harold B. Lee Library, Brigham Young University, Provo, Utah. Photographer George Edward Anderson, MSS P-1 #2280. 71

FIGURE 5.5: Crosses in stain glass of the Parowan (UT) 3rd ward building (built 1914), photographer Jonathan Kland, ldsarchitecture.wordpress.com, http://ldsarchitecture.wordpress.com/2011/12/21/parowan-3rd-ward-windows/, accessed 21 June 2012. 73

FIGURE 5.6: Crosses (on shields) in the stain glass of the Salt Lake Liberty Ward building (constructed at various stages 1908–1924), photographer Jonathan Kland, ldsarchitecture.wordpress.com, http://ldsarchitecture.wordpress.com/category/meetinghouses/united-states/utah/salt-lake-valley/salt-lake-liberty-ward/, accessed 21 June 2012. 73

FIGURE 5.7: Rose crosses in Whittier Ward chapel stained glass (built 1936-1938), photographer Jonathan Kland, ldsarchitecture.wordpress.com, http://ldsarchitecture.files.wordpress.com/2011/09/dsc_0752_adj.jpg, accessed 21 June 2012. 74

FIGURE 5.8: Cross detail outside the Odgen Deaf Branch building (built 1916), photographer Jonathan Kland, ldsarchitecture.wordpress.com, http://ldsarchitecture.wordpress.com/2011/04/01/ogden-deaf-branch-detail/, accessed 21 June 2012. 74

FIGURE 5.9: Memorial of "William Shanks Berry and John Henry Gibbs" (1884). Used by permission, Pioneer Memorial Museum (Salt Lake City), BER0001. 77

FIGURE 5.10: The floral arrangements for the funeral of 1887 funeral of LDS Church President John Taylor included a cross-and-anchor. "John Taylor [funeral]" (1887). Used by permission, Utah State Historical Society, photo #13916. All Rights Reserved. 78

FIGURE 5.11: "Amelia Folsom Young" (1895). Used by permission, Utah State Historical Society, photo #14195. All Rights Reserved. 80

FIGURE 5.12: "Talula Young Wood." Used by permission, Utah State Historical Society, photo #14159. All Rights Reserved. 80

FIGURE 5.13: "Nabby [Nabbie] Young Clawson." Used by permission, Utah State Historical Society, photo #11977. All Rights Reserved. 80

FIGURE 5.14: "Georgia C[Lawson] Foote" (c. 1880). Courtesy LDS Church History Library.

Photographer Charles Roscoe Savage, call #PH1700 238. 80

FIGURE 5.15: "Mary Ann Corlett Stewart." Used by permission, Utah State Historical Society, photo #13833. All Rights Reserved. 81

FIGURE 5.16: "[Ada] Afton Love." Used by permission, Utah State Historical Society, photo #12938. All Rights Reserved. 81

FIGURE 5.17: Dora Lowry wearing a cross on a chain. Used by permission, L. Tom Perry Special Collections, Harold B. Lee Library, Brigham Young University, Provo, Utah. Photographer George Edward Anderson, MSS P-1 #2835. 81

FIGURE 5.18: Caroline Ivins. Used by permission, Utah State Historical Society, photo #12595. All Rights Reserved. 81

FIGURE 5.19: "Mrs. J[ohn] W[hittaker] Taylor children" (1915). Used by permission, L. Tom Perry Special Collections, Harold B. Lee Library, Brigham Young University, Provo, Utah. Photographer George Edward Anderson, MSS P-1 #17860. 82

FIGURE 5.20: "John Loveless Girl, Springville [Utah]" (1880–1920). Used by permission, L. Tom Perry Special Collections, Harold B. Lee Library, Brigham Young University, Provo, Utah. Photographer George Edward Anderson, MSS P-1 #7115. 82

FIGURE 5.21: Family of "W[alter] K[illshaw] Barton, Sterling [Utah]" (c. 1888). Used by permission, L. Tom Perry Special Collections, Harold B. Lee Library, Brigham Young University, Provo, Utah. Photographer George Edward Anderson, MSS P-1 #2615. 82

FIGURE 5.22: Benjamin Franklin Johnson wearing a watch-chain with a cross (other images show him wearing the same), courtesy of Benjamin Franklin Johnson Family Organization. 82

FIGURE 5.18: "Tabernacle Choir" (1883). Courtesy LDS Church History Library. Photographer Charles Roscoe Savage, call #PH 2573. 83

FIGURE 5.19: "The Bishop, Superintendents and Teachers of the Sixteenth Ward Sunday School, Dec. 1883." Used by permission, L. Tom Perry Special Collections, Harold B. Lee Library, Brigham Young University, Provo, Utah. Photographer Charles Roscoe Savage, MSS P 24 Item 789. 83

FIGURE 5.20: 1852 European edition of the Doctrine and Covenants spine. Used by permission, L. Tom Perry Special Collections, Harold B. Lee Library, Brigham Young University, Provo, Utah. 85

FIGURE 5.21: "Elmeda Stringham Harmon." Used by permission, Pioneer Memorial Museum (Salt Lake City), HAR00o9a. 85

FIGURES 6.1 AND 6.2: Temporary cross monument in Emigration Canyon with an artist's reconstruction of the inscription. "Man standing next to marker 'where Brigham Young made the decision' to settle," Emigration

LIST OF ILLUSTRATIONS xiii

Canyon. Used by permission, Special Collections Dept., J. Willard Marriott Library, University of Utah, photo number P0893 #1_02_015. 100

FIGURE 8.1: The headstone of LDS General Authority, B. H. Roberts, erected in 1933, was inscribed with a prominent Latin cross. Centerville City Cemetery (Centerville, Utah), photo by Chad J. Stowell. 111

FIGURE 9.1: The headstone of US Navy Captain Lavell Bigelow, a Mormon veteran of World War II and the Korean War. Courtesy of John Hamer. 121

FIGURES 10.1 AND 10.2: Facsimiles of Strang's plates containing two prominent crosses. In the first diagram, the middle star below the man is marked with what Strang called a "cross pillar," while the hill of promise has a cross atop it. Courtesy Community of Christ Archives. 124

FIGURE 10.3: Emma Smith's Quilt. Photo by Val Brinkerhoff, courtesy Community of Christ Archives. 127

FIGURE 10.4: The RLDS First Presidency in the 1950s, F. Henry Edwards, Israel A. Smith, and W. Wallace Smith posing in front of a replica of the "Tablet of the Cross" — the most famous Pre-Columbian cross (see Figure 4.1). 130

FIGURE 10.5: Dora Burton (b. 1866–d.?). Journal of History 6 (Lamoni, Iowa: Reorganized Church of Jesus Christ of Latter Day Saints, 1913), 334. 132

FIGURE 10.6: Central Church of Kansas City Missouri. Courtesy Community of Christ Archives. 133

FIGURE 10.7: Stained glass with the image of a crown and a cross from the Stone Church in Independence, Missouri, preserved in the church's basement. Photo by author. 135

FIGURE 10.8: Stone Church stained glass window with a cross. Photo by Lachlan Mackay, courtesy Community of Christ Archives. 135

FIGURE 10.9: Advertisement for an RLDS Easter pageant staged in 1926. Elise M. Barraclough, "The Gate Ajar," Autumn Leaves 39, no. 3 (March 1926), 95-96. 136

FIGURE 10.10: Cross monument at Mount Rubidoux, California. Photo by Elbert A. Smith, courtesy of Community Christ Archives. 138

FIGURE 10.11: An RLDS church in Bryant, Texas. Courtesy of Community Christ Archives. 141

FIGURE 10.12: An RLDS church in Seattle, Washington. Courtesy of Community Christ Archives. 141

FIGURE 10.13: An RLDS church Berkeley, California. Courtesy of Community Christ Archives. 141

FIGURE 10.14: A cross inside the RLDS chapel in Berkeley, California. Courtesy of Community Christ Archives. 142

FIGURE 10.15: A large cross on the exterior of the Community of Christ Temple in Independence, Missouri. Courtesy of John Hamer. 143

Introduction

EVANGELICAL AND FUNDAMENTALIST Christians frequently argue that members of the Church of Jesus Christ of Latter-day Saints are "not Christian," in part because of Mormon opposition to the symbol of the cross.[1] Many Latter-day Saints adamantly deny this accusation, but their standard rebuttals can be self-contradictory. Neither group understands the actual basis for aversion to the cross in Mormonism. Thus, when this conflict arises, Mormons and their critics end up talking past one another, and, if anything, do little to facilitate profitable discourse.

Aversion to the symbol of the cross does not imply that Mormons are non-Christian. In fact, material display of the cross has not been a consistent or continuous custom in Christian history. Early Christians avoided displaying the cross because: (1) they worshiped surreptitiously for fear of persecution; (2) the image was a stumbling block to Jews and Gentiles, and therefore not a useful emblem for attracting converts; and (3) they feared that depicting the cross (or any other sacred symbol) materially was in violation of the second of the Ten Commandments.[2] Even

---

1. See James Walker, "Enemies of the Cross," *Internet Christian Library*, http://www.iclnet.org/pub/resources/text/apl/jw/jw-071.txt (accessed 29 December 2008). This is not to say, however, that the opposition to the cross is the sole reason why other Christians deny that Mormons are Christian.

2. It should not be concluded from these reservations that early Christians therefore believed (like Latter-day Saints today) the symbol of the cross to be an expression that is contrary to their faith. Although they avoided displaying the cross materially, they still embraced and promoted the acceptance of the symbol by actively searching out its hidden (and often natural) occurrence in the world around them, tracing the cross invisibly on their foreheads, praying in a cruciform

more relevant to the Mormon taboo, until the middle of the nineteenth century, American Protestants tended to avoid using the cross as a material symbol because of its association with Catholicism.³ This historical observation has been the basis for the standard scholarly explanation for Mormon cross aversion: early Mormons originally mirrored the contemporary Protestant view of the cross, retaining the taboo after Protestantism became more accepting of the symbol because of Latter-day Saint isolation in Utah.⁴

A common popular explanation for aversion to the cross was articulated by Gordon B. Hinckley, president of the LDS Church 1995–2008, who said "the cross is the symbol of the dying Christ, while our message is a declaration of the Living Christ."⁵ This argument is problematic be-

---

posture with arms extended, and even using crypto-crosses; such as those suggestive in the design of a ship's sail or anchor. See appendix.

3. See Ryan K. Smith, *Gothic Arches, Latin Crosses: Anti-Catholicism and American Church Designs in the Nineteenth Century* (Chapel Hill: University of North Carolina Press, 2006), and "The Cross: Church Symbol and Contest in Nineteenth-Century America," *Church History: Studies in Christianity and Culture* 70, no. 4 (2001): 705–734. "Lutherans and a smaller German-based sect, the Moravians, employed the cross as early as the eighteenth century without difficulties." Smith, *Gothic Arches*, 58.

4. David L. Paulsen and Cory G. Walker, for example, write, "While church policy does discourage using the cross, we believe the reasons are historical rather than theological. Early church members were drawn largely from communities whose churches bore no crosses.... Early Latter-day Saints simply followed suit. When Protestant America began using the cross again in the late 1800s, Latter-day Saints, culturally and geographically isolated from the rest of America, did not act similarly." David L. Paulsen and Cory G. Walker, "Work, Worship, and Grace," review of *The Mormon Culture of Salvation: Force, Grace and Glory*, by Douglas J. Davies, *FARMS Review* 18, no. 2 (2006), http://maxwellinstitute.byu.edu/publications/review/?vol=18&num=2&id=624 (accessed 30 October 2008). Richard Bushman concurs: "The cross was used by very few Protestant churches in 1830. It was a Catholic symbol that Protestants avoided. However, just as the Church was getting organized it began to seep into Protestant usage, following the lead of the Oxford Movement in England in the late 1830s and 1840s. Thus it required no decision on Joseph's part. No one around him used the cross." Richard Bushmen, email to Seth Payne, 17 November 2006, http://www.mormonstudies.net/html/faq/cross.html (accessed 30 October 2008). Terryl Givens likewise theorizes, "[The cross and crucifix have] always been scrupulously and positively shunned in LDS culture. The Puritans despised the cross as 'an idle apishe toye,' 'a part of deuill worship' for its evocation of Catholicism, and condemned 'the idolatrie of the Crosse, the Superstition of the Crosse, the Hipocrisie of the Crosse, the impietie of the Crosse, the injustice of the Crosse and the soule murther of the Crosse.' Mormons doubtless imbibed much of the anti-Catholicism pervasive on the (largely Protestant) frontier." Terryl L. Givens, *People of Paradox: A History of Mormon Culture* (New York: Oxford University Press, 2007), 114.

5. Gordon B. Hinckley, "The Symbol of Our Faith," *Ensign* (April 2005): 2. Elder Robert E. Wells also taught, "To us, the cross is a symbol of His passion, His agony. Our preference is to remember his resurrection. We seek to honor the living Christ who was brought forth in glory

cause it does not explain why other symbols of Jesus' torture and death are acceptable in the church.⁶ Additionally, the Mormon apologetic (however unintended it may be) carries the potentially offensive implication that mainstream Christianity has somehow lost focus of the tenet that Jesus was resurrected.

Both these explanations for the Latter-day Saint cross taboo are inadequate, and both speak from the assumption that aversion to the cross has always been embedded in Mormonism—that Mormons in the nineteenth century had the same feelings for the symbol as their twenty-first century heirs. This assumption is false. As this book will demonstrate, the cross taboo was a relatively late development in Mormon history. Contrary to conventional wisdom, members of the church in the first decades after its 1830 organization did not initially subscribe to the anti-cross rhetoric typical among contemporary American Protestants. Indeed, in the nineteenth and early twentieth centuries many Latter-day Saints individually used and promoted the symbol of the cross in its visual and material form. The current taboo emerged among Mormons at the grass-roots level around the turn of the twentieth century, and became institutionalized mid-century under the direction of David O. McKay, president of the LDS Church 1951–70.

---

from the tomb on the third day." *The Utah Evangel* 33 (May 1986): 8; as cited in Daniel C. Peterson and Stephen D. Ricks, *Offenders for a Word: How Anti-Mormons Play Word Games to Attack the Latter-day Saints* (Provo: FARMS, 1992), 131–132. Elder M. Russell Ballard of the Church's Quorum of the Twelve Apostles writes, "We rejoice in the knowledge of a living Christ, and we reverently acknowledge the miracles He continues to work today in the lives of those who have faith in Him. That is why we choose to place less emphasis on a symbol that can be construed to represent primarily His death." M. Russell Ballard, *Our Search for Happiness: An Invitation to Understand the Church of Jesus Christ of Latter-day Saints* (Salt Lake City: Deseret Book, 1993), 13. Mormon scholar Daniel H. Ludlow similarly taught, "Members of the Church of Jesus Christ of Latter-day Saints, however, emphasize the resurrected and living Jesus Christ: the symbol of the cross or crucifix, which depicts the dead or dying Christ, is therefore not part of our worship." Daniel H. Ludlow, *A Companion to Your Study of the New Testament: The Four Gospels* (Salt Lake City: Deseret Book, 1982), 56.

6. Every Sunday Latter-day Saints symbolically commemorate the death and suffering of Jesus as they perform and receive the communion. According to the New Testament, "For as often as you eat this bread and drink the cup, you proclaim the Lord's death until he comes" (1 Cor. 11:26 NRSV). Another conflicting symbol is the impression of the nails in the LDS endowment ceremony—a direct reference to one of the instruments used to torture and kill Jesus. See "The LDS Endowment: The Terrestrial World (1990)," *The LDS Endowment*, http://www.ldsendowment.org/1990terrestrial.html (accessed 24 October 2008).

Notes on Terminology

In order to make the case with precision, it is necessary to define a few terms. First, a "symbol," to put it simply, is "something [whether word or object] that stands for, represents, or denotes something else."[7] "Depictions" or "descriptions," on the other hand, are less abstract and more concerned with describing or portraying the thing itself, by matching the subject as it is perceived visually.

For example, if an artist paints Jesus as a fish, that painting is not a depiction of Jesus. It is a symbol of Jesus. If an artist chooses to paint a picture of Jesus on a cross between two crucified thieves (as the New Testament narratives describe), the cross portrayed will not (usually) be a symbol unless it is painted with the intent to communicate something beyond (or in addition to) the object of the cross. An exception to this is that artistic works may be used symbolically, even though the artist never intended them to be interpreted or used as such.

The same applies to symbolism and description in literature and spoken word. A Christian minister may say that he is "bearing the cross of Christ." By saying this, obviously the minister is not necessarily giving a mere description of an object of torture (or symbol of it) that he is literally carrying. The "cross of Christ" that he speaks of may instead symbolize the burdens and responsibilities he bears while preaching the gospel of salvation to the world. Perhaps additionally suggestive in this phrase is the notion that he is, as a messenger of that gospel, partners with Christ in bringing to pass the salvation of men.

These distinctions are important because although there has been intolerance and protocol against the display of the cross as a visual and material symbol in the LDS Church today, symbolic language and artistic depictions of the cross are more acceptable.[8] Although there seems to be some hesitancy among Latter-day Saints to depict the crucifixion in

---

7. *Oxford English Dictionary* (New York: Oxford University Press, 1989), http://dictionary.oed.com (accessed 24 October 2008). For an excellent introduction to semiotics see *Semiotics: An Introductory Anthology*, Robert E. Innis, ed., (Indiana University Press, 1985); and Terry Eagleton, *Literary Theory: An Introduction* (University of Minnesota Press, 2008), 79–109.

8. There appears to be little concern among Latter-day Saints today about using the word "cross" as a literary symbol, except when the literature promotes a visual (or material) symbol of the cross. More often than not, the literary symbol of the cross (when it is used) is given a negative connotation of gloom, burden, or death.

artwork[9] and even to use the word "cross" as a symbol,[10] these nuanced uses do not carry the same negative weight as the visual symbol itself.

To summarize, four categories have been defined: (1) Literary (or verbal) descriptions, (2) literary (or verbal) symbols, (3) material (or visual) depictions, and (4) material (or visual) symbols. Latter-day Saints have little or no concern for literary (or verbal) descriptions of the cross, only a mild concern for literary (or verbal) symbols and material (or visual) depictions of the cross, and a high concern for material (or visual) symbols of the cross. The scope of this book will primarily focus on attitudes toward this fourth category, explaining how and why an opposition to the material (and visual) symbol of the cross developed and became institutionalized into the LDS Church.

Finally, to provide comparative examples within Mormonism, this book will briefly examine two additional case studies: the evolving posi-

---

9. Douglas J. Davies observes, "LDS art, by sharp contrast has several important works on the sweating-blood feature [in the Garden of Gethsemane] but very few of the crucifixion." Douglas J. Davies, *An Introduction to Mormonism* (Campridge, UK: Cambridge University Press, 2003), 155. See also Douglas J. Davies, "Gethsemane and Calvary in LDS Soteriology," *Dialogue: A Journal of Mormon Thought* 34, no. 3–4 (2001): 19–30; Noel A. Carmack, "Images of Christ in Latter-day Saint Visual Culture," *BYU Studies* 39, no. 3 (2000): 47. Carmack mentions in his essay that "LDS artist Keith Eddington's version of *He Is Risen* has noticeably changed from his original 1960 version of the painting, entitled *The Ascension of Christ*.... The 1960 version, used for Church publications and tracts, includes the hill of Calvary and crosses on the horizon; in the 1994 version, painted for the Joseph Smith Memorial Building's Legacy Theater, the Calvary crosses were deleted." Ibid., 57.

10. The *Missionary Handbook*, published by The Church of Jesus Christ of Latter-day Saints in 1973, quoted Brigham Young saying, "If you go on a mission to preach the gospel with lightness and frivolity in your hearts, looking for this and that, and to learn what is in the world, and not having your minds riveted on the cross of Christ, you will go and return in vain." *Missionary Handbook* (Salk Lake City: The Church of Jesus Christ of Latter-day Saints, 1973), 19. The more recent 2006 edition of the handbook, however, edits out the symbol of the cross from Brigham Young's quote, and instead says, "If you go on a mission to preach the Gospel with lightness and frivolity in your hearts, looking for this and that, and to learn what is in the world,... you will go and return in vain.... Let your minds be centered on your missions." *Missionary Handbook* (Salk Lake City: The Church of Jesus Christ of Latter-day Saints, 2006), 7. Similarly, Elder Carlos E. Asay (of the Quorum of the Seventy) preached the following in 1978's fall General Conference: "We, like Israel of old, must rivet our eyes and minds upon the cross of Christ if we hope to gain eternal life, because through His resurrection we will gain the victory over physical death." Carlos E. Asay, "'Look to God and Live,'" *Ensign* (November 1978), 54. Asay's reference to the cross was omitted in the Old Testament Church curriculum manual, just as was done in the *Missionary Handbook* to Brigham Young's quote: "We, like Israel of old, must rivet our eyes and minds upon ... Christ if we hope to gain eternal life." *Old Testament Gospel Doctrine Manual* (Salk Lake City: The Church of Jesus Christ of Latter-day Saints, 2001), 71.

tion of the Community of Christ regarding the cross and the relationship Strangite Mormons have with the cross. It should be noted here that the umbrella of Mormonism (sometimes broadly referred to as the *Latter Day Saint* tradition), there are hundreds of competing denominations. The three under consideration here are:

(1) *The Church of Jesus Christ of Latter-day Saints (LDS Church)*. Headquartered in Salt Lake City, Utah, this is by far the largest Mormon denomination. After Joseph Smith Jr.'s death, this group followed Brigham Young to Utah, and hence have been called *Brighamites* or *Utah Saints*. Members identify themselves with the shortened title of *Latter-day Saints* (with the hyphen and lower case "d") or the acronym LDS.

(2) The *Community of Christ,* formerly known as the *Reorganized Church of Jesus Christ of Latter Day Saints (RLDS Church)*. Headquartered in Independence Missouri, the Community of Christ is the second largest denomination within the Latter Day Saint movement. This group did not follow Brigham Young's trek, but remained in the Midwest and eventually gave their allegiance to Joseph Smith III (the founder's son), and have therefore been called *Josephites*. In the late twentieth and early twenty-first centuries, the RLDS Church experienced a significant transformation in doctrine and practice, including ordaining women to the priesthood and changing of the organization's name. Thousands of disaffected members left forming their own independent *Restoration branches* because they believed these changes proved that the church had fallen into apostasy. Since the present work primarily examines the period prior to the church's name change, preference has been given to historic name of *RLDS Church*.

(3) The *Church of Jesus Christ of Latter Day Saints* (no hyphen, but with a capitalized "D") or *Strangite Church*. Headquartered in Voree, Wisconsin, the Strangite church is a relatively small Mormon denomination with a current membership of about two hundred or less. This group followed James Strang after Joseph Smith Jr.'s death, and was initially very successful, claiming many prominent members of the early church. Because James Strang did not appoint a successor on his deathbed, most *Strangites* in the 1860s rallied to the leadership of Joseph Smith III and the RLDS Church. Although the Strangite denomination is very

small today, they maintain a distinct tradition and their mass conversion also had a significant impact upon the RLDS tradition.

The subtle distinctions between the names of these related groups, relying on a single word, the capitalization of a "D," and the presence (or lack) of a hyphen, can be easily missed and consequently make comparative studies like this difficult to follow. To help minimize this difficulty, this book will confine the comparative study of the RLDS and Strangite traditions to the last chapter of this book (chapter 10). In the rest, the focus will be on the shared early Mormon tradition prior to 1844, and afterward on the Church of Jesus Christ of Latter-day Saints, headquartered in Utah.

Chapter One

Early Mormonism in Context

Joseph Smith Jr. (1805–1844), the founder of the *Latter Day Saint* movement, is identified by believers and non-believers alike as an "American Prophet." As historian Richard Bushman observes, Mormons use this title with an emphasis expressing patriotism towards the nation in which their church was born,[1] hoping to "win the affection of the American people." To many non-believers this title suggests that

---

1. Christian Nephi Anderson, for example, preached, "If there be an American religion, 'Mormonism' must be that one. No other religious system makes such claims for America as does 'Mormonism.' No other religion has made America such holy ground by its teachings and history. The 'Mormons' have placed America along with Palestine and made the Holy Land to share its honors with the Zion of the West. The Book of Mormon teaches that Jesus visited the ancient inhabitants of this continent, walked and talked with them and taught them the principles of the Gospel. The Lord's feet have pressed American soil. We 'Mormons' claim an American prophet. All other religions look to other lands for theirs. The founders of the Christian sects were German, or Scotch, or Swiss. The founder of 'Mormonism,' through God, was an American, a descendant of the Pilgrims. Other religionists limit angels' visits to a far eastern land. We claim that the West also has been sanctified by the presence of heavenly beings. Others confine apostles and inspired men to a past age, and an Old World nation. We say that God has raised up American apostles, and the inspiration of the Almighty can be and is given to Americans." Christian Nephi Anderson, "Are We Americans?" (October 1900), *Improvement Era* 3, no. 12, In *LDS Library 2006* [CD-Rom] (LDS Media, 2006).

the prophet's religious movement was the mere product of his environment.²

Although it would be unreasonable to expect Mormons and non-Mormons ever to see eye-to-eye about whether Joseph Smith was a visionary, a charlatan, or something in between,³ all parties can concur that the prophet, to one degree or another, made use of ideas from his immediate environment for the development of his church.⁴ All parties can additionally agree that certain key conditions within the United States were necessary for Mormonism to have been born, to have survived, and to become what it is today. This agreement about correlations does not extend to agreement about causes. As Bushman explains:

> Latter-day Saints are inclined to reverse the order and place American history in the history of the gospel. We think that Western civilization has been shaped in preparation for the Restoration.⁵

The time and space out of which Mormonism was born was one of transition and disarray. Citizens of the Second Great Awakening and residing in the Northeastern states, Joseph Smith and his family were wit-

---

2. Richard L. Bushman, "Joseph Smith's Many Histories," *The Worlds of Joseph Smith* (paper presented at an International Academic Conference at the Library of Congress, May 6, 2005), http://www.lds.org/library/display/0,4945,510-1-3067-1,00.html (accessed 20 January 2009). One of Joseph Smith's first critics, Alexander Campbell, for example, rejected the Book of Mormon as fabricated nineteenth century fiction, saying, "This prophet Smith, through his stone spectacles, wrote… in his book of Mormon, every error and almost every truth discussed in N. York for the last ten years." Alexander Campbell, "Delusions," *Millennial Harbinger*, vol. 2 (February 7, 1831), 93.

3. For an excellent resource exploring the ambiguous and complex character of Joseph Smith Jr., see *The Prophet Puzzle: Interpretive Essays on Joseph Smith*, ed. Bryan Waterman (Salt Lake City: Signature Books, 1999).

4. Historian Jan Shipps' following comments are worth noting here: "[I]t is not necessary to ignore the fact that Mormonism drew for inspiration not only the Old Testament and the New, but also the American experience in general, the experiences of the family of Joseph Smith in particular, and on Masonry and certain forms of magic and folk religion as well. But it is necessary to recognize that Mormonism is derivative and synthetic only insofar and in the same fashion that other religious traditions are derivative and synthetic. Locating and identifying its components can facilitate understanding, but this approach demands acknowledgement that Mormonism cannot be reduced to the sum of its parts any more than Christianity can be reduced to the sum of its parts or Judaism to the sum of its parts." Jan Shipps, *Mormonism: The Story of a New Religious Tradition* (Chicago: University of Illinois Press, 1987), 68–69.

5. Richard L. Bushman, "A Joseph Smith for the Twenty-First Century," *BYU Studies* 40, no. 2 (2001): 163.

nesses to a world of religious, intellectual, economic, political, social, and environmental turmoil. In the words of historian Robert V. Remini:

> Americans at this time were undergoing sudden, jolting change—again and again. In fact, the United States changed more profoundly in thirty years from 1790 to 1820 than during any other period in its history.[6]

From the tensions of this era and the years that followed, countless new religious movements emerged, a few of which have survived to this day: Seventh Day Adventists, Disciples of Christ, Pentecostals, and, of course, Mormons.

The American Context

In the generations immediately before the birth of Joseph Smith Jr., the Revolutionary War ended (1783), Americans succeeded in gaining independence from the British monarchial rule, the United States Constitution (1788) replaced the failed Articles of Confederation (1777), political parties took shape to govern the new nation, and the government steadily evolved from "a republican to a democratic form."[7]

The role of religion within the new nation and the relationship between churches and the state were not immediately settled questions. The United States Constitution said very little about religious freedoms explicitly; the only exception being the prohibition, "no religious test shall ever be required as a qualification to any office or public trust under the United states."[8] Three years later (1791), the Bill of Rights amended the Constitution in order to protect the nation from a future threat of theocracy: "Congress shall make no law respecting an establishment of religion, or prohibiting the free exercise thereof."[9]

The First Amendment, although a step forward toward church and state separation, did not complete the process. Rather, the amendment merely placed the authority to deal with matters of religion upon each

---

6. Robert V. Remini, *Joseph Smith* (New York: Viking Penguin, 2002), 2.
7. Ibid., 2.
8. United States Constitution, Article 6.
9. United States Constitution, Amendment 1.

individual state.[10] For the time being, it was within the rights of state government to establish their own state sanctioned church. The state-by-state disestablishment of religion was a separate process in itself, having happened at different points in time. Starting before the constitution was drafted, formal disestablishment occurred first in North Carolina (1776), followed by New York (1777), Virginia (1776–1779), and Maryland (1785). After the Constitution and Bill of Rights were created, disestablishment of state churches followed in South Carolina (1790), Georgia (1798), Vermont (1807), Connecticut (1818), New Hampshire (1819), Maine (1820), and finally Massachusetts (1833).[11]

Hand in hand with disestablishment came the decline of the traditionally dominant Anglican and Puritan denominations. Anglicanism (Episcopalianism) fell into disrepute due to the Revolutionary War and the church's association with the oppressive King of England.[12] But in New England, Puritanism (or Congregationalism) also lost much influence upon the minds and souls of Americans.

The increasing separation of church and state and the decline of traditional state denominations in America does not imply that the populace abandoned faith. Indeed, the period c. 1790–1830 has been identified by historians as a great revival of religious interest, known as the "Second Great Awakening." Without the support of state authorities, conditions for survival changed for denominations: Denominations must live or die upon their own merits. Consequently, in a capitalist, democratic, and romantic spirit, denominations competed fervently against one another in order to win converts. The greatest successes were among the previously tiny Methodist and Baptist denominations whose memberships experienced phenomenal growth.

The Industrial Revolution also became part of the American experience (1820–1870), propelling the breakdown of what had been the traditional family model. Instead of family farms and household manufacturing, the economy came to be driven by commercial farming and factory

---

10. Carl H. Esbeck, "Dissent and Disestablishment: The Church-State Settlement in the Early American Republic," *Brigham Young University Law Review* 4 (2004): 1449.

11. Esbeck, *Dissent and Disestablishment*, 1458.

12. According to historian Jon Butler, "Fifty Anglican priests were working in Pennsylvania, New York and New England before the Revolution; only nine remained." Butler, *Awash in a Sea of Faith*, 206.

production. One consequence of this transformation was the intensification of gender role distinctions. As historian Mark C. Carnes observed:

> Men generated wealth and created the economic and political institutions on which civilization depended; women raised children and cultivated moral and religious values, so the civilization would retain a modicum of civility.[13]

It should be noted that the responsibilities of "family religion" fell upon the shoulders of women even before the Industrial Revolution began. This development was partly due to "the seventeenth-century Puritan emphasis on the woman's role in family religion," and may have additionally "reflected a shift in the timing and, perhaps, in the substance of male spiritual awakening." In short, while married men had a tendency to undertake "full membership only before assuming local political office," single men remained aloof and unconverted. Women, on the other hand, tended to join churches while still in their twenties.[14]

This gender gap resulted in what has been called the "feminization" of Protestant churches, a process which was reinforced and accelerated by the Industrial Revolution. Female adherents soon outnumbered males two-to-one in Protestant congregations. Mark C. Carnes sees a correlation between this shift and a shift in Protestant preaching styles. According to Carenes, ministers adjusted, tailoring and adapting their sermons to what they perceived to be the concerns and needs of their feminine audience by turning to consolation and emotion.[15] Carnes also argues that ministers, in finding themselves in "feminine" churches, reaffirmed their masculinity with aggressive preaching.[16]

There may be some substance to this argument, but shifts in preaching styles should also be understood from the perspective of another important factor leading up this period, such as the rise of secularism and the popularity of Deism. Protestant ministers revived the spiritual outpourings of the previous (First) Great Awakening (1730-1750), and did so in a wake of confusion and doubt that followed the American

---

13. Mark C. Carnes, *Secret Ritual and Manhood in Victorian America* (New Haven: Yale University Press, 1989), 77.

14. Jon Butler, *Awash in a Sea of Faith: Christianizing the American People* (Cambridge: Harvard University Press, 1992), 170.

15. Carnes, *Secret Ritual and Manhood*, 77.

16. Ibid.

Enlightenment (1750–1800). Works like Thomas Paine's *Age of Reason* (1794–1795) further disenchanted believers, convincing many that God was no longer involved in the lives of humanity.

The religious revivals of the Second Great Awakening directly challenged the Deist views as Protestant ministers and their congregations placed emotion and the manifestations of the Holy Spirit on center stage, amplifying both with great theatrics. Ironically, the emphasis of feeling and intuition over learning undermined ecclesiastical authority. The implication was that any pious man, woman, or child, "though unschooled in theology, could better discern the will of a loving God than could a hard-hearted doctor of divinity."[17] It is within this context that women obtained a more dominant role in the churches, and many men developed feelings of alienation and resentment towards organized religion in general.[18]

The Smith Family Context

Joseph Smith's earliest ancestors were respected citizens, well adjusted to the colonial life of Massachusetts—a strictly Puritan colony with little or no tolerance for heretics that preserved the sanctioned religion by expelling those out of step with the faith.[19] By the generation of Joseph Smith's grandfather, Asael Smith, adherence to Puritanism had broken down. Asael Smith was a rather independent thinker who eventually came to "oppose established churches, and [so he] left his father's community [in Massachusetts] to make a new, freer life in Vermont."[20] In Vermont, Asael and others who settled the new state sought out and obtained the freedom "to avoid religious establishments elsewhere."[21]

---

17. Ibid., 78.
18. One man vented his frustrations, saying that the religious services had "stuffed my wife with tracts, and alarmed her fears, and nothing short of meetings, night an day, could atone for the many fold sins my poor, simple spouse had committed, and at the same time, she made the miraculous discovery, that she had been 'unevenly yoked.' From this happy period, peace, quiet, and happiness have fled from my dwelling, never, I fear, to return." *Liberal Advocate* (September 29, 1832); as cited in Carnes, *Secret Ritual and Manhood*, 78-79.
19. Esbeck, *Dissent and Disestablishment*, 1415.
20. Hill, *Joseph Smith: The First Mormon*, 7.
21. Esbeck, *Dissent and Disestablishment*, 1526.

One by-product of the denominational competition during the Second Great Awakening was feeling of extreme sectarianism. In vying for converts, Methodists, Baptists, and other Protestants insisted that even the smallest points of doctrinal difference were essential to salvation. While many were attracted by these arguments, many others (including members of the Smith family) were put-off by intensified competition between sects.[22]

Alternative spiritual paths were available to those who felt disheartened by this religious conflict. Popular options included Universalism, Primitivism, Seekerism,[23] Freemasonry (for men), and the practice of folk-magic. Joseph Jr.'s parents, Joseph Smith Sr. and Lucy Mack Smith, and their family were involved in all five of these alternatives. Lucy was a Primitivist, and Joseph Sr. was a Seeker with Universalist leanings.[24]

---

22. Lucy Smith recalled reading the "Bible, and praying; but, notwithstanding my great anxiety to experience a change of heart, another matter would always interpose in all my meditations:— If I remain a member of no church, all religious people will say I am of the world; and, if I join some one of the different denominations, all the rest will say I am in error. No church will admit that I am right, except the one with which I am associated. This makes them witnesses against each other." *Lucy's Book: A Critical Edition of Lucy Mack Smith's Family Memoir* (Salt Lake City: Signature Books, 2001), 258.

23. Dan Vogel makes an important observation when describing the differences between Seekers and Primitivists: "[Seekers] anticipated new apostles who would be divinely commissioned to 'restore' the true Christian worship. Seekers shared with Primitivists the belief that there had been an 'apostasy' from an original church established by Jesus and that a 'restoration' was necessary. But Seekers differed on matters of authority and restoration. They disagreed with Campbell and others that the Bible provided all necessary authority to establish a church. Seekers believed that ordinances would be inefficacious until there was a new, literal, and evident dispensation of divine power." Dan Vogel, *Religious Seekers and the Advent of Mormonism* (Salt Lake City: Signature Books, 1988), http://www.signaturebookslibrary.org/seekers/Introduction.htm (accessed 4 February 2009).

24. Joseph Smith Sr. had Universalist leanings that he inherited from his father (Asael) as a boy. After the death of Joseph Sr.'s oldest son, Alvin (d. 1823)—and after a minister preached a sermon at the funeral intimating "very strongly that he had gone to hell, for Alvin was not a church member"—the Smiths had all the more reason to accept Universalist doctrines. William Smith, "Deseret News" (1894), *Early Mormon Documents* vol. 1, ed. Dan Vogel (Salt Lake City: Signature Books, 1996), 513. After the death of Alvin and the minister's sermon, the Smith family became further disaffected from organized religion. This experience later motivated Joseph Smith Jr. to introduce a revelation to his church, allowing the possibility for salvation to all but perhaps a handful of the world's most wicked (See Doctrine and Covenants 19:6–12; 76:50–70; 137:1–10). See Richard L. Bushman, *Joseph Smith: Rough Stone Rolling* (New York: Alfred A. Knopf, 2006), 196–202.

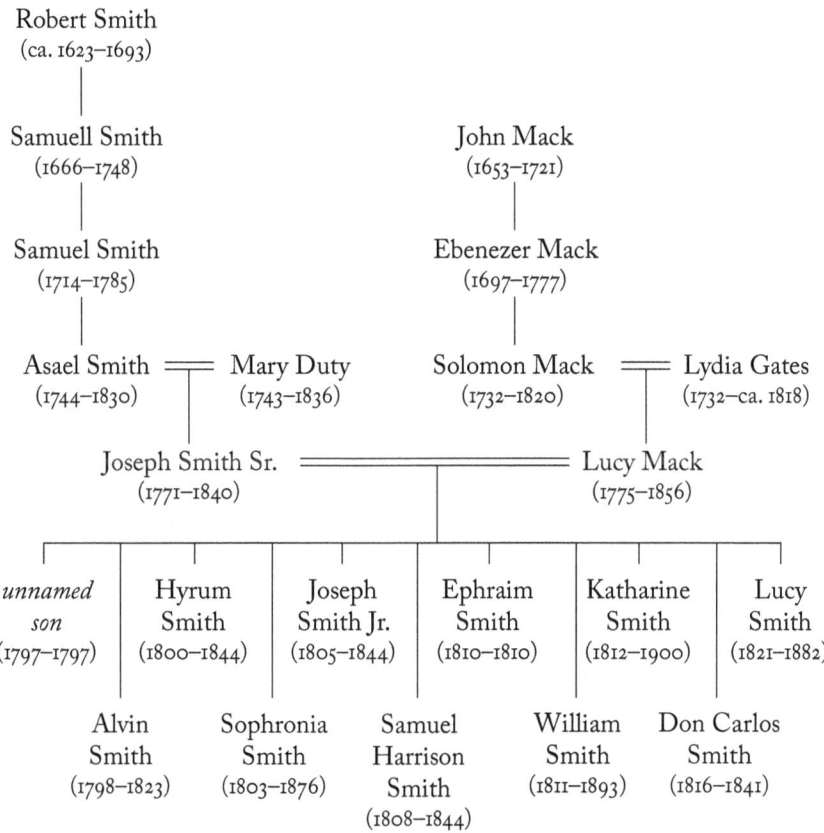

FIGURE 1.1: *Ancestors of Joseph Smith Jr. and the immediate family of Joseph Sr. and Lucy Mack Smith.*

The entire family dabbled in folk-magic; and both Hyrum and Joseph Jr. became Masons.[25]

Nature was also turbulent and unpredictable, burdening many Americans with continuous calamities. The state of Vermont—where Joseph Smith Jr.'s parents had met (1791), married (1796), and raised their children (for the majority of the time) up until 1816—was hit particularly hard:

---

25. Michael W. Homer, "'Similarity of Priesthood in Masonry': The Relationship Between Freemasonry and Mormonism," *Dialogue* 27, no. 3 (Fall 1994): 15–16.

> Two-thirds of the mills in Rutland and Windsor counties [in Vermont] were destroyed by flash floods in 1811, which also drowned livestock, washed away soil, and carried off bridges.

Spotted fever (cerebro-spinal meningitis) spread throughout the state killing over 6,000 between 1813 and 1814.²⁶

The Smiths temporarily moved to New Hampshire between 1811 and 1813. During the first winter of their stay, an epidemic of typhoid fever killed 6,000 more Americans in just five months while spreading from Connecticut Valley into New Hampshire.²⁷ All of Joseph Smith's siblings were infected, and his sister Sophia nearly died of the disease. Young Joseph was also infected, and due to a misdiagnosis and complications that followed, he almost lost his leg.²⁸ After a successful surgery to save Joseph Smith Jr.'s leg and life, the Smith family (being nearly bankrupted from medical expenses) moved back to Vermont for another attempt at livelihood, but sadly natural calamity stuck again.

The Year Without a Summer (1816) brought seasonal temperatures that were (and still are) among the lowest ever recorded in the area's history, when "snow and ice remained present in parts of New England for twelve consecutive months." From June 6 to June 11:

> The snow line ran from a point just north of Troy, New York, diagonally northeastward to Brunswick, Maine, encompassing almost all of Vermont and New Hampshire and most of Maine.

Frosts followed the snow in the months of July and August, contributing further destruction to crops.²⁹

Many Americans reacted to the extreme cold summer (and other natural disasters) with increased religiosity and apocalyptic expectation:

> There were many supplications to the heavens for relief from the cold and drought. Prayer days and fast days were held, begging for relief and 'a more copious outpouring of the Holy Spirit.'

---

26. In 1810, Vermont had a population of only 217,000. This means that nearly three percent of Vermont's population died. Michael Barkun, *Crucible of the Millennium: The Burned-Over District of New York in the 1840s* (New York: Syracuse University Press, 1986), 108.
27. Bushman, *Joseph Smith: Rough Stone Rolling*, 20.
28. Richard L. Bushman, *Joseph Smith and the Beginnings of Mormonism* (Chicago: University of Illinois Press, 1984), 32.
29. Barkun, *Crucible of the Millennium*, 108-109.

Other pious Christians, on the other hand:

> submitted to the judgment from the 'Great First Cause,' and they quoted from the Bible which said: 'By the breath of God frost is given, and the breath of the waters is restrained.'[30]

A mass westward migration followed these calamities. "Between 1810 and 1820 Vermont alone lost 10–15,000 people, many because of the summer of 1816."[31]

Although unrealized in Joseph's day, the main factor contributing to this anomalous weather was the volcanic eruption of Indonesia's Mount Tambora on the first week of April, 1815.[32] Twenty-five cubic miles of debris and dust blocked sunlight so severely that sunspots could be seen with the naked eye.[33] Many people attributed the extreme weather to these sunspots, and others theorized that lightning rods interfered with nature's electric currents.[34] Both of these explanations, incidentally, would have given credence to natural magic beliefs about animal magnetism and astrology common to American folk religion at the time.[35]

---

30. C. Edward Skeen, "'The Year without a Summer': A Historical View," *Journal of the Early Republic* 1, no. 1 (Spring 1981): 63.

31. Barkun, *Crucible of the Millennium*, 109-110.

32. Latter-day Saint Peter K. Bellville writes, "The exact date of the eruption is given variously as April 5 or 7, depending on the source of information and what is defined as an eruption. If April 7 is used and time zones considered, the volcano erupted April 6, 1815, North American time." Peter K. Bellville, "A Year Without a Summer," *Ensign* (January 1983), 65. This possibility is of interest to the Saints because April 6 is the date the Church was officially organized, and is also commonly believed to be the date of Jesus' birth (based on a literal interpretation of D&C 20:1). See John P. Pratt, "The Restoration of Priesthood Keys on Easter 1836, Part 1: Dating the First Easter," *Ensign* (June 1985), 59.

33. "[T]he dry fog reddened and dimmed the sun to such an extent that sunspots became visible to the naked eye. This apparently took place over a 'long' period in the day both before and after sunrise. Sunspots can normally be seen with the naked eye only if the sun lies less than about 2.5° in apparent altitude above the horizon." Richard B. Stothers, "The Great Tambora Eruption in 1815 and its Aftermath," *Science—American Association for the Advancement of Science* 223, no. 4654 (June 15, 1984): 1194–95.

34. Barkun, *Crucible of the Millennium*, 109.

35. Divining rods (such as those used by the Smith family) were believed to have magnetic solar power charged into them: "It must be new wood and it must have grown upon the tree in such a position that the rising and setting sun looked between the prongs.... If the rod is in the right hands, as soon as the bearer passes over a vein of metal or an underground spring it will move on its own accord and will twist over till the foot of the Y points toward the ground." Another author has explained: "[I]n the early days in America, witch hazel was used in local witchery, to find water or even mineral deposits. You took a forked branch, one whose points grew north and south so that they felt the influence of the sun at its rising and setting.... Any downward tug of

To the Smith family, like many others, the crop failure of 1816 was the last straw, convincing them that it was time to leave Vermont and move to Palmyra, a bustling town along the route of the Erie Canal in western New York.[36] They soon discovered that the area hot-spot of competitive revivalism,[37] which consequently came to be known as the "Burned-over District."[38] Joseph Smith Jr. reported that shortly after the move, he "pondered many things in my heart concerning the situation of the world." The "contentions and divisions[,] the wickedness" he saw pervaded his mind to the point that he had "become exceedingly distressed"—distressed not only about the state of society, but also about his unworthy standing before God. He therefore turned to the Bible for answers, and came to realize that mankind "apostatized from the true and living faith." Young Joseph concluded that "there was no society or denomination that built upon the gospel of Jesus Christ as recorded in the new testament."[39] In an account dictated six years later in 1838, Joseph described other details of the religious conflict he had seen in his youth:

> Great multitudes united themselves to the different religious parties, which created no small stir and division amongst the people.... Some were contending for the Methodist faith, some for the Presbyterian, and some for the Baptist.[40]

---

the stem was caused by the flow of hidden water or the gleam of buried gold." Both authors are quoted in Edmund H. Fulling, "American Witch Hazel: History, Nomenclature and Modern Utilization," *Economic Botany* 7, no. 4 (October–December 1953): 369–370.

36. Construction of the Erie Canal began the year after the Smith family's arrival and the waterway was officially opened for business on 26 October 1825.

37. According to Lucy Smith, "In [Vermont] we established ourselves on a farm belonging to one Esquire Moredock. The first year our crops failed; yet, by selling fruit which grew on the place, we succeeded in obtaining bread for the family, and by making considerable exertion we were enabled to sustain ourselves. The crops the second year were as the year before—a perfect failure. Mr. Smith now determined to plant once more, and if he should meet with no better success than he had the two preceding years, he would then go to the state of New York, where wheat was raised in abundance. The next year an untimely frost destroyed the crops, and being the third year in succession in which the crops had failed, it almost caused a famine. This was enough; my husband was now altogether decided upon going to New York." Lucy Smith, "Biographical Sketches of Joseph Smith the Prophet," *Early Mormon Documents*, 1: 270.

38. "Between 1816 and 1820 more revivals were reported in New York than in any previous period." Donna Hill, *Joseph Smith: The First Mormon*, 49.

39. Joseph Smith, "1832 History," *The Papers of Joseph Smith: Autobiographical and Historical Writings* vol. 1, ed. Dean C. Jessee (Salt Lake City: Deseret Book, 1989), 5.

40. *Joseph Smith—History* (1838), 1: 5.

EARLY MORMONISM IN CONTEXT 19

FIGURE 1.2: *Vermont, New York and vicinity (boundaries as of 1816).*

Concerned about his own spiritual standing before God, and (according to later accounts) not knowing if it would be best for him to join a Church, Joseph Smith Jr. turned to God in prayer. "I cried unto the Lord for mercy for there was none else to whom I could go... and the Lord heard my cry in the wilderness."[41] Joseph's account published in 1838 described him being attacked by an evil presence while attempting to petition God.[42] But then, he said, as he poured his heart out to God, a "pillar of light above the brightness of the sun at noon day come [sic] down from above and rested upon me." Joseph Smith reports that he was visited by the Lord, who confirmed that all other denominations were corrupt, and commanded that he "must join none of them."[43] The vision closed promising to "bring to pass that which hath been spoken by the mouth of the prophets and Apostles behold and lo I come quickly."[44]

41. *1832 History.*
42. *Joseph Smith—History* (1838), 1: 15–16.
43. Ibid., 1: 19.
44. *1832 History.*

What exactly would be "brought to pass" was not made entirely clear. Surely the second coming was to be expected, but was there something more, such as the Restoration that many Seekers and Primitivists of the day were waiting for?

As exceptional as this story may sound, reported visions like Joseph's were fairly common during his day. The language Smith used, even the order of the events he described, reveal strong parallels to reports given by other visionaries. Latter-day Saint scholar Donna Hill sees these parallels with contemporaries as evidence validating that Joseph Smith was neither psychotic nor a fraud.[45] Other Latter-day Saints dismiss the parallels as mere coincidence, and therefore unimportant and hardly worth noting. Skeptics, on the other hand, perceive the parallels, as well as apparent contradictions among Joseph Smith's various accounts, as strong evidence undermining his credibility.[46]

Whatever may have actually been the case, soon a series of events followed that (collectively) set young Joseph apart from the other visionaries of his generation: An angel, he reported, directed him to an ancient record buried in a hillside near where he lived. Written by prophets of the New World, and engraved upon gold plates in "reformed Egyptian," the record was translated by young Joseph Smith. He claimed to do so through the power of God by looking into his seer-stones. The record was to be a second witness of Jesus Christ, a sacred account of a group of Israelites who sailed to the new world while fleeing Jerusalem, just prior to the Babylonian invasion (c. 600 BCE). The crowning event of the narrative is the appearance of Jesus Christ, just after his crucifixion and resurrection, at which time he preached his Gospel and established his Church among them. From these gold plates Joseph Smith averred that he had produced the Book of Mormon.

---

45. According to Donna Hill, "The religious fervor of the times, the then not uncommon reports of dreams and visions, the intense conversions not infrequently experienced by adolescents and the fact that Joseph sustained his testimony ever afterward, lived fully in accordance with it and died a martyr to his conviction suggests that he spoke the truth." Hill, *Joseph Smith: The First Mormon*, 54.

46. See H. Michael Marquardt and Wesley P. Walters, *Inventing Mormonism: Tradition and the Historical Record* (Salt Lake City: Smith Research Associates, 1994); see also Richard L. Bushman, "Just the Facts Please," *FARMS Review* 6, no. 1 (1994), 122–133, http://farms.byu.edu/publications/review/?vol=6&Num=2&id=156 (accessed 4 February 2009).

The Early Development of Mormonism

In March 1829, before the Book of Mormon was completed and published, Joseph reported receiving another revelation, this time announcing that God intended to "restore" the primitive Christian church. The Lord informed him:

> If the people of this generation harden not their hearts, I will work a reformation among them, and I will put down all lyings, and deceivings, and priestcrafts, and envyings, and strifes, and idolatries, and sorceries, and all manner of iniquities, and I will establish my church, like unto the church which was taught by my disciples in the days of old.[47]

This newly established church would not only be purified from the iniquities listed, but it would also have a restored apostolic order of Priesthood. According to Smith's later account, John the Baptist appeared as an angel to confer the Aaronic Priesthood upon his and his friend Oliver Cowdery's[48] heads, commanding them to baptize each other. Afterwards apostles of the early Christian church, Peter, James, and John, visited and ordained Smith and Cowdery to the higher Melchizedek priesthood.[49]

Smith's church brought in thousands of converts, increasing in size exponentially. Within the first couple of years missionaries succeeded in converting entire congregations of believers. Early converts, including the prophet's immediate family, tended to be Seekers and Primitivists, who were drawn to the claims of apostolic authority, the spiritual gifts of New Testament times, and the concept of restoring of Christ's original church. In all these cases, Joseph Smith offered precisely what Seekers and Primitives sought.

---

47. *A Book of Commandments, for the Government of the Church of Christ* (W.W. Phelps, 1833), 4:5 [original spelling and punctuation retained].

48. Oliver Cowdery served as one of Joseph Smith's scribes for the translation of the Book of Mormon, and was among the three witnesses who formally declared that he had seen the gold plates.

49. There is much controversy over early Mormon claims for the restoration of the Melchizedek priesthood. See D. Michael Quinn, *The Mormon Hierarchy: Origins of Power* (Salt Lake City: Signature Books, 1994), 7–32; and Brian Q. Cannon et. al, "Seventy Contemporaneous Priesthood Restoration Documents," *Opening the Heavens: Accounts of Divine Manifestations 1820–1844* (Salt Lake City: Brigham Young University Press, 2005), 215–263.

Building upon this foundation, the prophet envisioned and organized a utopian community ("the city of Zion")[50] where the Saints of the Latter-days would soon gather to live the "United Order,"[51] a communitarian economic system, under the political direction of what Smith described as a "theodemocracy."[52] As Apostle George A. Smith later put it (1865), "Our system should be Theo-Democracy—the voice of the people consenting to the voice of God."[53]

Among other innovations, Smith constructed temples and developed an elaborate, quasi-Masonic ritual to be performed therein. Contemporary Mormons essentially believed this ritual (known as the "endowment") "restored" Masonry to its original form,[54] as it supposedly

---

50. "Hearken, O ye elders of my church, saith the Lord your God, who have assembled yourselves together, according to my commandments, in this land, which is the land of Missouri, which is the land which I have appointed and consecrated for the gathering of the saints. Wherefore, this is the land of promise, and the place for the city of Zion. And thus saith the Lord your God, if you will receive wisdom here is wisdom. Behold, the place which is now called Independence is the center place; and a spot for the temple is lying westward.... Behold, this is wisdom, that [my disciples] may obtain it for an everlasting inheritance." Doctrine and Covenants 57:1–7; see also Moses 7:62.

51. "VERILY I say unto you, my friends, I give unto you counsel, and a commandment, concerning all the properties which belong to the order which I commanded to be organized and established, to be a united order, and an everlasting order for the benefit of my church, and for the salvation of men until I come.... And I now give unto you power from this very hour, that if any man among you, of the order, is found a transgressor and repenteth not of the evil, that ye shall deliver him over unto the buffetings of Satan; and he shall not have power to bring evil upon you." Doctrine and Covenants 104:1, 10.

52. The prophet said, "As the 'world is governed too much' and as there is not a nation or dynasty, now occupying the earth, which acknowledges Almighty God as their law giver, and as 'crowns won by blood, by blood must be maintained,' I go emphatically, virtuously, and humanely, for a THEODEMOCRACY, where God and the people hold the power to conduct the affairs of men in righteousness. And where liberty, free trade, and sailor's rights, and the protection of life and property shall be maintained inviolate, for the benefit of ALL." Joseph Smith, "For the Times and Seasons. The Globe," *Times and Seasons* 5, no. 8 (April 15, 1844), 510, In *New Mormon Studies: A Comprehensive Library* [CD-ROM] (Smith Research Associates, 1998).

53. *Deseret News* 14: 338, Journal History of the Church of Jesus Christ of Latter-day Saints, vol. 64, 13 July 1865, 1, In *Selected Collections from the Archives of The Church of Jesus Christ of Latter-day Saints* [DVD] (Provo: Brigham University Press, 2002), 2: 4. This quote is also (erroneously?) cited under the date of July 12th in several publications.

54. According to Joseph Smith's close and trusted friend, Benjamin F. Johnson, "[Joseph Smith] told me Freemasonry, as at present, was the apostate endowments." Benjamin F. Johnson, *My Life's Review: Autobiography of Benjamin Franklin Johnson* (Provo: Grandin Book, 1997), 85. Heber C. Kimball reported in 1842 essentially the same thing in a letter written to Apostle Parley P. Pratt: "Bro. Joseph Ses Masonry was taken from the preasthood but has become degenerated. But menny things are perfect" [original spelling and punctuation retained]. Later Kimball de-

existed when the Lord first endowed Adam and Eve, providing a way for their redemption from the fall through the atoning blood of Jesus Christ.[55]

Theocracy in the political arena and communitarianism in the economic arena both generated opposition among non-Mormon Americans, but no practice was met with more antagonism than Smith's challenge to basic social norms with his restoration of the practice of polygamy.[56] Taken together, these three practices made Mormonism appear dangerous and even treasonous to some Americans. As a result, whenever Mormons gathered together in vast numbers, in Ohio, in Missouri, and in Illinois, they aroused determined opposition from their neighbors. As a result, they were continually forced to relocate and start anew. These persecutions resulted in much hardship and loss of property, and a number of the faithful lost their lives, including the prophet Joseph Smith himself in 1844.

---

clared in a public discourse, "We have the true Masonry. The Masonry of today is received from the apostasy which took place in the days of Solomon and David." In Edward H. Ashment, "The LDS Temple Ceremony: Historical Origins and Religious Value," *Dialogue* 27, no. 3 (Fall 1994): 291–292.

55. Historian Richard Bushman draws a distinction between the LDS endowment and Freemasonry, saying, "The Masonic elements that appeared in the temple endowment were embedded in a distinctive context—the Creation instead of the Temple of Solomon, exaltation rather than fraternity, God and Christ, not the Worshipful Master. Temple covenants bound people to God rather than to each other. At the end, the participants entered symbolically into the presence of God. Endowment, Joseph's name for the temple ceremony, connected it to promises made long before his encounter with Freemasonry.... On the surface, the temple resembles the cloistered, brotherly world of the lodges. But the spiritual core of the Nauvoo endowment was not male bonding. By 1843 women were sitting in the ordinance rooms and passing through the rituals. Adam and Eve, a male-female pair, were the representative figures rather than the Masonic hero Hiram Abiff. The aim of the endowment was not male fraternity but the exaltation of husbands and wives." Richard Lyman Bushman, *Joseph Smith: Rough Stone Rolling* (New York: Knopf, 2005), 450–51. Although it may be true that Masonic orders did not generally utilize the biblical narratives of the creation and the fall and redemption of Adam and Eve in their rituals, it should also be understood that many Christian Masons in Joseph Smith's day *interpreted* their rituals in this way, as they believed their rituals and the characters (the initiate and Hiram Abiff, etc.) of the drama to be *types and shadows* of greater religious truths. See Salem Town, *A System of Speculative Masonry* (New York, 1818), 75–82; see also my conference presentations on "The Mormon Endowment and the Christianization of Freemasonry" at the Mormon History Association (St George, Utah, 2011) and Sunstone Symposium (Ogden Utah, 2011).

56. To the list of beliefs that provoked negative responses in non-Mormons, Hill added one other belief to the list: "An infallible prophet." Marvin S. Hill, "A Note on Joseph Smith's First Vision and Its Import in the Shaping of Early Mormonism," *Dialogue* 12, no. 1 (Spring 1979): 95–96.

Mormonism after Joseph Smith Jr.

Joseph Smith's death was unexpected and was a terrible blow. The founding prophet had left no clear successor appointed to unify and, in the words of historian Steven L. Shields, "the church simply blew apart at the seams."[57] Rival claimants soon emerged, assumed the mantle, and eventually severed into distinct groups of competing organizations.[58] For example, James J. Strang insisted that he was ordained through angelic ministry immediately at the time of Smith's death. Strang also distributed a "Letter of Appointment" allegedly written by Joseph Smith, assigning him to gather the faithful to a new center of the church in Voree, Wisconsin. Sidney Rigdon led a group of Mormons to Pennsylvania and Lyman Wight brought another to Texas. William Smith came forward as the last surviving brother of the fallen prophet, Alpheus Cutler claimed leadership through his membership in Joseph Smith's elite "Council of Seven," and David Whitmer claimed leadership based on an 1834 appointment as Smith's successor.[59] After some successes, the movements of all of these successors effectively faltered and most of the Mormons who remained in the Midwest were eventually gathered into the Reorganized Church of Jesus Christ of Latter Day Saints under the leadership of the deceased prophet's eldest son, Joseph Smith III.

As president of the Quorum of the Twelve Apostles in 1844, Brigham Young was also a strong candidate for succession as church president. Beyond his rank, as a polygamist, Brigham Young appealed to the core of Mormon leaders in Nauvoo, who were also engaged in the practice. As historian D. Michael Quinn noted, Brigham Young's followers naturally did not want "a new church president who would brand polygamous wives as whores."[60] Young eventually decided that his followers would have to leave the Midwest and find refuge in the Great Basin. After a long, hard, and treacherous journey, the first pioneers arrived at the Salt Lake Valley in 1847. At last, these Mormons hoped, they could live their

---

57. Steven L. Shields, "Foreword," *Scattering of the Saints: Schism within Mormonism* (Independence: John Whitmer Books, 2007), viii.

58. Explains Stephen Shields, "Each of these leaders, and those who united with them, was faithful to the vision and mission of Joseph Smith, Jr. However, the vision was expressed differently. Each group was representative of, but not identical with, the original church." Ibid.

59. Ibid.

60. Quinn, *The Mormon Hierarchy: Origins of Power*, 152.

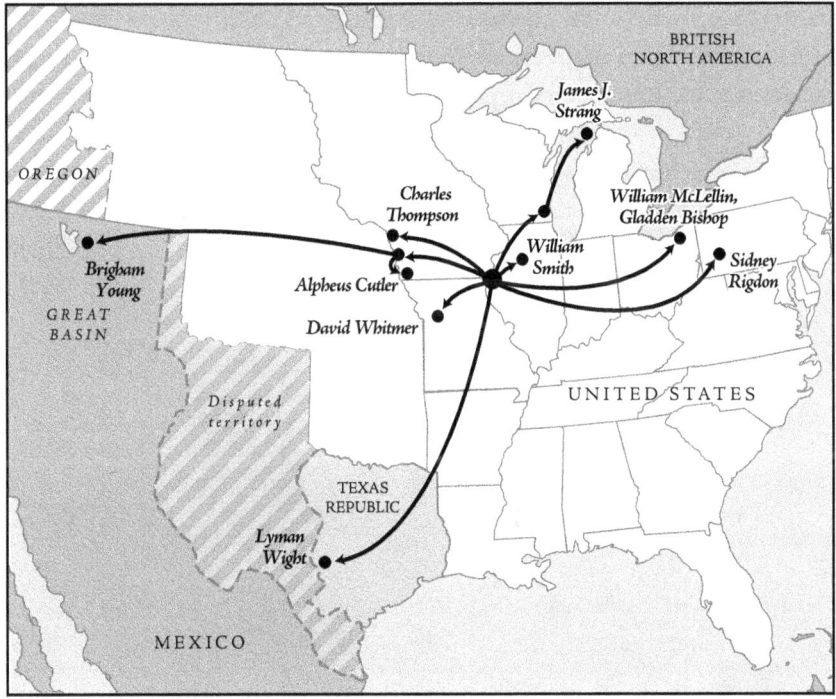

FIGURE 1.3: Competing Mormon leaders and factions (boundaries as of 1844).

religion in peace and prosperity, isolated from the persecutions and influence of outsiders, while laboring to build up their utopian "Zion" once again. But this hope quickly faded a few years later as the United States' westward expansion brought the Great Basin (that included the Salt Lake Valley) into American territory by the establishment of the Territory of Utah (1850). Utah Mormons fell under federal control and soon anti-polygamy laws were enforced upon them.

Despite legal persecution, many Mormons continued to practice polygamy secretly. Some avoided the law by moving to Mexican and Canadian territory. Gradually, however, church leaders came to realize (albeit in different stages) that for the church to survive, it would have to accommodate the government and abandon controversial practices including polygamy, utopian communalism, and theocracy.

As a result of this accommodation, the end of the nineteenth century marked a major shift for the Church of Jesus Christ of Latter-day

Saints, beginning a long process of enthusiastic assimilative movement into the American mainstream.[61] As Mormons assimilated, opposition declined substantially, and by the second decade of the twentieth century, the Mormon self-image made an about-face. No longer playing the role of a rebellious sect standing apart from American norms and lifestyles, suddenly Mormons wanted to show the world that they were even more American than Americans, and that they were just as Christian as Catholics and Protestants. This self image has continued into the twenty-first century today.

---

61. See Armand L. Mauss, *The Angel and the Beehive: The Mormon Struggle with Assimilation* (Chicago: University of Illinois Press, 1994).

Chapter Two

The Cross in Early Nineteenth Century Catholic and Protestant America

At the time Joseph Smith Jr. officially organized his church in 1830, many citizens of the United States held deep contempt for Catholicism. Mainstream Protestants generally regarded the Catholic Church to be both a threat to democracy and true Christianity, as they perceived it to be theocratic and full of corrupt elements of paganism. Tensions increased when Catholics immigrated with great numbers into what was essentially a Protestant nation, bringing "new schools, parishes, and missions throughout the country, introducing this faith into countless communities for the first time."[1] The change was rapid and massive, as historian Ryan K. Smith explains:

> From 1820 to 1850, the Catholic Church grew from about 195,000 members—less than four percent of the nation's total number of Christians—to 1.75 million, becoming the largest religious body in the United States.[2]

Smith also notes that:

> Canon law prescribed specific architectural locations for Catholic crosses and crucifixes, thereby bolstering their prominence.

---

1. Ryan K. Smith, *Gothic Arches, Latin Crosses: Anti-Catholicism and American Church Designs in the Nineteenth Century* (Chapel Hill: University of North Carolina Press, 2006), 9.
2. Ibid.

These qualities made the cross a regular target for anti-Catholic mobs.³

To Protestant Americans, the cross was perceived to be a strictly Catholic symbol. Reports a Boston Episcopalian in 1847:

> When a stranger enters a city, and passes a church with a cross upon it, his impression is that it is Roman Catholic; and when one visits the cemetery... and sees a stone embellished with the same symbol, he takes it for granted that a Roman Catholic sleeps underneath.⁴

Additionally, in 1847 a Presbyterian magazine insists that the cross is "not a symbol of redemption through the blessed Savior, but a perverted, abused symbol of a great system of superstition and imposture."⁵

Protestants were unwilling to risk the threat of mob violence and internal dissent, and so they generally avoided crosses that would have otherwise made their churches appear Catholic. Most protestant denominations, "including the Methodists, Congregationalists, Episcopalians, Presbyterians, and Baptists, rigorously avoided any use of 'Catholic' art."⁶ One exception was in Burlington, New Jersey, in 1834. George Washington Doane, the Bishop of New Jersey and rector of St. Mary's Episcopal Church decided to renovate his congregation building with an "ambitious new design [that] featured a cruciform plan with Greek details." The completed project alarmed both the vestry, "as well as that of many in the community, of all 'denominations'—lo! A cross made quite a Catholic appearance on the apex of the pediment!" Controversy continued to stir and soon "one of the Vestry... declared that unless the Cross was taken down very soon, it should be pulled down." A carpenter was therefore hired to remove the cross in the middle of the night. But by the next day, the cross was returned to "the apex of the pediment"—presumably indicating that Bishop Doane and his congregation had quickly resolved the conflict.⁷

---

3. Ryan K. Smith, "The Cross: Church Symbol and Contest in Nineteenth-Century America," *Church History: Studies in Christianity and Culture* 70, no. 4 (2001): 706.
4. Ibid.
5. Ibid.
6. Ibid., 713. General exception: "Lutherans and a smaller German-based sect, the Moravians, employed the cross as early as the eighteenth century without difficulties." Ryan K. Smith, *Gothic Arches*, 58.
7. Smith, "The Cross: Church Symbol and Contest," 705.

Other congregations were less successful than Doane's in avoiding violent confrontation. For example, the St. Augustine's Church was destroyed by arson in the Philadelphia riots of 1844, and the Boston chapel was attacked by mobs in 1854, having its cross pulled down from the steeple and set ablaze.[8] This extreme opposition to the cross is graphically illustrated in a pamphlet published in Boston, 1855, entitled "The Satanic Plot, or, Awful Crimes of Popery in High and Low Places." Ryan Smith describes the pamphlet as follows:

> In this pamphlet championing free schools and Protestant churches, the cover art centered on a discussion between the seated figures of the Pope and Satan over a map of the United States. Not only did the cross appear prominently on the back of the Pope's chair, but it adorned the back of Satan's chair as well. Such a scene left little doubt that Protestant loyalties to the symbol were thin. In these and other images, the cross served as a Catholic trademark, a piece of visual shorthand representing the sensual tools of Catholicism and the oppressive authority of the Catholic church.[9]

Early Mormon Attitudes toward Catholicism

Early Mormons had their own share of anti-Catholic sentiment, echoing from time to time many of the same criticisms that Protestants had leveled against the Roman Church. Historian Matthew J. Grow explains, "Mormons initially described Catholicism in language nearly indistinguishable from that used by their Protestant friends and families," identifying the Catholic Church as "Babylon the Great, the Mother of Harlots and [the] Abominations of the Earth."[10]

In a language of apocalyptic dualism, the Book of Mormon declares that there are only two churches in the world, the "Church of the Lamb of God" and the "Church of the Devil" (also known as the "Great and Abominable" and "Mother of Harlots"). This Great and Abominable Church would be politically and spiritually oppressive and motivated

---

8. Ibid., 706.
9. Ibid., 708-709.
10. Matthew Grow, "The Whore of Babylon and the Abomination of Abominations: Nineteenth-Century Catholic and Mormon Mutual Perceptions and Religious Identity," *Church History: Studies in Christianity and Culture* 73, no. 1 (March 2004): 143.

by worldly praise, riches, and sexual promiscuity. Furthermore, it would stand in direct opposition to "the Church of the Lamb of God" by interfering with their missionary efforts, polluting scripture, and persecuting the Saints (even unto death).[11] The Book of Mormon identifies this abominable Church as the very same "mother of Harlots" described in the book of Revelation: "And the angel said unto me: Behold one of the twelve apostles of the Lamb [John]... he shall see and write the remainder of these things."[12] These "remaining" details that the book of Revelation describes include the "Whore" riding upon the back of a Beast (whose number is 666[13]):

> I saw a woman sit upon a scarlet coloured beast, full of names of blasphemy, having seven heads and ten horns. And the woman was arrayed in purple and scarlet colour, and decked with gold and precious stones and pearls, having a golden cup in her hand full of abominations and filthiness of her fornication: And upon her forehead [was] a name written, MYSTERY, BABYLON THE GREAT, THE MOTHER OF HARLOTS AND ABOMINATIONS OF THE EARTH.[14]

Many early Mormons, like contemporary Protestants, identified the foretold "Abominable Mother of Harlots" with the Catholic Church. Oliver Cowdery, who was among Joseph Smith's Jr.'s closest associates and confidants, was no exception.[15] In the church's official newspaper, *The Evening and the Morning Star*, Oliver Cowdery published an article denouncing the persecution of Mormons in Jackson County Missouri,

---

11. 1 Nephi 13-14; 22:13-14.
12. 1 Nephi 14:20-21, 27.
13. Rev. 14:20.
14. Rev. 17:3-5 KJV.
15. "[Reverend Ethan Smith] was minister of Poultney's Congregational church where he served from 21 November 1821 until December 1826. Cowdery's stepmother and three of his sisters were members of the congregation, according to Poultney church records." Richard Van Wagoner, *Sidney Rigdon: A Portrait of Religious Excess* (Salt Lake City: Signature Books, 1994), 465. Reverend Ethan Smith wrote, "Q[uestion]. 188. What is denoted by a harlot, or whore? A[nswer]. An apostate church; a system of religious imposition, or of real idolatry, under the Christian name. See Rev. xvii. 1-5 16. 18; where Popery is the mother of harlots;' and 'the great whore, with which the kings of the earth have committed fornication.' See also chap. xiv. 8. xviii. 9. On the other hand, chastity is an emblem of the purity of the protestant doctrines and worship from Papal corruption. See Rev. xiv. 4; where the true worshippers of God are said to be 'not defiled with women,' because they were pure from idolatry, the idolatry of the papal see." Ethan Smith, *A Key to the Figurative Language Found in the Sacred Scriptures* (New Hampshire: C. Norris & Co., 1814), 65, http://olivercowdery.com/texts/ethn1814.htm (accessed 30 October 2008).

while simultaneously associating the Catholic Church with the "Whore of Babylon," and rebuking it for a number of sinful acts:

> The popes and priests of the Romish church have sought, (more particularly perhaps in former days,) to keep the true knowledge of the word of God from their flocks.... And instead of teaching their congregations the doctrine of the bible, they have taught them a long round of whims and fabulous traditions.

Ultimately Cowdery blames Catholic influence for the persecutions Mormons had experienced, despite the fact that they had largely come from Protestant hands. "A strange notion has almost invariably pervaded the minds of men—a wild desire to seek the blood of the innocent. What urges men on to the commission of such inhuman acts?" asks Cowdery. "Did the Lord Jesus in all his communications from heaven to earth ever command it? No! Who does, or ever did? *POPES* and *PRIESTS!*"[16]

Eliza R. Snow, polygamous wife to both Joseph Smith Jr. and Brigham Young, and sister to Apostle (and later LDS Church President) Lorenzo Snow, also saw the Catholic Church as a major obstacle to missionary work. "I can see no hope for millions of people under the training of the 'Mother of Harlots,' and the influence of priestcraft, but through the ordinance of the dead."[17]

Apostle John Taylor, also a future LDS Church president, reported the common Protestant disregard for Catholicism, saying:

> The Protestants believe the Catholics are all in error, and pack the whole church off to hell as the mother of harlots, without any trouble, or without a sigh.

Like mother, like daughters, claims Taylor:

---

16. Oliver Cowdery, "The Outrage in Jackson County Missouri," *Evening and Morning Star* 2, no. 18 (March, 1834), 137, In *LDS Library 2006*. The phrase "Popes and Priests" is further notable here, due to its appearance in the LDS endowment ceremony. Prior to its 1990 deletion from the LDS temple ceremony drama, the character of Satan declared his plan to purchase "popes and priests," and rule the earth with violence and horror. See "The LDS Endowment: The Garden (1990)," *The LDS Endowment*, http://www.ldsendowment.org/garden.html (accessed 30 October 2008).

17. Eliza R. Snow in a letter to Mrs. Jane S. Richards (January 1, 1873); as cited in Grow, *Whore of Babylon*, 146.

The old mother is just as charitable towards her daughters, for they are her offspring, and she sends the whole of them unceremoniously to the same place.[18]

Apostle Parley P. Pratt expressed anti-Catholic views in a letter written to Brigham Young (1852), describing his missionary struggles in Chile, and blaming Catholicism for his failures. Pratt found it difficult to convince investigators the truthfulness of "the Book of Mormon... the evils of adultery, drunkenness, gambling, and other sins, and the wickedness of the Catholic abominations." He lamented:

> For three centuries, all intellect has slept, and all freedom of thought been crushed-buried-under the incubus of the horrid institutions of the great Mother of Abominations.[19]

Apostle Orson Pratt held equal—if not greater—contempt for Catholicism than his older brother Parley. In a missionary periodical of which he was editor, Orson Pratt posed the direct question, "Who founded the Roman Catholic Church?" He answered the question bluntly:

> The Devil, through the medium of Apostates, who subverted the whole order of God by denying immediate revelation, and substituting in the place thereof, tradition and ancient revelations as a sufficient faith and practice.

He further argued that Protestant denominations could not be true Christianity either, since these denominations derived their corrupt authority from the "Mother of Harlots."[20] Orson Pratt, however, later expanded this appellation of the Great and Abominable Mother of Harlots to include all Protestants,[21] the United States, and the European nations together.[22] This eventual amalgamation to include all organizations (both secular and religious) that stood in opposition of the Church be-

---

18. John Taylor (1853), *Journal of Discourses*, 1: 154; as cited in Grow, *Whore of Babylon*, 147.
19. Parley P. Pratt, *Autobiography of Parley P. Pratt* (Salt Lake City, Deseret Book, 1985), 366, 368.
20. Orson Pratt, *The Seer* (1853-54; repr., Salk Lake City: Eborn Books, 2000), 205.
21. Pratt believed that Protestantism consisted of "666 different Christian denominations," the number of the Beast! Orson Pratt (1872), *Journal of Discourses*, 14 : 347; as cited in Grow, *Whore of Babylon*, 146.
22. Pratt, *The Seer*, 246, 255.

came a popular trend among Latter-day Saints. Mormon scholar Matthew Grow explains:

> As the national campaign to crush polygamy intensified in the 1870s and 1880s, Latter-day Saint leaders further broadened the definition of the 'great and abominable' church to include American society.[23]

Some Latter-day Saints, however, like the early Mormon pioneer Benjamin F. Johnson, were resistant to this shift. In a letter to George F. Gibbs in 1903, Johnson reports that early Mormons had "regarded the Catholic church as the great head of priestcraft and hypocracy [sic]." Johnson then says:

> And so far as I am personally concerned, I am hardly rid of that view and feeling yet, that they are really but 'garnished sepulchers' filled with the bones of a dead and rotten past.[24]

Condemning Catholics, not the Cross

It is significant to note that despite their employment of Protestant anti-Catholic rhetoric, the condemnation of the cross is noticeably absent in the early years of Mormonism. Contrary to what one would expect all commentary on the symbol seems to have been neutral or positive. Even while condemning idolatry the Saints refrain from making targeted rejections of the cross.

Parley P. Pratt, for example, condemns idolatry but makes a distinction between American Catholicism and the kind of Catholicism that exists outside the United States. He asserts that because of the "influence" of Protestantism, Catholics in the States are not as guilty of the

---

23. Grow, *Whore of Babylon*, 147. For a contemporary LDS interpretation, see Stephen E. Robinson, "Nephi's 'Great and Abominable Church,'" *Journal of Book of Mormon Studies* 7, no. 1 (Provo: FARMS, 1998): 32-39.
24. Benjamin F. Johnson, Letter to George F. Gibbs (1903). Moses Thatcher alluded to a belief that the Roman Catholic church was this abominable Church, charging that the Mexicans had "become gross, dark and dull, having for nearly four hundred years been fettered with such bondage of body and soul, as only the 'mother of harlots' can invent and inflict." Moses Thatcher, Mexico City, to Junius F. Wells, 4 August 1881, "Correspondence," *The Contributor* 2 (September 1881): 381; as cited in Grow, *Whore of Babylon*, 145. A year later, however, he asked, "Who shall decide which is the 'man of sin,' the Roman Church or the Protestant Christian nation of the United States?" Moses Thatcher, "Mormon Polygamy and Christian Monogamy," *The Contributor* 3 (June 1882): 263; as cited in Grow, *Whore of Babylon*, 147.

sin—unlike those in other nations who live under the close theocratic control of the Roman Church. "[G]o to Chili, Spain, or any other of the states or nations where the Roman cross... is the standard," says Pratt, "where there are no Protestant influences and Protestant dissensions to interfere with the prevailing power.... In such countries... you will see more fully exhibited the practice of worshipping images."[25]

Brigham Young, while also speaking against idolatry, expressed a more nuanced and sympathetic view that rather judiciously undermined flagrant iconoclasm:

> [Catholics] have paintings and images in their chapels.... But those representations were introduced in the same way that a father would show his children that Jesus Christ is actually a man like their father, by showing them a [crucifix]... and saying, "This gives you, my children, an idea that he was a man." Now... how long would it be before some of their neighbours' children would tell their mothers that those children were worshipping a picture or image? This is the way that idolatry has sprung up in the world, through a method established to keep the people in remembrance of the God they once worshipped and were acquainted with.[26]

In other words, according to Brigham Young, the use of images (like the cross or crucifix) is not the problem. The problem exists in forgetting that a symbol is a representation of something far greater, and believing

---

25. Parley P. Pratt (1855), *Journal of Discourses*, 3: 39.
26. Brigham Young (1858), *Journal of Discourses*, 6: 195. Brigham Young also taught, "The secret of their [Catholicism's] great success is no doubt in their strict observance of outward ordinances and ceremonies. But while they go to one extreme in the observance of ceremony, making bigots of their children, (for one of the earliest recollections of the child, who is reared in Catholicism, is the use of the sign of the cross) many of the Latter-day Saints go to the other, failing entirely to impress the minds of their children with that degree of reverence and sacredness that belongs to the ordinances of our Church." Brigham Young (1877), *Journal of Discourses*, 19: 222. It is unlikely that Brigham Young's claim—that Catholic children are "bigots" for making the sign of the cross—is a condemnation of the symbol of the cross itself, since (as shall be discussed later in this book) Brigham Young's wife Amelia Folsom Young and a few of his daughters (Nabby, Talula Young, etc.) openly wore crosses, the official Church brand was a cross, and several church buildings were built in a cruciform design. Rather, it seems Young is simply criticizing the excessiveness of the Catholic ritual (as he perceives it), regularly crossing oneself. The 1828 Webster's Dictionary defines "Bigot" as "A person who is obstinately and unreasonably wedded to a particular... practice or ritual." *Webster's Dictionary* (1828), http://1828.mshaffer.com/d/word/bigot (accessed 20 November 2008).

that the symbol is the end itself. He warns his followers that if they are not careful, they can just as easily forget and do the same.[27]

Taking a slightly different approach, Apostle Charles W. Penrose taught that Catholic idolatry lies not in the mere use of images, since they (perhaps speaking specifically of the American flavor) do not worship them. Rather, idolatry happens when God is perceived inaccurately; in a way that has little or no revelatory basis:

> When [a Roman Catholic] bows down before the image of... the Savior upon the cross, he does not profess to worship the picture or the image; these are merely methods to lead the mind to something beyond what the natural eye sees.... But then, these various deities which people worship are, after all, the emanation of their own minds; they are gods of their own invention.[28]

Paradoxically, *The Times and Seasons,* an official Mormon newspaper based in Nauvoo, published an article (1845) speaking favorably of the cross while condemning the actions of anti-Catholic iconoclasts. Titled "The Cross of Our Savior," the article describes a scene of outrage over a simple "cross (+)" that a young boy drew on "a sheet of printing paper, and hung it out the window."

> It had not hung there five minutes, when a... mob surrounded our office, hooting like incarnate fiends as they pointed to the cross, and clamoring madly for the destruction of the building in front of which it hung! And this, because an Emblem of the Death and Redemption

---

27. Brigham Young states, "Yet it can readily be understood that if this people should backslide, they would, as others have, introduce an idolatrous worship." Ibid. Young's relatively friendly and diplomatic approach in addressing Catholic issues during his leadership of the Church earned him a reputation of being an admirer of the Church of Rome. One writer even quoted Brigham Young as saying the following about an early Catholic Priest: "I am certain I did all a man could do to convert your priest to my religion, and without any success. But I am not so certain that he could not have converted me to the Catholic faith had he remained long enough and tried hard enough." Mother Austin Carrol, "Forty Years in the American Wilderness," *American Quarterly Catholic Review* 15 (1890): 145; as cited in Grow, *Whore of Babylon,* 158. Historian Matthew Grow comments, "In addition, several authors described the friendly relations of the Scanlan era, especially the assistance and kindness of Young to Catholic priests and nuns, to argue that Catholicism was in a unique position to assist the Saints." Grow, *Whore of Babylon,* 158. Catholic Father Lawrence Scanlan came to Utah in 1873, appointed as pastor of the Catholic Church. He became the first Bishop of Utah (1887) and died in 1915. See Robert J. Dwyer, "Pioneer Bishop: Lawrence Scanlan, 1843-1915," *Utah Historical Quarterly* 20 (1952): 135-58.

28. Charles W. Penrose (1883), *Journal of Discourses,* 23: 343-44.

of the LORD JESUS was hung from the window! The CROSS, which symbols universal love, became the object of the hatred of a mob, who are ripe for any deed of blood, any act of outrage!... [A] sudden gust of wind tore the paper on which the cross was pasted, from the bricks of the building, and it fell into the hands of the mob. The tore it to fragments, with curses and yells. Ere an instant a hundred hands grasped the symbol of Salvation, and shook its fragments in the air with brutal hurrahs and frenzied yells.... This little incident speaks for itself."[29]

Exactly why early Mormons omitted[30] targeted criticisms of the cross from the anti-Catholic polemics they echoed isn't entirely clear, but evidence suggests at least three contributing factors. They were reluctant to condemn the cross symbol because: (1) Early Latter-day Saints were involved in folk-magic, and (2) Freemasonry, which encouraged the use of symbols like the cross; (3) Pre-Columbian natives used the symbol, and this (in the minds of Mormons) validated the authenticity of the Book of Mormon.

---

29. "The Cross of Our Savior," *Times and Seasons* 6, no. 1 (15 April 1845), 874-875, In *New Mormon Studies*.

30. The earliest Mormon negative view of the cross that the author has found dates 1877: "The Hebrew symbol is not the cross, but the sceptre. The Hebrews know nothing of the cross. It is the symbol of heathenism, whence Rome received her signs and her worship. Rome adopted the cross and she has borne it as her mark." Edward W. Tullidge, *Women of Mormondom* (New York, 1877), 79, http://www.archive.org/details/womenofmormondomootullrich (accessed 7 April 2009). Ironically, a symbol of the cross (and serpent) is displayed on the title page of this edition. Although he was officially a Brighamite at the time of this volume's publication, Tullidge had a history of instability in the Church, and soon joined the Reorganized Church. President John Taylor rebuked Tullidge, saying, "[W]hen in the East, you are an apostate, because it is expected your book will sell better, and here you are a Saint, because to be a Saint pays better." Tullidge replied, "I repudiate your remarks." Taylor then forbade him from accessing the historian's office. *Messages of the First Presidency of the Church of Jesus Christ of Latter-day Saints* (Salt Lake City: Bookcraft, 1965-75), 2: 316; see Ronald W. Walker, "Edward Tullidge: Historian of the Mormon Commonwealth," *Journal of Mormon History* 3 (1976): 55-72.

CHAPTER THREE

Mormon Magic, Freemasonry, and the Cross

MORMONS WERE RELUCTANT to condemn the cross, in part, because of their involvement in folk-magic and Freemasonry. It can be argued persuasively that one reason why magic and masonry were so popular in the United States was because they provided outlets for those who felt unsatisfied and restricted by the sterilization of Protestantism. "When Protestant leaders deinstitutionalized mystical, magical, and sensory aspects of religion," says Mormon commentator Val Rust, "the common, ordinary believer simply turned to sources of mystical experiences outside the church."[1] Arthur M. Schlesinger, similarly remarks:

> The plain citizens sometimes wearied of his plainness and, wanting rites as well as rights, hankered for the ceremonials, grandiloquent titles, and exotic costumes of a mystic brotherhood.[2]

---

1. Val D. Rust, *Radical Origins: Early Mormon Converts And Their Colonial Ancestors* (Chicago: University of Illinois Press, 2004), 118. Thomas Wentworth Higginson, a Spiritualist who had converted from Unitarianism, reported in 1859, "When the minister of a cold, conservative church preaches his last closing climax of sermons against spiritualism, he little knows that the church membership who sit patiently beneath him, more than one half are spiritualists already in their hearts." Thomas W. Higginson, *The Results of Spiritualism* (New York, 1859), 19; as cited in Jon Butler, "Magic, Astrology, and the Early American Religious Heritage, 1600-1760," *American Historical Review* 84, no. 2 (April 1979): 346.

2. Arthur M. Schlesinger, "Biography of a Nation of Joiners," *American Historical Review* 50, no.1 (October 1944): 15.

Early Mormonism and Folk-Magic

Scholars have published a vast amount of material that leave little room for doubt that early Latter Day Saints were involved in a certain level of magic and other esoteric practices. The point of disagreement between historians, critics, and apologists, however, is the exact nature of those beliefs and practices, and the impact that they had on the Church.[3] We know that Joseph Smith Jr.'s family, while living in Vermont, Massachusetts, New Hampshire, and New York, had exposure to occult arts commonly practiced at the time.[4] In his ground-breaking work on the topic, *Early Mormonism and the Magic World View*, D. Michael Quinn asserts that the Smith family "was typical of many early Americans who practiced various forms of Christian folk magic."[5] Corroborating evidence (weak and strong) confirms this about Joseph Smith and his family.

Affidavits accused the Smith family of being so involved in magical treasure hunting that they neglected the upkeep of their farm and the fulfillment of their daily duties. Joseph Smith's mother, Lucy Mack Smith, defended her family against the claim that they were irresponsible neighbors, but then she simultaneously concedes implicitly (while using language that indicates a familiarity with magical practices) that they were indeed involved in less time consuming magical activities:

> [L]et not my reader suppose that because I shall pursue another topic for a season that we stopt our labor and went <at> tryin=g to win the faculty of Abrac[,] drawing Magic circles or sooth saying to the neglect of all kinds of bu<i>sness we never during our lives suffered one important interest to swallow up every other obligation but wilst we

---

3. Faithful Mormon historian Richard Bushman expresses concern in an interview about the more conservative Latter-day Saints who are uncomfortable with this magical influence in early Mormonism, saying, "They think my book [*Rough Stone Rolling*] gives altogether too much credit to magic. I hope we can overcome that. There is nothing malicious about magic. It is a form of supernaturalism that the people the world over have believed in; and the people who have studied magical practices from times past find much that is admirable. Like there is in Freemasonry. It is not the devil's tool. It is a form of human questing for powers beyond themselves." Richard L. Bushman, "Joseph Smith and the Translation of the Book of Mormon," *Mormon Stories Podcast* 049 (interview by John Dehlin, 2007), http://mormonstories.org/ (accessed 21 August 2008).

4. D. Michael Quinn, *Early Mormonism and the Magic World View* (Salt Lake City: Signature Books, 1998), 39.

5. Ibid., 30.

worked with our hands we endeavored to remmember [sic] the service of & the welfare of our souls.⁶

Historian Richard Bushman agrees that Lucy Smith's statement confirms the Smith family's involvement in folk magic:

> Lucy's point was that the Smiths were not lazy—but she showed her knowledge of formulas and rituals and associated them with the "welfare of our souls." Magic and religion melded in Smith family culture.⁷

Before and after initiating his prophetic career, Joseph Smith used seer-stones ("peep-stones"),⁸ divining rods, and healing objects. He also wore talismanic protective undergarments, practiced forms of necromancy, married several (if not all)⁹ of his polygamous wives on days that had favorable astrological significance, was involved in treasure hunting in his youth,¹⁰ and may have practiced alchemy.¹¹

---

6. Lucy Mack Smith, "Preliminary Manuscript" (1845), *Early Mormon Documents*, 1: 285 [original spelling and punctuation retained].

7. Bushman, *Joseph Smith: Rough Stone Rolling*, 50-51.

8. Joseph Smith was summoned to court, and tried and convicted for a misdemeanor offence of "glass looking" and (presumably) treasure hunting in 1826. The court record reads:

    same vs Joseph Smith
    The Glass Looker
    March 20, 1826
    Misdemeanor
    To my fees in examination of the above cause 2.68

Robert N. Hullinger, *Joseph Smith's Response to Skepticism* (Salt Lake City: Signature Books, 1992), 104. "Alva Hale, a son in the household where the Smiths in Harmony while digging for Stowell, said Joseph Jr. told him that the 'gift in seeing with a stone' was 'a gift from God' but that 'peeping was all d—d nonsense'; he had been deceived in his treasure-hunting, but he did not intend to deceive anyone else," explains Richard Bushman. "By this time [1825], Joseph apparently felt that 'seeing' with a stone was the work of a 'seer,' a religious term, while 'peeping' or 'glass-looking' was fraudulent." Bushman, *Joseph Smith: Rough Stone Rolling*, 51.

9. We only have evidence of exact or probable dates for seventeen of Smith's wives. All seventeen of these marriages have dates of favorable astrological significance. See Quinn, *Early Mormonism and the Magic World View*, 76.

10. Joseph Smith's interest in treasure hunting seems to have also shown up in the Book of Mormon: "Yea, we have hid up our treasures and they have slipped away from us, because of the curse of the land" (Helaman 13:33-36); "[T]he inhabitants thereof began to hide up their treasures in the earth; and they became slippery, because the Lord had cursed the land, that they could not hold them, nor retain them again" (Mormon 1:18).

11. See John L. Brooke, *The Refiner's Fire: The Making of Mormon Cosmology, 1644-1844* (Cambridge: Cambridge University Press, 1996); Lance S. Owens, "Joseph Smith and Kabbalah: The Occult Connection," *Dialogue* 27, no. 3 (Fall 1994): 117-194.

FIGURES 3.1 AND 3.2: *Image (top) from Heinrich Cornelius Agrippa's* Occult Philosophy *(1655) and image (bottom) from Francis Barrett's* The Magus *(1801).*

Much evidence also shows that several other early church members similarly practiced folk magic and were attracted to Mormonism because of the occult elements it possessed.[12] The depth and breadth of this topic is beyond the scope of this book, but it suffices to say that the standard ceremonial magic manuals likely available to the early Mormons all agree that the symbol of the cross has magical significance (see figures 3.1-3.4).

Treasure seekers in particular believed in the magical powers of the cross. According to treasure lore, "The mines in the valley of Ohio" were be protected by a "spell" or "charm" of the "single and double Spanish cross" placed by the "Spaniards, when they were forced to leave the country." "This was a common belief among the old mineral hunters of the West," explained a report in 1850. Upon finding the location with a divining instrument, treasure seekers would make:

> a circle on the surface of the ground round the spot, so large that the earth thrown out of the hole should not roll over the ring—nine new nails were then dropped into the ring at equal distances; while the operator, reading the chapter in the Apocrypha, where Raphael exorcises the devil, walked round the circle with the course of the sun. This... would entirely overcome the charm of "the Spanish cross," and the mine be brought to light.[13]

---

12. Quinn, *Early Mormonism and the Magic World View*, 239-42. See also Marvin S. Hill, "Money Digging Folklore and the Beginnings of Mormonism: And Interpretive Suggestion," *BYU Studies* 24 (Fall 1984): 473-488.

13. "History of the Divining Rod: With the Adventures of an Old Rodsman," *The United States Magazine and Democratic Review* (March 1850), vol 26, no 141, p. 225, http://books.google.com/books?id=C2MAAAAAYAAJ&pg=PA225 (accessed 18 March 2010).

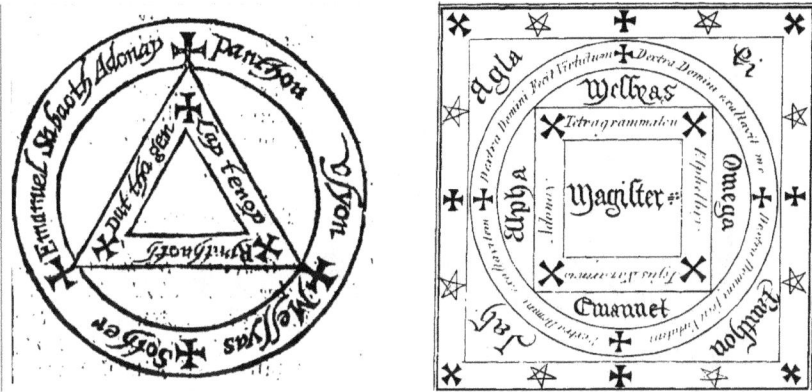

FIGURES 3.3 AND 3.4: *Image (left) from Reginald Scot's 1584 exposé entitled* Discovery of Witchcraft *and image (right) from Ebenezer Sibl[e]y's* New and Complete Illustration of the Occult Sciences *(c. 1795).*

A neighbor to the Smith family, William Stafford, participated in a treasure hunt with the Smiths, and although he made no mention of the "Spanish Cross," he reported many other similar details about their expedition:

> Joseph, Sen. first made a circle, twelve or fourteen feet in diameter. This circle, said he, contains the treasure. He then stuck in the ground a row of witch hazel sticks, around the said circle, for the purpose of keeping off the evil spirits. Within this circle he made another, of about eight or ten feet in diameter. He walked around three times on the periphery of this last circle, muttering to himself something which I could not understand. He next stuck a steel rod in the centre of the circles, and then enjoined profound silence upon us, lest we should arouse the evil spirit who had the charge of these treasures.[14]

---

14. John Cook Bennett, *The History of the Saints: or, An exposé of Joe Smith and Mormonism* (Boston, 1842), 65, http://books.google.com/books?id=WGU0AAAAYAAJ&pg=PA65 (accessed 18 May 2010). Another variation of treasure seeking ritual describes the use of steel nails (or sharp rods) instead of witch hazel sticks, two circles instead of one, and even animal sacrifice: "Tak nine Steel Rods about ten or twelve inches in Length Sharp or Piked to Perce into the Erth, and let them be Besmeared with fresh blood from a hen mixed with hogdung. Then mak two surkels round the hid Treasure one of Sd surkles a Little Larger in Surcumference than the hid Treasure lays in the Erth the other Surkel Sum Larger still, and as the hid treasure is wont to move to the North of South, East or West Place your Rods as is

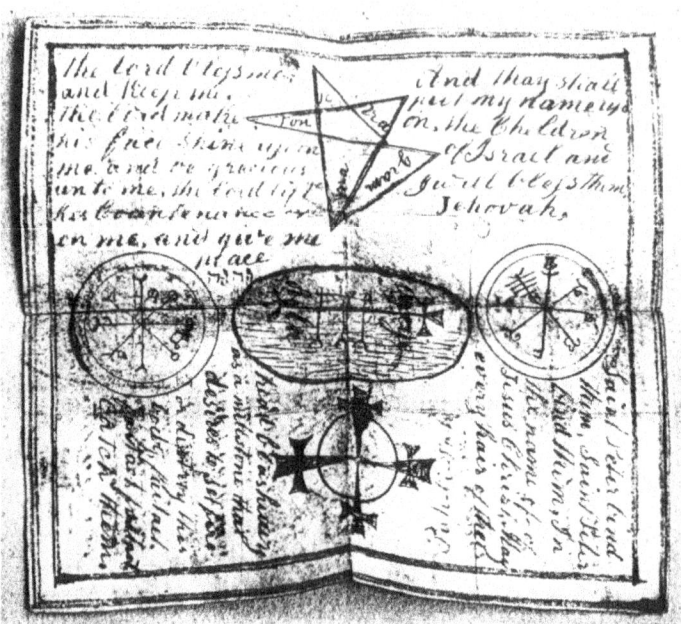

FIGURE 3.5: Smith family "Saint Peter Bind Them" parchment.

FIGURE 3.6: The Smith family's "Holiness to the Lord" parchment contains a number of symbols believed to have magic power, including three crosses (see detail at right).

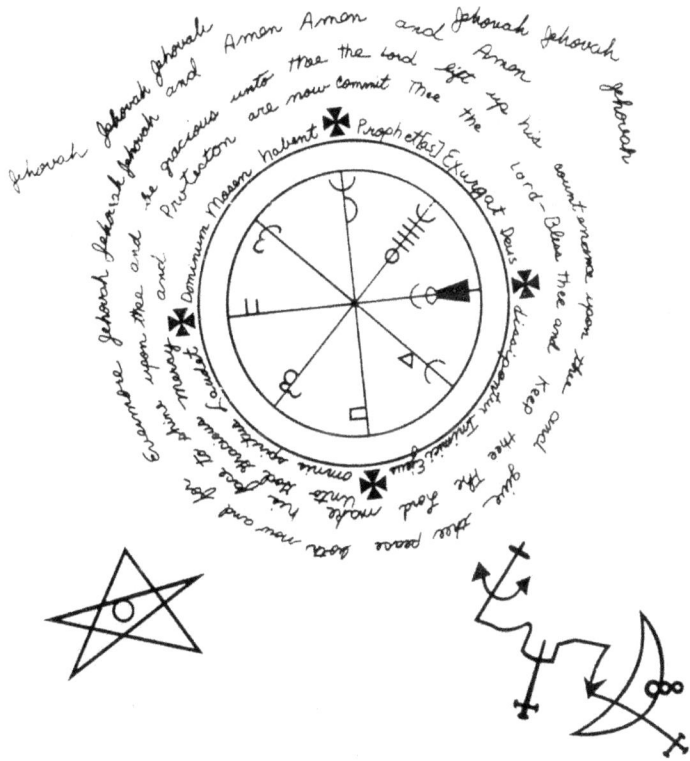

Figure 3.7: The Smith family's "Jehovah Jehovah Jehovah" parchment contains several crosses amid other symbols.

The "muttering" Stafford heard may have been Smith's recitation from the "Apocrypha, where Raphael exorcised the devil." But what of the cross? Did Smith's group believe the powers of the cross in any way play a role in their treasure seeking quests? Although Stafford does not answer this question, Smith family artifacts indicate that they did. Three magic parchments, which were almost certainly designed based on instructions and illustrations given in the aforementioned occult manuals, all have crosses drawn on them.

Discribed on the other Sid of this leaf." Clark Jillson, *Green Leaves from Whitingham, Vermont: A History of the Town* (Worcester, 1894), 119, http://books.google.com/books?id=G7ATAAAAYAAJ&pg=PA119 (accessed 18 May 2010).

Notable among these is the "Holiness to the Lord" parchment (see figure 3.6) that not only has three crosses drawn side by side, but these three crosses are adjacent to a Raphael figure. Quinn comments on the three crosses and Raphael figure, while arguing persuasively that the Smith family indeed used these artifacts for treasure seeking and divination:

> Another symbol shows that this "Holiness to the Lord" magic parchment was for invoking "good spirits" in connection with treasure-seeking. Directly to the right of the Raphael figure and above the Tetragrammaton figure are three crosses [see the image to the right for a magnified view].... These faintly drawn crosses could refer to the crucifixion at Golgotha, yet [Reginald] Scot specified that three crosses were used for treasure-seeking.[15]

Regarding the use of the cross to "invoke good spirits," an anecdote reported in the diary of early Mormon Zebedee Coltrin may have some relevance. According to Coltrin, he and Oliver Cowdery were walking with Joseph Smith outside one day when Smith stopped by some wild grape vines and said, "Let us kneel down here and pray." After the completion of the prayer, "Joseph stretched himself on his back upon a grassy spot with his arms extended like one upon a cross. He told me to lie by his side with my head resting upon his arm, and Oliver in like manner upon the other side"—thereby making the form of three crosses. "We did so," said Coltrin, "all three looking heavenwards. As I looked I saw the blue sky open. I beheld a throne, and upon the throne sat a man and a woman. Joseph asked us if we knew who they were. We answered 'no,' Joseph said, 'That is father Adam and mother Eve.'"[16]

Back to Quinn's statement that the three crosses were "used for treasure-seeking." This symbolism appears in a collection of short stories about "Money-Diggers," written pseudonymously by the American author Washington Irving. Published in 1824, and claiming the stories to have been originally "found among the papers of the late [Dutch historian] Diedrich Knickerbocker,"[17] Washington Irving weaved elaborate

---

15. Quinn, *Early Mormonism and the Magic World View*, 112.
16. Zebedee Coltrin, "Diary Excerpts of Zebedee Coltrin" (1878), In *New Mormon Studies*.
17. Geoffrey Crayon (pseud.), *Tales of a Traveller* (London, 1824), 2:231. Washington Irving published the two volumes under a second pseudonym Geoffrey Crayon. These volumes includ-

details related to the treasure seeker activity and folklore of antebellum America.[18] Among the narratives, the story of *The Adventure of the Black Fisherman* describes a band of treasure seekers who come upon an area marked by "three mystic crosses."[19] A member of the band created divining rod, manipulated it to find the exact location of the treasure, drew a circle, and then instructed his associates to dig at the designated spot.[20]

Utah folklore collections contain several catalogued traditions illustrating beliefs in the cross having magical binding power. One such example pertains to the action of four people simultaneously shaking hands in the form of a cross. According to the superstition, when this is done, someone in that group "is going to get married." Eighty-seven year old Latter-day Saint, Eliza Zollinger (1884–1978), born of pioneer ancestry and living in Providence Utah, reported this, claiming, "She didn't believe it, but her parents did."[21] Another VeNeal J. Jenkins (1912–1992) of Cachem, Utah reported how her cousins would tell her, "To make a man love you, you should somehow get his hat. Then you must turn the inside sweatband down and place two needles crossed inside where he won't find them. When he wears his hat again, he'll love you."[22]

---

ed the section (part iv) about "Money-Diggers" that was purportedly a compilation of articles/stories originally written by a Dutch historian named Diedrich Knickerbocker. People read these stories with great interest, not realizing that they were actually fictional narratives.

18. Among such details that may be of particular interest to Mormon history scholars, Washington Irving notes the folk-belief that the spiritual guardians of buried treasure could take on the form of animals, such as toads. "Wild vines entangled the trees, and flaunted in their faces; brambles and briers caught their clothes as they passes; the garter snake glided across their path; the spotted toad hopped and waddled before them; and the restless cat-bird mewed at them from every thicket. Had Wolfert Webber [a man in search of treasure, but who had no expertise in folk-magic] been deeply read in romantic legend, he might have fancied himself entering upon forbidden enchanted ground; or that these were some of the guardians set to keep watch upon buried treasure." Diedrich Knickerbocker (pseud.), "The Adventures of the Black Fisherman," *Tales of a Traveller*, 2: 356. According to Willard Chase, Joseph Smith Sr. told him that angel Moroni initially had the form of "something like a toad, which soon assumed the appearance of a man, and struck him on the side of his head." Willard Chase (1833); as quoted in Eber D. Howe, *Mormonism Unvailed* [sic] (Painesville Ohio: Telegraph Press, 1834), 242, http://solomonspalding.com/docs/1834howf.htm#pg221 (accessed 1 July 2010).

19. Knickerbocker (pseud.), "The Adventures of the Black Fisherman," *Tales of a Traveller*, 2: 375.

20. Ibid., 369.

21. Folklore Collection 8a: group 2, box 8 folder 25 (item 7.3.0.1), Utah State University Special Collections and Archives.

22. Ibid., folder 21 (item 7.1.13), Utah State University Special Collections and Archives.

Unfortunately, certain biographical information is lacking in many of these catalogued entries, thereby making it difficult (if not impossible) to determine which of the traditions Mormons believed and circulated, and how early such folklore may have existed in Mormon circles.[23]

Early Mormons and Freemasonry

The Smiths and several early Saints were also involved in (and influenced by) Freemasonry—which perhaps should not be treated as a mutually exclusive influence, as several branches of Freemasonry were experimenting with folk magic, at times adopting various elements into their fraternities.[24] One Masonic official observed that some of the younger Masons "were 'so in love with mysteries' that they did not care where they came from,"[25] and it is quite telling that Ebenezer Sibley even dedicated his occult manual to "the Ancient and Honourable fraternity of Free and Accepted Masons."[26] Lucy Smith's previously noted statement about her family's treasure seeking adventures, and "winn[ing] the faculty of Abrac," may indicate a conflation of Freemasonry and folk-

---

23. Most entries that pertain to the cross in the USU folklore collection predict favorable outcomes.

24. Some artifacts, such as the Jupiter talisman that Joseph Smith reportedly wore at the time he was killed, have been identified as having both Magical and Masonic significance. See Homer, "Similarity of Priesthood," 3, 96; and Reed C. Durham, Jr., "Is there No Help for the Widow's Son?" *Presidential Address at the Mormon History Association Convention* (April 20, 1974), http://www.cephasministry.com/mormon_is_there_no_help.html (accessed 20 May 2010).

25. Carnes, *Secret Ritual and Manhood*, 6. This eclecticism fits the prophet Joseph Smith like a glove. The prophet taught, "One of the grand fundamental principles of 'Mormonism' is to receive truth, let it come from whence it may." Joseph Smith (July 9, 1843), *History of the Church of Jesus Christ of Latter-day Saints*, 5: 499.

26. Allen G. Debus, "Scientific Truth and Occult Tradition: The Medical World of Ebenezer Sibley (1751-1799)," *Medical History* 26 (1982): 261. A French anti-Mason reports, "To captivate their [Ginii's/angels] favor, the Cabalistic Mason is to study what we should call the Conjuring-book. He must be well versed in the names and signs of the planets and constellations; he must also know whether it be a good or evil Genius which presides over it, and which are the numbers that represent them... [T]he Cabalistic Mason will be favoured by these good and evil Gennii, in proportion to the confidence he has in their power; they will appear to him, and they will explain more to him in the magic table, than the human understanding can conceive." Abbe Baurrl, *Memoirs, Illustrating the History of Jacobinism: A Translation from the French of The Abbe Barruel* 2 (New York, 1799): 182-83, http://books.google.com/books?id=v-wvAAAAMAAJ (accessed 16 November 2008).

magic in the minds of the Smith family, as this particular phrase was quite uncommon anywhere outside of Masonic discourse.[27]

Although Joseph Smith may not have been directly involved with Freemasonry until he was raised a Mason "on sight" with Sidney Rigdon in 1842, he almost certainly would have had much exposure to it decades before in the "Burned-over District" where he and his family lived during his childhood.[28] As one historian of the period notes:

> Countless churches during the late 1820s and 1830 in the "burned-over district" of western New York featured exposés of Masonic secrets.[29]

It is reasonable to assume that these exposés would have been of particular interest to young Joseph, since his brother Hyrum joined Freemasonry in the 1820s.[30]

---

27. John E. Thomson, "The Facultie of Abrac: Masonic Claims and Mormon Beginnings," *The Philalethes Society* (December 1982), http://www.masonicmoroni.com/Philalethes/facultie_of_abrac.htm (accessed 29 June 2011). John L. Brooke reports that at least one member of Smith's treasure digging comrades was a Royal Arch Mason who had been "expelled for 'unmasonic conduct' in 1825. Given the subsequent history of William Morgan, the Antimasonic martyr, one wonders whether this conduct involved the divulging of the ritual secrets of the Royal Arch to the money-digger circles." Perhaps Smith's associates even incorporated certain Masonic elements into their treasure-digging rituals. John L. Brooke, *The Refiner's Fire*, 158.

28. Independent scholar Nick Literski writes, "While it is true that Joseph was initiated as a Mason in 1842, he already had a lifetime of exposure to the Fraternity and its legends. Several family members were Masons. Joseph was a mere 9 miles from the epicenter of the Morgan scandal, and was exposed to considerable media attention on the subject, not to mention public re-enactments of masonic ceremonies. It may be technically correct to say Joseph was not 'involved' in Masonry until his initiation, but to do so is a half-truth at best, which can only mislead the reader." Nick Literski, *Re: Search for the Truth, Anti-Mormon DVD* (March 25, 2007), http://www.millennialstar.org/2007/03/24/search-for-the-truth-anti-mormon-dvd/ (accessed 6 November 2008).

29. Carnes, *Secret Ritual and Manhood*, 96-97. "Masonic publications, including Masonic newspapers, transplanted English- or American-born commentaries, and exposés by those opposing the Craft, enabled initiates and students of Freemasonry to become familiar with the philosophy [and rituals] of Freemasonry" before ever becoming a member of a particular order. Homer, *Similarity of Priesthood*, 16.

30. Homer, *Similarity of Priesthood in Masonry*, 15-16. Hyrum's given name may be an indication that Freemasonry had an appeal to the Smiths even before he was born in 1800. Says historian Steven Bullock about (non-Mormon) Hiram Hopkins, "The growing popularity of Hopkin's given name—Hiram, after the Masonic notables King Hiram or Tyre and Hiram Abiff—further suggest the growing appeal of the fraternity. Rare before the revolution, the name became common after the war." Steven C. Bullock, "A Pure and Sublime System: The Appeal of Post-Revolutionary Freemasonry," *Journal of the Early Republic* 9 (Fall 1989): 366. Hyrum Smith's official birth record (1803) records his given name as "Hiram": "Hiram son to Joseph & Lucy

Several future converts were also interested in Freemasonry. Scholar Michael W. Homer observes:

> Many others who eventually embraced Mormonism, joined Freemasonry during the 1820s, including...Heber C. Kimball (Victor Lodge No. 303, Victor, Ontario County, New York), Newell K. Whitney (Meridian Orb Lodge No. 10, Painesville, Lake County, Ohio), and George Miller (Widow's Son Lodge No. 60, Albemarle, Milton County, Virginia).[31]

And after Joseph Smith and Sidney Rigdon were formally initiated in 1842, many more Latter Day Saints became Masons, as Homer records:

> Within five months the Nauvoo Lodge had initiated 256 candidates and raised 243 others, which "was six times as many initiations and elevations as all the other lodges in the state combined."[32]

Five Mormon Lodges were established in Nauvoo—having a total of 1,366 Master Masons[33]—and by the time the Saints had left Nauvoo and arrived in Salt Lake (1847), says Homer, "most of the Mormon hierarchy were Master Masons."[34]

Joseph Smith and Brigham Young, believing that Freemasonry had a corrupt version of divinely instituted priesthood ordinances that derived from Solomon's temple, "expanded, revised, and restored the rituals of Freemasonry," and adapted them to LDS temple worship.[35] Joseph Smith and Brigham Young also adopted Masonic symbols as visual expressions of the Mormon faith, as Homer acknowledges:

> Mormons were hardly discreet in their depictions of symbols long associated with Freemasonry, including the square, the compass, the sun, moon, and stars, the beehive, the all-seeing eye, ritualistic hand grips, two interlaced triangles forming a six-pointed star (known as

---

Smith was born February ninth 1800 Likewise Sophrona daughter to the Joseph & Lucy Smith was born May 17th 1803 Certified by Joseph Smith Attest Saml Austin Town Clerk." *Record of Births, Deaths, Marriages, and Miscellaneous Items*, Book A, 402, Tunbridge Town Clerk's Office, Tunbridge, Vermont, in *Early Mormon Documents*, 1:638.

31. Homer, *Similarity of Priesthood in Masonry*, 15-16.
32. Ibid., 28-29.
33. Ibid., 32-33.
34. Ibid., 97.
35. Ibid., 38.

the seal of Solomon), and a number of other Masonic symbols on endowment houses, temples, cooperatives, grave markers, tabernacles, church meetinghouses, newspaper mastheads, hotels, residences, money, logos, and seals.[36]

Although the influence of Freemasonry on Mormonism is self-evident, some LDS scholars have attempted minimize or even deny the connections. For example, one Mormon apologist insists in a tract that Joseph Smith could not have possibly gotten the inverted pentagram for the Nauvoo Temple (1846) from Freemasonry, since the Order of the Eastern Star logo was not developed until after the construction of the temple.[37] This argument is false. It is true that the emblem of the Order of the Eastern Star was not created by Robert Morris until 1850, however, Freemasonry used the inverted star long before this creation.[38] In fact, Robert Morris had clearly explained that he got the idea of using the pentagram (pentagon) from the Masonic "Masters Carpet".[39]

---

36. Ibid.,73-74. According to Mormon historian Reed C. Durham, "There is absolutely no question in my mind that the Mormon ceremony which came to be known as the Endowment, introduced by Joseph Smith to Mormon Masons initially, just a little over one month after he became a Mason, had an immediate inspiration from Masonry. This is not to suggest that no other source of inspiration could have been involved, but the similarities between the two ceremonies are so apparent and overwhelming that some dependent relationship cannot be denied." Reed C. Durham, Jr., "Is there No Help for the Widow's Son?"

37. Matthew B. Brown asserts, "Some anti-Mormons claim that Joseph Smith 'stole' the inverted star design from the Freemasons. But the Order of the Eastern Star, which utilizes the inverted five-pointed star as its emblem, was not even conceived by Robert Morris until 1850—long after Joseph Smith's death." Matthew B. Brown, *Inverted Stars on LDS Temples* (FAIR, 2002), fn 8, http://www.fairlds.org/pubs/ Stars.pdf (accessed 6 November 2008).

38. For several examples, see *Masonic Symbols in American Decorative Arts*, ed. Louis L. Williams and Alphonse Cerza (Lexington: Scottish Rite Masonic Museum and Library, 1976).

39. Writes Robert Morris, "About the first of February, 1850, I was laid up for two weeks with a sharp attack of rheumatism, and it was this period which I gave to the great work at hand. By the aid of my papers and the memory of Mrs. Morris, I recall even the trivial occurrences connected with the work, how I hesitated for a theme, how I dallied over the name, how I wrought face to face with the clock that I might keep my drama within due limits of time, etc. The name was first settled upon—The Eastern Star. Next the number of points, five, to correspond with the emblem on the Master's carpet. This is the pentagon, 'The signet of King Solomon,' and eminently proper to Adoptive Masonry." Albert G. Mackey, *Encyclopedia of Freemasonry and Its Kindred Sciences* vol. 2 (New York: The Masonic History Company, 1921), 909. Matthew B. Brown's book, "Exploring the Connection Between Mormons and Masons" (Covenant Communications, Inc, 2009), is also overly concerned with disassociating the LDS temple endowment from Freemasonry. For a good review of this book, see Nick Literski's "Book Review: Exploring the Connection Between Mormons and Masons," *Mormon Matters*, http://mormonmatters.

FIGURE 3.8: *Pentagram windows on the replica Nauvoo Temple, surrounded by cruciform stonework (see detail at right).*

Joseph Smith left no direct statements to the effect that the pentagrams adorning the exterior of the Nauvoo Temple were derived from Freemasonry. However, it is possible to infer the migration of the symbol by considering the other symbols found in the temple's design, including the moonstones, sunstones, square and compass, and the angel atop the weather vane with trumpet in hand. None of these symbols had figured in the previous temple that Smith and his followers had constructed in Kirtland, Ohio. Just as the Nauvoo Endowment ritual only became a part of Mormon temple practice after Smith's induction into Freemasonry, so too these common Masonic symbols only figured in temple design after that induction.

Among the symbols adorning the Nauvoo Temple are cruciform stoneworks surrounding the pentagram windows in the building's upper frieze (see figure 3.8). Unlike the stoneworks around the temple's other windows and doors, the cruciform stoneworks project out from the temple wall. This projection is not necessary structural; the purpose

---

org/2009/10/29/book-review-exploring-the-connection-between-mormons-and-masons/ (accessed 15 March 2010).

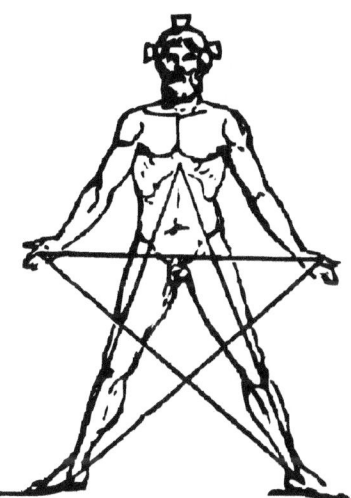

FIGURE 3.9: *The "Five Wounds of Christ" from George Oliver's "The Theocratic Philosophy of Freemasonry, in Twelve Lectures" (1840).*

is therefore decorative. The resulting effect calls special attention to the shape of the cross and connects it with the symbol of the pentagram.

There is reason to believe this correlation of symbols—pentagram and cross—is neither arbitrary nor coincidental. Christian Masons have argued that the pentagram symbolizes the "five wounds" that Jesus suffered while hanging on the cross. The pentagram has also been used to signify the "Five Points of Fellowship" used to raise Hyrum Abiff from the grave in Masonic mythology.[40] Likewise, in the Nauvoo endow-

---

40. Albert G. Mackey explains, "Freemasons of this country [the United States] have, by tacit consent, referred to it [the five-pointed star] as a symbol of the Five Points of Fellowship.""The early Christians referred it to the five wounds of the Saviour, because when properly inscribed upon the representation of the human body, the five points will respectively extend to and touch the side, the two hands, and the two feet." Albert G. Mackey, *Encyclopedia of Freemasonry*, 279, 570 (Philadelphia: Moss & Company, 1879), http://books.google.com/books?id=fAgIAAAAQAAJ&pg= (accessed 7 November 2008). See also George Oliver, *The Theocratic Philosophy of Freemasonry* (1853), 183, http://books.google.com/books?id=30MBAAAAQAAJ&pg=PA183 (accessed 10 May 2010); and Albert G. Mackey, "The Triangle as a Symbol," *The Masonic Eclectic: Gleanings from the Harvest Field of Masonic Literature* 1, no. 8. (April 1861), 376. http://books.google.com/books?id=z-E2AAAAMAAJ&pg=PA376 (accessed 10 May 2010). William Morgan gave the following details of this portion of the Masonic ritual: "He [the candidate] is raised on what is called the five points of fellowship.... This is done by putting the inside of your right foot to the inside of the right foot of the person to whom you are going to give the word, the inside of your knee to his, laying your right breast against his, your left hands on the back of each other, and your mouths to each other's right ear [in which position you are alone permitted to give the

ment, the initiate receives secret handshakes representing the wounds of Christ, and then assumes the position of the "Five Points of Fellowship" to obtain a password and pass through the veil—symbolic of resurrection and entering into the celestial kingdom of heaven.[41]

In 1845, Mormon Apostle Amasa Lyman explained that the tokens he received in the endowment directly correlate with the nail wounds that were inflicted on Jesus during the crucifixion:

> This is the Key by which to obtain all the glory and felicity of eternal life. It is the key by which you approach God. No impression which you receive here should be lost. It was to rivet the recollection of the tokens and covenants in your memory like a nail in a sure place, never to be forgotten.[42]

The connection in the temple endowment between the "Five Points of Fellowship" and the five wounds of the crucifixion, coupled with the common use of the pentagram to symbolize the "Five Points" and of the cross to symbolize the crucifixion, imply that their connection in the

---

word], and whisper the word MAH-HA-BONE." William Morgan, *Light on Masonry*, ed. David Bernard (1829), 69, http://books.google.com/books?id=QlIZAAAAYAAJ&pg=PA69&lpg=PA69 (accessed 7 November 2008).

41. The description of the position in the LDS ceremony (before the 1990 editing) is nearly identical to what exists in Freemasonry. See "The LDS Endowment: The Veil (1990)," http://www.ldsendowment.org/veil.html (accessed 8 November 2008). Joseph Smith was not alone in reinterpreting the Masonic ceremonies in a Christian context. One Masonic publication reports, "Our continental brethren identified Hiram Abiff with Jesus Christ, and endeavoured to prove that his history was an allegory of the Crucifixion." *The Freemasons' Quarterly Magazine and Review* (London, 1843), 16, http://books.google.com/books?id=mq8EAAAAQAAJ&q=&pgis=1 (accessed 2 April 2009). This same statement is quoted in the *Universal Masonic Library* vol 7, ed. Robert Macoy (New York, 1855), 72, http://books.google.com/books?id=IgBKAAAAMAAJ&pg=RA1-PA72&lpg=RA1-PA72&dp= (accessed 2 April 2009).

42. George D. Smith, *An Intimate Chronicle: The Journals of William Clayton* (Salt Lake City: Signature Books, 1995), 225. Brigham Young may have also alluded to this "riveting," when he stressed to missionaries the importance of having an appropriate frame of mind: "If you go on a mission to preach the gospel with lightness and frivolity in your hearts, looking for this and that, and to learn what is in the world, and not having your minds riveted on the cross of Christ, you will go and return in vain." Brigham Young (1867), *Journal of Discourses*, 12: 33. On a related note, George Miller (who was ordained the Second Bishop of the Church, and had become the Worshipful Master of the Masonic Nauvoo lodge) "spoke of the design and purpose for which all the Symbols in the garden [of Eden] were given &c. Paul said he bore in his body the marks of the Lord Jesus Christ, which was as plainly as he dare allude to these things in writing. But the marks Paul alluded to were just such as we now have on our garments. He spoke of the signs, tokens and penalties and of the work in general, said it was the work of God, by which he designs to reinstitute man into his presence &c." Ibid., 223.

temple's exterior is no accident. Instead, the pentagrams inscribed on windows within cruciform stoneworks appear pregnant with meaning, together symbolizing the endowment ritual itself.[43]

Another example of Joseph Smith using the cross in a magical or Masonic context is on his serpent walking cane (see figure 3.11). D. Michael Quinn comments on the engraved shield containing Smith's initials, and argues that the symbolism reveals a belief and involvement in astrology and talismanic magic. Quinn notes an "x" on the crown above the shield and says that although some may think this is Saint Andrew's cross, there are no other Christian symbols on the cane—unless you in-

---

43. At least one report even claimed that sign associated with the fourth token was called "the crucifixion." See J.H. Wallis, Sr. testimony in the Reed Smoot Hearings (13 December 1904). Congressional Edition vol. 4933 (Washington: Government Printing Office, 1906), p. 78, http://books.google.com/books?id=nABHAQAAIAAJ&pg=PA78 (accessed 4 February 2012). Wallis allegedly went through the endowment approximately twenty times between 1895 and 1898. Identifying this sign in such a way, however, is not explicit in the ritual today. See also Stuart Martin, *The Mystery of Mormonism* (London, 1920), 261. Since this sign also functions as an animated prayer posture during the endowment, the previous section's commentary on the Zebedee Coltrin visionary account, and the cross being used for invoking "good spirits," may be connected. Wandle Mace, an architect who had designed the wooden framework for the Nauvoo Temple, described the temple as representing the *Bride of Christ* in Revelation 12: "The order of architecture was unlike anything in existence; it was purely original, being a representation of the Church, the Bride, the Lamb's wife. John, the Revelation in the 12 chapter, first verse says, 'And there appeared a great wonder in heaven; a woman clothed with the sun, and the moon under her feet, and upon her head a crown of twelve stars.' This is portrayed in the beautifully cut stone of this grand temple." Wandel Mace, *Autobiography of Wandle Mace*, p.207, In *New Mormon Studies*. It should be observed that Mace is specifically talking about the symbols "cut in stone," illustrated on the temple's stone pilasters. The pentagram windows are not mentioned in his description. Incidentally, some Masons, who were especially influenced by the teachings of Emmanuel Swedenborg, associated Freemasonry with the New Jerusalem and the Bride of Christ. They quoted Emanuel Swedenborg's prophetic declaration, "[T]he Lord has opened the eyes of my mind; he has reveled to me the inward meaning of the Holy Scriptures, and he has ordered me to announce the approaching establishment of his new church, which is the New Jerusalem." The Mason authors then supported Swedenborg's claim, saying, "We find the following, written down in the rituals of that heaven in whose secret places Swedenborg learnt all we have just heard: 'The New Jerusalem represents ancient Freemasonry, which comes down from heaven to replace the ancient Temple.'... [T]he twelve stars, round the head of the candidate [being initiated], are the very same twelve stars which shine round the head of the august lady of the Revelations; who is here transformed into a man.'Twelve golden stars on the fillet of the candidate.''A woman clothed with the sun, and the moon under her feet, and upon her head a crown of twelve stars.'—(Rev. xii. 1.)" Bishop Gabriel P. Rossetti, *Disquisitions on the Antipapel [sic] Spirit Which Produced the Reformation* vol. 2, translated by Caroline Ward (London, 1834), 181-182, http://books.google.com/books?id=gdcAAAAAcAAJ&pg=PA181&dq=#PPA181,M1 (accessed 30 March 2009).

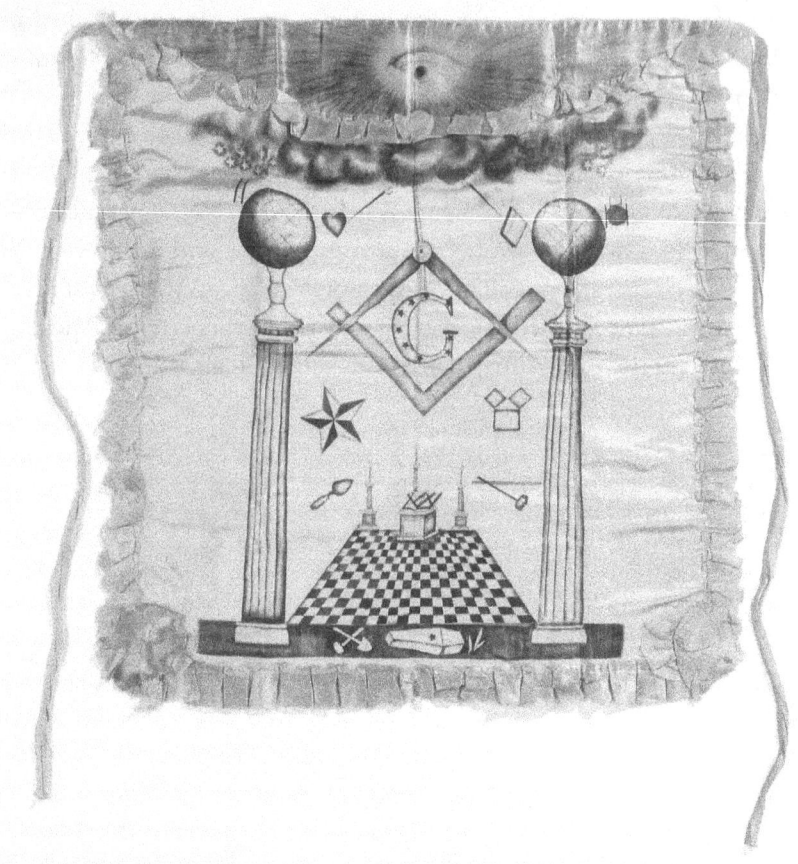

FIGURE 3.10: *Joseph Smith's Masonic apron.*

terpret the serpent as a symbol of the devil (which he thinks is unlikely)—and so it is more probable that the "x" is the magic sigil of Jupiter.[44]

Although Quinn is surely correct that Smith's cane was at least partially related to folk magic, his interpretation of the symbolism is open to question. Contrary to Quinn's implication, the serpent is not exclusively a motif for Satan in Christianity. The serpent can also be a symbol for Christ, especially in allusion to the bronze serpent of Moses. According to scriptural accounts, this bronze serpent had the power to heal those

---

44. See Quinn, *Early Mormonism and the Magic World View*, 90-91.

FIGURE 3.11: *Joseph Smith's serpent walking cane is decorated with a shield emblazoned with a cross (see detail at right).*

who had been bitten by the poisonous vipers, if only they would look to it and live.[45] The Gospel of John states:

> And as Moses lifted up the serpent in the wilderness, even so must the Son of man [Jesus Christ] be lifted up: That whosoever believeth in him should not perish, but have eternal life.[46]

The Book of Mormon remarks further:

> As he [Moses] lifted up the brazen serpent in the wilderness, even so shall he be lifted up who should come. And as many as should look upon that serpent should live, even so as many as should look upon the Son of God with faith, having a contrite spirit, might live, even unto that life which is eternal.[47]

---

45. Numbers 21:6-9, KJV.
46. John 3:14-15, KJV.
47. Helaman 8:15.

Christian Masons often promoted this imagery, illustrating in their artwork the serpent on the staff (or cross). Even more significantly for Smith's cane, Freemasonry regularly employed the imagery of the rod of Aaron (and Moses) in their rituals. According to the Book of Exodus, this rod transformed into a serpent to devour the serpent-rods owned by the Pharaoh's magicians.[48] David Bernard's widely circulated 1829 Masonic exposé explains the relevance of the serpent rod in Royal Arch Freemasonry:

> After traveling the rugged paths till all are satisfied, they arrive at the first Veil of the Tabernacle, give the pass word, and pass on to the second, give the pass words, and present the sign. This, it will be recollected, is in imitation of the sign which Moses was directed to make to the children of Israel. He threw his rod upon the ground and it became a serpent; he put forth his hand and took it by the tail, and it became a rod in his hand. The conductor is provided with a rod, made in the form of a snake, and painted to resemble one. This he drops upon the floor, and takes up again.[49]

Royal Arch Masons also lowered initiates through a secret passageway, into a vault where they would find a chest:

> "having on its top several mysterious characters." Inside were a pot of manna, Aaron's rod, and the "long lost book of the law."[50]

The Book of Numbers says the rod "was budded, and brought forth buds, and bloomed blossoms, and yielded almonds."[51] Thus, Royal Arch Masons sometimes designed their "rod of Aaron" with artificial (or real) buds. This description of the rod of Aaron may explain the curious circular protrusions carved out of the knots on Smith's cane, seemingly suggestive of the buds/almonds on Aaron's rod. As can be seen in figure 3.4, many of these bumps (several of which are even almond shaped) cover the cane from the shield down.

---

48. Exodus 7:9-12, KJV.
49. David Bernard, *Light on Masonry*, 141. A photograph of a similar Masonic serpent staff/rod (1890) can be found in *Material Culture of the American Freemasons*, ed. John D. Hamilton (Lexington, Massachusetts: Museum of Our National Heritage, 1994), 85.
50. Carnes, *Secret Ritual and Manhood*, 44.
51. Numbers 17:8.

The "x" carved into the crown is also symbolically appropriate for a cane designed to evoke the rod of Aaron and Moses. Masonic mythology included the belief that when Aaron was appointed High Priest, Moses marked his forehead with a cross, shaped either as a "+" or an "x." Mason Albert Mackey writes that in ancient Hebrew the figure of the *tau* "x, or +, was that of the cross":

> This *tau*, *tau cross*, or *tau mark*, was of very universal use as a sacred symbol among the ancients... It is a sign of salvation; according to Talmudists, the symbol was much older than the time of Ezekiel, for they say that when Moses anointed Aaron as the high priest, he marked his forehead with this sign.[52]

When a Mason was initiated into "the order of High Priesthood as practiced in America," explains Mackey:

> Oil was poured on the head in the form of a crown, that is, in a circle around the head; while in the ointment of the priest it was poured in the form of the Greek letter X, that is, on the top of the head, in the shape of a St. Andrew's cross.[53]

One final cross (that has thus far escaped notice by scholars) is also found on Smith's serpent cane: a large inverted cross fills the carved

---

52. Albert G. Mackey, *Encyclopedia of Freemasonry*, 791 (Philadelphia: Moss & Company, 1879), http://books.google.com/books?id=fAgIAAAAQAAJ&pg= (accessed 7 November 2008). Smith's first and second anointing rituals consecrated various body parts in ways that were quite similar to Catholic and Masonic anointing rituals. The seventeenth degree ("Knights of the East & West") of the Southern Jurisdiction of the U.S. (1801) describes an anointing ritual as follows: "The All Puissant then takes the ewer filled with perfumed ointment, and anoints his Head, Eyes, Mouth, Heart, the tip of his right Ear, hand, and foot, and says—'You are now, by dear Brother, received a member of our society. You will recollect to live up to the precepts of it, and also remember that those parts of your body, which have the greatest power of assisting you in good or evil, have this day been made Holy.'" *Ordo ab Chao: The Original and Complete Rituals, 4th-33rd Degrees of the first Supreme Council, 33rd Degree at Charleston, South Carolina* (Kessinger Publishing, 1995), 189. Joseph Smith noted a distinct difference between his ritual and Catholic tradition, however, saying, "[S]ealing of the servants of God on the top of their heads. tis not the cross as the catholics would have it." Joseph Smith (1843), *The Words of Joseph Smith: The Contemporary Accounts of the Nauvoo Discourses of the Prophet Joseph*, ed. Andrew F. Ehat and Lyndon W. Cook (1996), 239, In LDS Library 2006. Joseph Smith did not state why he concluded this, but considering the examples given of this book verifying Joseph's acceptance of the symbol, it seems that we can safely rule out the possibility that the prophet was implying an anti-cross view.

53. Ibid., 72.

shield.⁵⁴ This is almost certainly the cross of Peter; an intriguing addition to the symbolic context of the cane, testifying further (it seems) of Joseph Smith's priesthood power and authority. One reading of these symbols is that the serpent-rod of Aaron and the "x" on the crown illustrate that Smith was a high priest of the Aaronic order (thereby having the "gift of Aaron"), while the inverted petrine cross testify of Smith's apostolic power and authority to "bind on earth" and "in heaven."

Although these symbolic interpretations differ from those Quinn has suggested, his overall conclusion that the symbols can be connected with folk magic surely still stands. As already noted, some Masons were very willing to incorporate folk magic into their orders.⁵⁵ A connection could be posited between the petrine cross on the serpent cane and the "Saint Peter Bind Them" parchment owned by the Smith family. As treasure seekers often appealed to the Angel Raphael's power to bind the spirits guarding the buried treasure, so too they sometimes called upon St. Peter's power to "bind on earth" and "in heaven." It is possible that the cane's inverted cross should also be understood within this context. Finally, it should be noted that it was not uncommon for treasure seekers to identify their divining rods with the "rod of Aaron." As explained in an article (1850) entitled, "A History of the Divining Rod; With the Adventures of an Old Rodsman":

> With a large portion of the simple-hearted people in the agricultural districts of the country, from the earliest ages there has been an implicit belief in the powers and virtues of the Divining Rod—either for the discovery of water, mines, or hidden treasures. This belief, it would seem, has originated from the wonderful powers of the miraculous rod in the hands of Moses and Aaron, imparted to it by the Almighty.

---

54. After reading a preliminary draft of this book, D. Michael Quinn gave the following remark in a panel discussion at Sunstone: "While [Michael Reed's] book acknowledges that Joseph Smith's serpent-cane 'was either inspired by Freemasonry, folk-magic, or both,' he discovered a symbol in it that I did not recognize in my book about *Early Mormonism and the Magic World View*. In what I regarded as simply carved compartments on the cane, Reed perceives an inverted cross. Now I see it, too. Pointing out the previously unperceived is the role of ongoing historical analysis." D. Michael Quinn, *Sunstone West Symposium* (Claremont Graduate University, 2010).

55. Scholar Clyde R. Frosberg Jr. argues in favor of this understanding of Joseph Smith's cane. Not only does it depict what appears to be a Masonic insignia on it, he says, but the cane also "resembles a Masonic divining rod, or 'pedum.'" Clyde R. Frosberg Jr., *Equal Rights: The Book of Mormon, Masonry, Gender, and American Culture* (New York: Columbia University Press, 2004), 47. Frosberg also overlooks the inverted cross.

Their rod was made from a simple twig of the almond tree; with this, water was discovered and brought forth from the flinty rock.[56]

In the Latter Day Saint context, the 1833 Book of Commandments reported that Oliver Cowdery possessed a "gift" to use the divining rod:

> Now this is not all, for you [Oliver Cowdery] have another gift, which is the gift of working with the rod: behold it has told you things: behold there is no other power save God, that can cause this rod of nature, to work in your hands, for it is the work of God.[57]

The passage was later modified in Doctrine and Covenants, changing the phrase "rod of nature" to "gift of Aaron":

> Now this is not all thy gift; for you have another gift, which is the gift of Aaron; behold, it has told you many things; Behold, there is no other power, save the power of God, that can cause this gift of Aaron to be with you. Therefore, doubt not, for it is the gift of God; and you shall hold it in your hands, and do marvelous works; and no power shall be able to take it away out of your hands, for it is the work of God.[58]

The recent publication of the *Joseph Smith Papers* volume (*Revelations and Translations—Manuscript Revelation Books*) renewed interest in this specific passage, when scholars realized that the verse initially

---

56. "A History of the Divining Rod; With the Adventures of an Old Rodsman," *The United States Democratic Review* 26, no. 141 (March 1850): 218, http://cdl.library.cornell.edu/cgi-bin/moa/moa-cgi?notisid=AGD1642-0026-66 (accessed 27 March 2009); as also quoted in Seth L. Bryant, "Latter-Day Anguish and the Epic of greater Mormonism," (master's thesis, University of Florida, December 2008), 91. For more information on divining rods and Joseph Smith's activities in treasure hunting, see Ronald W. Walker, "The Persisting Idea of American Treasure Hunting," *BYU Studies* 24, no. 3 (Fall 1984): 429-59. Some also associated the American Indian "sanctified rod" tradition with the *Rod of Aaron*: "The Indians have an old tradition, that when they left their own native land, they brought with them a *sanctified rod*, by order of an oracle, which they fixed every evening in the ground, and were to remove from place to place on the continent towards the sun rising, till it budded in one night's time.... Instead of the miraculous direction, to which they limit it, in their western banishment, it appears more likely that they refer to the ancient circumstance of the rod of Aaron." Barbara Anne Simon, *Hope of Israel: Presumptive Evidence that the Aborigines of the Western Hemisphere are Descended from the Ten Missing Tribes of Israel* (London, 1829), 92; as cited and quoted in Rick Grunder, *Mormon Parallels: A Bibliographic Source* [CD-ROM] (La Fayette, New York: Rick Grunder Books, 2008), 1574.
57. Book of Commandments 7:3.
58. Doctrine and Covenants 8:6-8.

identified the divining instrument as a "sprout" and a "thing of Nature."⁵⁹ The passage evolved in the following sequence:

> "which is the gift of working with the sprout" → "which is the gift of working with the rod" → "which is the gift of Aaron"
>
> "thing of nature" → "rod of nature" → "gift of Aaron"

Editing of this passage removed wording that would have otherwise helped readers to understand that Oliver Cowdery was actually using a divining-rod during the translation process. Consequently, many readers now assume that the "gift" was merely the Aaronic Priesthood, and nothing more. Although inaccurate, this interpretation is certainly more consistent with current LDS orthopraxy, which has rejected obvious folk-magic practices. Whether or not this distortion of the record is intentional, it is clear that Joseph Smith identified Oliver Cowdery's divining rod with the Rod of Aaron.

Whether ultimately derived from folk-magic, from Freemasonry, or from both in combination, the symbol of the cross can be found inscribed in Smith's parchments, carved his cane, and even decorating the Nauvoo Temple itself. It is apparent, therefore, folk-magic and Freemasonry were both contributing factors to early Mormon acceptance and use of the symbol of the cross during Smith's lifetime.

---

59. *The Joseph Smith Papers: Revelations and Translations, Manuscript Revelation Books*—Facsimile Edition (Church Historian's Press, 2009), 16. Identifying the rod as "sprouts" is consistent with terminology used by other divining rod practitioners: "They take a long sprout of hazel, or any other wood straight and smooth, like an ordinary cane... and when they pass over a water source, the rod turns and the arc twists toward the ground." Abbé Vallemont, *Occult Physics or Treatise on the Divining Rod* (Paris, 1693), as quoted in Christopher Bird, The Divining Hand (New York: E.P. Dutton, 1979), 101. The Rod of Aaron is also described as a "sprout" in David Bernard's *Light on Masonry*, "The H[igh] Priest then takes from the ark a bit of an apple tree sprout, a few inches long, with some withered buds upon it, or a stick of a similar length with some artificial buds upon it, which, after consulting with the King and Scribe, he pronounces Aaron's Rod." *Light on Masonry* (1829), 143.

Chapter Four

Pre-Columbian Crosses

Following Joseph Smith's reported visit from the angel Moroni, and approximately two years before he began translating the gold plates, Joseph Smith shared with his family stories about the Pre-Columbian natives. Joseph Smith's mother, Lucy Mack Smith, gave the following account:

> In the course of our evening conversations Joseph would give us some of the most ammusing recitals which could be im=magined[.] he would describe the ancient inhabitants of this continent[,] their dress[,] their maner of traveling[,] the animals which they rode[,] The cities that were built by them[,] the structure of their buildings[,] with eve=ry particular of their mode of warfare[,] their religi=ous worship as particularly as though he had spent his life with them.[1]

Lucy Mack Smith does not say where her son learned this information. Some believing Mormons propose that young Joseph must have received these details from the Angel Moroni;[2] by contrast, skeptics con-

---

1. Quote comes from 1845 manuscript of Lucy Mack Smith's autobiography, as published in *Early Mormon Documents*, ed. Dan Vogel (Salt Lake City, Signature Books, 1996–2003), 1:296.
2. This proposal is supported by Joseph Smith's claim in 1832 that the angel Moroni had "revealed unto me many things concerning the inhabitants of the earth." Joseph Smith, "1832 History," *The Papers of Joseph Smith*, 1: 7-8. Likewise John Taylor states: "Why, there was a young man [Joseph Smith] in Ontario county, New York, to whom the angel of God [Moroni] appeared and

clude that Smith himself composed the stories from his own imagination. In the latter view, Smith's earlier stories were a rehearsal or a rough draft for his later composition of the Book of Mormon.

While the source of the Book of Mormon is ultimately a question of faith, its contents attempt to create a place for native Americans within the Biblical world-view. According to common Nineteenth-century Biblical exegesis, derived from Medieval European geography, all peoples of the Old World were descended from the three sons of Noah, described in the Book of Genesis. In the most common formulation, Asians were said to be descended from Shem, Africans from Ham, and Europeans from Japeth.[3] This traditional interpretation left open the question: how do native Americans fit into this scheme?

The Book of Mormon answered the question by narrating the story of three migrations from the Old World. The earliest were a people called the Jaredites who crossed the ocean shortly after the Biblical story of the Tower of Babel, while the two subsequent migrations, the Mulekites and the Nephites and Lamanites, were Israelites who came to the New World in the wake of the destruction of Jerusalem in 587 BCE. A connection between native Americans and Israelites (such as the "Lost Tribes of Israel") were relatively commonplace at the time. See, for example, *View of the Hebrews: Or the Tribes of Israel in America*, published in 1825 by Ethan Smith (no relation to Joseph Smith).

The Book of Mormon narrative, however, goes further, explaining that the Nephites considered themselves "Christians," were aware of the Christian gospel, and were even visited by Jesus Christ here in the New World after his crucifixion in Jerusalem. As a result of these details, early Latter Day Saints naturally viewed any evidence of Christian practice among the Indians or, for example, in the ruins of Pre-Columbian civilizations, as supportive of the authenticity of the Book of Mormon.

Although non-Mormon historians and archaeologists today have universally dismissed these connections, they were widely accepted in past centuries. For example, Dan Vogel notes that early Spanish explorers of Central and South America often searched the ruins they found

---

gave an account of the whole. These majestic [Pre-Columbian] ruins bespeak the existence of a mighty people." John Taylor (1857), *Journal of Discourses*, 5: 241.

3. See, for example, Robert D. Mayo, *A View of Ancient Geography and Ancient History* (Philadelphia: John F. Watson, 1813) 165-66.

for parallels with their own Christian beliefs. Vogel explains that "large stone crosses found in Central America...were cited as evidence that Christianity had been preached in ancient America." He further writes:

> Cortez reported seeing a cross ten feet high near a temple in Central America. The Indians, he reported, "could nevre know the original how that God of Crosse came amongst them.... There is no memorie of anye Preaching of the Gospell." Although the natives had no memory of Christianity, the stone crosses, according to early writer Francesco Clavigero, proved to many that "the Gospel had been preached in America some centuries before the arrival of the Spaniards." Antonio del Rio included in his 1822 book a plate showing a codex of a Mayan offering sacrifice to one of these large stone crosses.[4]

Early Latter Day Saints read with great interest the discoveries made by John L. Stephens and Fredrick Catherwood during their 1837 expedition to Central America, documented and published in their *Incidents of Travel in Central America, Chiapas, and Yucatan* (1841). Interest was so high, in fact, that the Mormon periodical *Times and Seasons* published several lengthy excerpts from the book. One such excerpt from this series included their findings of curious symbols in certain pre-Columbian sites:

> Some were of this form "T," and some of this "+," which has been called the Greek Cross and the Egyptian Tau, and made the subject of much learned speculation.[5]

Other details given by Stevens and Catherwood illustrated the remains of advanced civilizations that once thrived in Central America. Mormon Apostle (later president of the LDS Church) Wilford Woodruff recorded in his journal:

---

4. Dan Vogel, *Indian Origins and the Book of Mormon* (Salt Lake City: Signature Books, 1986), www.signaturebookslibrary.org/indian/indian4.htm (accessed 10 October 2008).

5. "Extracts From 'Incidents of Travel in Central America,'" *Times and Seasons* 3, no. 22 (15 September 1852), 912, In New Mormon Studies. The *Times and Seasons* quoted the *New York Herald Weekly* the year before as follows: "Inside the building there are recesses which contain stone tablets of rich and beautiful workmanship. The principal ornaments is a cross, but it has no resemblance to the cross of the Christians." "American Antiquities: More Proofs of the Book of Mormon," *Times and Seasons* 2:16 (15 June 1881), 442, In *New Mormon Studies*. Presumably what made this cross appear unlike the "cross of Christians" is that it was of Greek form.

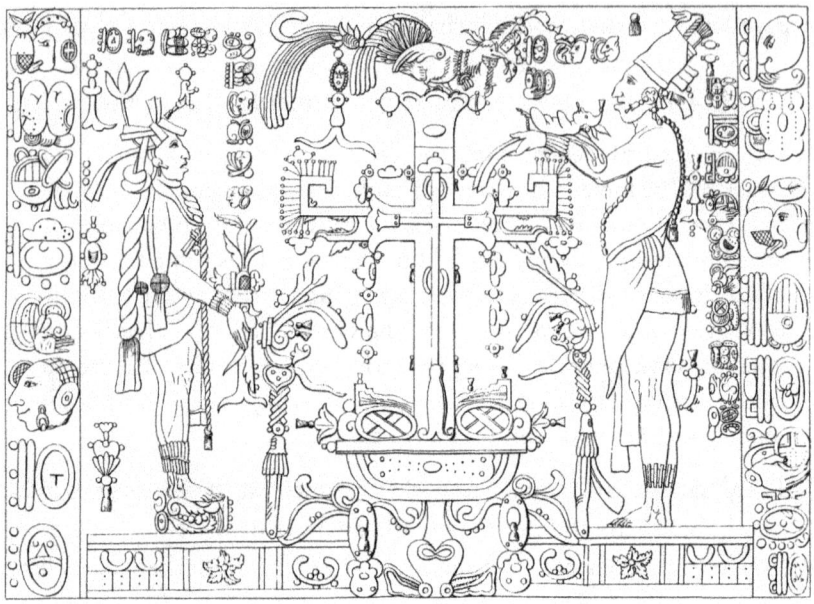

FIGURE 4.1: *A facsimile of the "Tablet of the Cross," a Mayan carving in Palenque.*

> I spent the day in reading the 1st vol of INCIDENTS OF TRAVELS.... I felt truly interested in this work for it brought to light a flood of testimony in proof of the book of mormon.[6]

The prophet Joseph Smith himself remarked that:

> Stephens and Catherwood have succeeded in collecting in the interior of America a large amount of relics of the Nephites, or the ancient inhabitants of America treated of in the Book of Mormon.[7]

The prophet's younger brother, Apostle William Smith (who later joined the Strangites, became disaffected, and then ultimately joined the RLDS Church), declared in a letter to W. W. Phelps that:

> The Book of Mormon was published in 1830, and the discoveries and facts proved by Stephens and Catherwood in 1837, proving to a demonstration the inspiration of the prophet, and the divinity of the book.[8]

---

6. *Willford Woodruff's Journal* (September 13, 1841), ed. Scott G. Kenny (Midvale, Utah: Signature Books, 1983), 2.126, In *New Mormon Studies.*

7. Joseph Smith (June 25, 1842), *History of the Church*, 5: 44.

8. William Smith, *Times and Seasons* 5, no. 24 (November 10, 1844), 755, http://www.centerplace.org/history/ts/v5n24.htm (accesses November 10, 2008).

In a similar vein, Apostle John Taylor (later president of the LDS Church) claimed in an 1857 discourse that Stephens and Catherwood's discoveries "bespeak the existence of a mighty people. The Book of Mormon unfolds their history."[9] Several years later, Taylor specifically noted the Pre-Columbian depiction of Quetzalcoatl being crucified on a cross, as described in Lord Kingsborough's *Antiquities of Mexico* (1831):

> He [Kingsborough] observes:... "The seventy-third plate of the Borgain MS. is the most remarkable of all, for Quetzalcoatl is not only represented there as crucified upon a cross of Greek form, but his burial and descent into hell are also depicted in a very curious manner."[10]

In 1879, Utah Mormon elder W. H. H. Sharp wrote an article that appeared in the *Deseret News*, entitled: "The Divine Authenticity of the Book of Mormon." In it, he cited a number of perceived supporting evidences, including "at Marietta, Ohio, a mound in the form of a Maltese Cross, 188 feet square, top measurement."[11]

LDS general authority B. H. Roberts also believed the Pre-Columbian cross was evidence confirming that American Indians received the Christian gospel.

> Holding the cross as an object of veneration, the rite of baptism as celebrated among them, and the notion of three states of existence in the future life.

This parallel, wrote Roberts in 1888:

> Leads one inevitably to the conclusion that by some means or other the forefathers of the Mexicans must have been acquainted with the leading principles of the Christian religion.[12]

---

9. John Taylor (1857), *Journal of Discourses*, 5: 240-41.

10. John Taylor, *An Examination into and an Elucidation of the Great Principle of the Mediation and the Atonement of Our Lord and Savior Jesus Christ* (Salt Lake City: Deseret News Co., 1882), 202, http://books.google.com/books?id=eERCAAAAIAAJ&printsec=toc&source=gbs_summary_r&cad=0#PPA202,M1 (accessed 10 November 2008).

11. Elder W. H. H Sharp, "The Divine Authenticity of the Book of Mormon" *Deseret News*, 6 August 1879, http://udn.lib.utah.edu/u?/deseretnews3,2230434 (accessed 26 March 2009).

12. B. H. Roberts, "A New Witness for God," *The Contributor* 9, no. 11 (September 1888), In *LDS Library* 2006.

The Contributor, a Mormon periodical, republished in 1892 an article originally written by a non-Mormon that evidently appealed to Mormon thought at the time. The article declared, "The sign of the cross in all the ages previous to the time of the Savior was a common and most sacred symbol." Listing various cultures that revered the cross throughout history, the author included mention of the symbol illustrated on "hundreds of the temples and pyramids in America found by the Spaniards in the conquest of Mexico and Central America." Upon seeing these crosses, Spanish missionaries supposed that "St. Thomas the Apostle had at some time preached in America."[13]

Throughout the nineteenth century, it is clear that Mormons perceived Pre-Columbian crosses as evidence vindicating the Book of Mormon narrative that Christianity was practiced among native Americans in ancient times. Since the Nephites of the Book of Mormon were said to have practiced the Christian faith correctly for many centuries, the clear implication is that Mormons saw the cross as a legitimate symbol of that Christian faith.

---

13. "The Cross," *The Contributor* 13, no. 11 (September 1892), In *LDS Library 2006.*

Chapter Five

Mormon Crosses before the Institutionalized Taboo

When the plat for the City of Zion was originally drawn in the summer of 1833, Joseph Smith Jr. marked the location of the temple with a cross. "This temple is to be built in the square marked figure 1," said Smith, "and to be built where the circle is which has a cross on it on the north end." Looking closely at the cross on the drawing of the plat, there appears to be an italicized slant to it, which has led some scholars to believe that it is really just an "x" marking the spot. This view seems unlikely, however, since the angle matches the slant of the handwriting on the drawing.

Many (if not all) of the earliest church authorities, believed that it was okay to associate the cross with Zion. The following summer, after Smith marked the location of the temple with a cross on the plat, the "leading elders in the church of the Latter Day Saints" envisioned a heavenly cross monument, as they wrote in an appeal addressed to "the people and constituted authorities of this nation, and to the ends of the earth, FOR PEACE." Their vision predicted:

> When time is no longer, he, with all the ransomed of the Lord, may stand, in the fullness of joy, and view the grand pillar of heaven, which was built by the faith and charity of the saints, beginning at Adam, with this motto in the base: "Repent and live;" surrounded with a

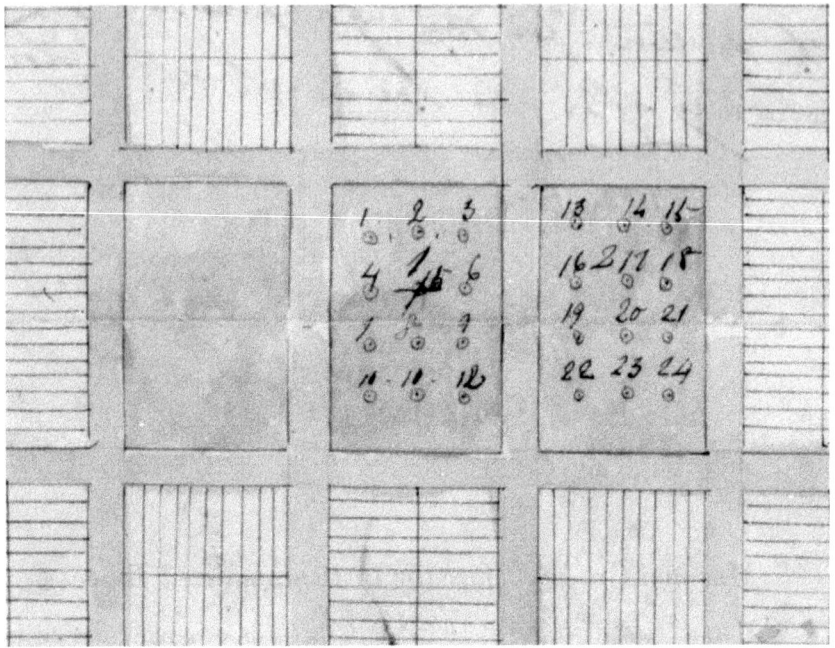

FIGURE 5.1: *The cross marking the first of the twenty-four temples to be built at the centerplace of the City of Zion (detail from the first Plat of Zion).*

beautiful circle sign, supported by a cross, about midway up its lofty column, staring the world in letters of blood: "The kingdom of heaven is at hand," and finished with a plain top, towering up in the midst of the celestial world, around which is written, by the finger of Jehovah: "Eternal life is the greatest gift of God."[1]

The appeal was signed by the twelve "leading elders": W.W. Phelps, David Whitmer, John Whitmer, Edward Partridge, John Corrill, Isaac Morley, Parley P. Pratt, Lyman Wight, Newel Knight, Thomas B. Marsh, Simeon Carter, and Calvin Beebe; and appeared again in a second edition (1840), "revised by authority of said Church, Joseph Smith, Jun., Sidney Rigdon, Hyrum Smith, Presidency."[2] Evidently, none of these church authorities agreed with the anti-cross views common in mainstream Protestantism.

---

1. "An Appeal" (June 1834), *History of the Church*, 2: 133.
2. *History of the Church*, 4: 255.

Crosses among the Utah Saints

The general acceptance of the cross by Utah Saints continued under the leadership of Brigham Young (1844–1877). The symbol "+" was the first brand owned by the Church, and was recorded in 1850, later being cataloged in Legislative Assembly's *Book of Recorded Marks and Brands* (1874).[3] The LDS Church's design choice likely had precedent from Biblical, early Christian, and perhaps also Masonic traditions. According to scholar Richard Viladesau:

> In the vision of the prophet Ezekiel (Ez. 9:4-6), those who are to be saved from the wrath of God are marked with the cross (i.e., the letter tav [+ or x])…. The early Christians connected the passage from Ezekiel with the cross of Christ…. Hence in marking themselves with the "sign of the cross"… Christian[s] expanded on the Old Testament symbol of God's protection and possession. In baptism, the forehead of a new Christian was anointed with oil in the form of a cross, symbolizing both the sharing in the paschal mystery of Christ's death and resurrection and a "branding" of the person with the Lord's mark as the sign of belonging to Him and of being under His protection against the powers of the world.[4]

As late as 1927, Mormon scholar Janne M. Sjodahl (1853–1939), while citing the pre-Columbian use of symbols resembling the *tav* [T or +] as evidence validating the Book of Mormon, explained that the symbol was anciently associated with branding property:

---

3. *Book of Recorded Marks and Brands* (Salt Lake City: Deseret News, 1874), 140, http://images.archives.utah.gov/cdm4/document.php?CISOROOT=/540&CISOPTR=2597&REC=4 (accessed 10 November 2008). The Church's brand being a cross is confirmed by Robert Baskin's Mountain Meadow's Massacre court trial report, saying, "Klingensmith testified that Bishop-Major John M. Higbee cut one man's throat; that women were lying around with their throats cut, and some with their heads smashed in; that he branded some of the cattle about fifty head with a cross, which was the church brand." Robert Baskin, *Reminiscences of Early Utah* (Salt Lake City, Tribune-Reporter Printer Co., c.1914), 110, http://www.archive.org/details/reminiscencesofe-oobaskrich (accessed 10 November 2008).

4. , Richard Viladesau, *The Beauty of the Cross: The Passion of Christ in Theology and in the Arts—From the Catacombs to the Eve of the Renaissance* (Oxford: Oxford University Press, 2005), 42-43.

FIGURES 5.2 AND 5.3: *Hair art (left) from the officer ladies of the 20th Ward Relief Society surrounding a cross and an anchor, and (right) a cross and an anchor on a marriage certificate of Matthew Urie Bailey and Mary Isabella Hales.*

> The Hebrew "T" (tav) means a "mark," and especially a "signature." It was the "brand" that marked a human being as somebody's property. In the early Hebrew the *tav* was written as a cross [+].

Sjodahl then offers a rhetorical question to his readers, asking where the pre-Columbian natives got the idea to mark their property with crosses, "if not from a Nephite ancestry?"[5]

It should be pointed out that Masons were also aware of this practice of branding with the sign of the cross, and some even incorporated it into their rituals, claiming:

> Every mason, who shall attain the third degree, shall be burnt in the posterior with a cross, as being symbolical of the cross, upon which

---

5. Janne M. Sjodahl, *Introduction to the Study of the Book of Mormon* (Kessinger, 2003), 239-240, http://books.google.com/books?id=GxBLdgrLCkEC&printsec=frontcover&dq=#PPA239,M 1 (accessed 10 November 2009). In the Book of Mormon narrative Nephites were a fair skinned people, allegedly of Israelite decent, who were generally regarded as the righteous inhabitants of the New World (as opposed to the Lamanites, who were of a darker complexion, and generally considered wicked).

FIGURE 5.4: *Framed cross hanging in Manti Temple.*

our blessed savior died, and if such brothers has received the HOLY BRAND should, through age or infirmities, forget the grip, or any other inaugural part of masonic ceremony, this shall stand as a note of reference to the end of their lives.[6]

---

6. Ephraim Smooth, "To Richard Carlile Dorchester Goal," *The Republican* 12 (1825), 253, http://books.google.com/books?id=Cx8rAAAAYAAJ&pg=PA253&dq= (accessed 25 March 2009). Although this report comes from an anti-Masonic publication, the Masonic practice of branding initiates is confirmed by other sources. According to George Oliver, for example, "In the last century our Brethren introduced many tests of fortitude to prove the candidates before they were initiated; and hence the *brand*, which in those times referred to the initiation fee, was often considered in a much more formidable point of view, and was an object of dread to the nervous candidate, and his initiation frequently produced more entertainment to the Brethren than the Order would fairly justify. His fortitude was severly tested in some of the Lodges; but such practices form no part of the system of Freemasonry, and have been many years abolished." George Oliver, "The Masonic Manual," ed. Robert Macoy, *Universal Masonic Library* (New York, 1855), 49, http://books.google.com/books?id=gflJAAAAMAAJ&pg=RA1-PA49&dq= (accessed 25 March 2009).

The account goes on to say that the brand in the initiation ceremony had previously been used to mark sheep.

Although Mormons did not brand themselves in their temple rituals,[7] given the context provided above, it is nevertheless understandable that the Church would have chosen crosses to mark their livestock. Brand marks were the owner's sign, and since the owner of the LDS Church's livestock was theoretically Jesus Christ himself, the Lord's sign—the cross—was used.

Mormons designed religious meeting houses (which were also considered the Lord's "property") and other buildings in the form of crosses. On the trek west, one tabernacle was erected in 1849 in Pigeon Creek, Iowa, "constructed of oak logs hewn on the inside" with the floor-plan "taking the form of a Greek cross."[8] A couple years later, another meeting house built in a cruciform design in Parowan, Utah. Apostle George Albert Smith reported that it was built:

> In the winter of 1850–1...in the shape of a Greek cross, and was of hewn logs. It served the town which we named Parowan, for fifteen years.[9]

The original plan for the Utah state capital building in Fillmore City also had a cross form. In the *Atlantic Monthly* (1859) Colonel Albert G. Brown Jr. praised LDS Church Architect Truman Angell's plan for the building, noting that it was:

> A magnificent edifice in the shape of a Greek cross, with a rotunda sixty feet in diameter. Only one wing has been completed, but this is spacious enough to furnish all needful accommodations.[10]

The capital building never was finished, however. Historian C. Mark Hamilton explains that federal funding troubles interrupted and delayed

---

7. Mormons instead had their temple undergarments cut and stitched to serve as a reminder of the endowment and their temple covenants made therein.
8. Andrew Jenson, *Encyclopedic History of the Church of Jesus Christ of Latter-day Saints* (Salt Lake City: Deseret Book, 1941), 860.
9. George A. Smith, *The Contributor* 4, no. 6 (March 1883), In *LDS Library 2006*.
10. *A Comprehensive History of the Church of Jesus Christ of Latter-day Saints* (Provo: Brigham Young University, 1965), 4:23, In *LDS Library 2006*.

MORMON CROSSES BEFORE THE TABOO

FIGURE 5.5: *Crosses in stain glass of the Parowan (UT) 3rd ward building (built 1914).*

FIGURE 5.6: *Crosses (on shields) in the stain glass of the Salt Lake Liberty Ward building (constructed at various stages 1908–1924).*

FIGURE 5.7: *Rose crosses in Whittier Ward chapel stained glass (built 1936–1938).*

FIGURE 5.8: *Cross detail outside the Odgen Deaf Branch building (built 1916).*

further construction; then construction "ceased altogether when the capitol was officially moved back to Salt Lake City on December 15, 1856."[11]

In the following decade, cruciform plans increased in popularity, in part due to the influence of architects Obed Taylor and William Folsom who joined the LDS Church and served as assistants to Angell. Taylor is credited with the design of the Salt Lake Assembly Hall, a cruciform building on Temple Square.[12] Folsom later "adopted a similar cruciform plan," when "church leaders in Provo asked him to pattern their new tabernacle after the Salt Lake Assembly Hall."[13] As additional examples, Hamilton notes:

> The cruciform plan continued into the first decade of the twentieth century with tabernacles in Vernal (1901–7) and Loa (1906–9), Utah.[14]

And these examples do not mark the end of the practice. Both the Laie, Hawaii (1919), and the Cardston, Alberta (1923), temples were built in the shape of a cross.[15] Crosses were also incorporated into the stonework of church buildings, at times surrounding windows or attic vents. They were also occasionally included in stained-glass windows, engraved on pulpits, and hung on walls.

Crosses in Quilts and Floral Arrangements

Beyond their use in architecture, Utah Mormons drew crosses as notational marks, wore crosses as jewelry, used crosses decoratively during celebrations, sewed crosses into quilts, assembled funeral floral arrangements in cross form, and etched them onto gravestones.[16]

Early pioneer Matilda Caroline Fuller made a quilt before her conversion to the Church some time between 1835 and 1845, and brought

---

11. C. Mark Hamilton, *Nineteenth-Century Mormon Architecture & City Planning* (New York: Oxford University Press, 1995), 137.
12. Ibid., 70.
13. Ibid., 72.
14. Ibid., 74.
15. "The Hawaiian temple… is built in the shape of a Grecian cross," and the Cardston, Alberta, Canada temple "is built in the shape of a Maltese cross." Andrew Jensen, *Conference Report* (October 1923), 131-32, In *LDS Library 2006*.
16. In addition to images provided here in this book, other photographs of Mormon crosses can be viewed in Michael G. Reed, "The Development of the LDS Church's Attitude Toward the Cross," (master's thesis, California State University of Sacramento, Spring 2009).

it across the plains before settling in the Salt Lake Valley. Each of the quilt's squares has a large yellow cross in the center.[17] The Salt Lake City 14th Ward relief society produced a quilt in 1857, piecing together squares made by various women in the Church. The squares have stars, flowers, birds, a beehive, and crosses on them. Although several of the crosses on this quilt are less obvious, due to their floral depiction, a more obvious square with a cross was contributed to the ward quilt by Sarah Ann Ballo.[18] Pioneer Ann Sewell Hawkins made a quilt (sometime between 1885 and 1890) that included a cross.[19] A similarly styled quilt was made by Lydia Rebecca Baker Price late in 1915, showing crosses (rose-cross, Maltese cross, and simply stitched Greek crosses).[20]

Crosses were particularly common in funerals. Newspaper reports specifically mention that crosses were displayed at funeral services for martyr Joseph Standing (d. 1879);[21] Joseph Young (d. 1881), Brigham Young's brother who served as first counselor of the Quorum of the Seventy;[22] Eliza R. Snow (d. 1888), a polygamous wife of both Joseph Smith and Brigham;[23] Daniel H. Wells (d. 1891), Brigham Young's first

---

17. Quilt Historian Mary Bywater Cross comments about this quilt, saying that there is "clear evidence of a cross in the yellow fabric pieces, the more appropriate pattern name is Christian Cross, a popular early pattern named in Ohio and New England." Mary Bywater Cross, *Quilts & Women of the Mormon Migrations: Treasures of Transition* (Nashville: Routlege Hill Press, 1996), 40-41.
18. Carol Holindrake Nielson, *The Salt Lake City Album Quilt, 1857: Stories of the Relief Society Women and Their Quilt* (Salt Lake City: University of Utah Press, 2004), 146.
19. Cross, *Quilts & Women*, 92-93.
20. Ibid., 31.
21. "A few floral offerings, including a wreath, an anchor, and a cross, were placed on the top of the coffin." "The Martyr Saint," *Salt Lake Daily Tribune*, 5 August 1879, 4, http://udn.lib.utah.edu/u?/slt4,20343 (accessed 26 March 2009).
22. "The casket containing the remains was profusely ornamented with exquisite flowers, artistically arranged in crosses, crowns, anchors and bouquets, and a sheaf of wheat fully ripe, emblematical of the full life, was bound with a white ribbon, on which was printed, in gold letters, the appropriate words, 'Well done, good and faithful servant.' Above it was a sickle decorated with white flowers. It was a beautiful tribute to the memory of the departed." "Joseph Young," *The Contributor* 2, no. 12 (September 1881), In *LDS Library*. "[Joseph Young's casket] was made of solid walnut with French burl walnut panels, and was chastely decorated with flowers, arranged in the form of a cross and chaplet, with the initials of the deceased and several fine bouquets." "Funeral Services," *Deseret News*, July 27, 1881, 8, http://udn.lib.utah.edu/u?/deseretnews3,195886 (accessed 26 March 2009). The Quorum of the Seventy is a priesthood office ranked just below the Quorum of the Twelve Apostles.
23. "The various stands were, in accordance with the wish of the departed, draped in white, nothing black being introduced. There was a great variety of floral offerings, contributed by lov-

FIGURE 5.9: *Memorial of "William Shanks Berry and John Henry Gibbs" (1884).*

counselor in the First Presidency of the Church;[24] Elder Jacob Gates (d. 1892), one of the Seven Presidents of Seventy;[25] and Barbara Ann Evans (d. 1898).[26] We likewise know the funeral for the third president of the LDS Church, John Taylor (d. 1887), had a cross-and-anchor floral

---

ing hearts. They were of various forms, such as wreaths, crosses, hearts and other suggestive and appropriate devices." "Funeral Services" (December 7, 1888), *Collected Discourses: Delivered by President Wilford Woodruff, His Two Counselors, The Twelve Apostles, and Others*, ed. Brian H. Stuy (B.H.S. Publishing, 1999), 1: 178.

24. "The casket was then decorated with ornaments of flowers. One was a beautiful harp of ivy and lilies. Another represented the cross and crown. Bouquets and sprays were strewn appropriately around the casket while a beautiful white dove with outstretched wings as if ready to soar to the realms on high, carrying an olive leaf in its beak, surmounted the whole." "We Mourn the Dead," *Ogden Standard Examiner*, March 31, 1891, 1, http://udn.lib.utah.edu/u?/ogden3,57355 (accessed 26 March 2009).

25. "The [Provo] Tabernacle was draped in white, was ornamented with beautiful wreaths, boquets [sic], and cross and anchor and vessel, an emblem of faith, hope and charity and was filled to overflowing." "Funeral of Elder Jacob Gates," *Deseret News*, April 23, 1892, 16, http://udn.lib.utah.edu/u?/deseretnews4,25397 (accessed 26 March 2009).

26. "[T]he flowers were more numerous and artistically arranged than at any service ever before held in Lehi. The most beautiful design was a large cross of white flowers which supported a pair of scales, likewise composed of flowers. The one side of the scales, which contained her good deeds, greatly outbalanced the other, which was truly emblematic of her whole life." "Funeral of Mrs. Evans," *Ogden Standard Examiner*, July 1, 1898, 2, http://udn.lib.utah.edu/u?/ogden6,13064 (accessed 26 March 2009).

FIGURE 5.10: *The floral arrangements for the funeral of 1887 funeral of LDS Church President John Taylor included a cross-and-anchor (far left).*

arrangement, since it is visible in a photograph of the service (see figure 5.10). However, while a report states that "the stands were decorated with beautiful flowers, tastefully arranged,"[27] it fails to specifically mention either crosses or anchors. This omission illustrates the likely possibility that many more Mormon funerals included flowers arranged in the form of crosses, but the information simply went unreported.[28]

---

27. "Laid to Rest" (1887) *Collected Discourses*, 1: 40.

28. Granted, these reports quoted above do not tell us exactly who had donated the floral arrangements, and so the possibility remains that the crosses did not actually come from Latter-day Saints. But, whatever the source of these gifts may be, it is quite telling that the authors of these reports never imply even the slightest hint of controversy about them. Instead, the crosses are praised as being "appropriate," "truly emblematic," "tasteful," "a beautiful tribute to the memory of the departed," and "an emblem of faith." Besides, a funeral for a Latter-day Saint named Charlie Brown (1891) displayed arrangements given by "the employes [sic] of Z. C. M. I., a broken column, sickle, pillow and cross." "Funeral of Charlie Brown," *Deseret News*, September 12, 1891, 31, http://udn.lib.utah.edu/u?/deseretnews4,21534 (accessed 26 March 2009). Zion's Cooperative Mercantile Institution was a department store owned and controlled by the Church. Those from Z. C. M. I. who attended Brown's funeral included "Bishop [of the SLC Twentieth Ward] George Romney, one of the directors of Z. C. M. I.; Superintendent T[homas] G. Webber, A[ugust] W. Carlson, treasurer of the institution." Ibid.. All three of these men were prominent

Crosses as Jewelry

Many Mormons also wore crosses as jewelry, a practice that increased in popularity at the turn of the twentieth century.[29] Brigham Young's polygamous wife, Harriet Amelia Folsom Young, wore a cross brooch in more than one photograph (c. 1895),[30] as did some of Brigham Young's daughters. At least two daughters were children from another of Young's wives Clara Decker Young: Charlotte Talula Young wore a chain necklace with a cross (c. 1880),[31] and Nabbie Howe Young wore cross earrings and a necklace in two separate photographs (c. 1873; 1885).[32] Daughter of polygamist and pioneer Hiram B. Clawson, Georgia, wore a cross necklace in a portrait (c. 1880).[33] Her father Hiram was quite close

Latter-day Saints. See Andrew Jensen, *LDS Biographical Encyclopedia* (1901), 1: 670-71, 678; 4: 368.

29. Not only did Mormons become increasingly concerned with projecting themselves as Christian at this period in time, but the turn of the twentieth century was also the heart of Utah's consumer revolution. See Greg Umbach, "Learning to Shop in Zion: The Consumer Revolution in Great Basin Mormon Culture, 1847-1910," *Journal of Social History* 38, no. 1 (Fall 2004): 29-61. These two factors together seem to be largely responsible for the increased popularity of cross jewelry among Latter-day Saint women.

30. Besides the photograph of Amelia Folsom Young wearing a cross brooch in figure 5.11, another photo of her wearing the brooch can be seen at the following source: Utah State Historical Society Classified Photo Collection, no. 14192, http://content.lib.utah.edu/u?/USHS_Class,4126 (accessed 12 April 2009).

31. Photograph of Talula is archived in the Utah State Historical Society Classified Photo Collection, no. 14159, http://content.lib.utah.edu/u?/USHS_Class,4071 (accessed 10 October 2010). The writing on the back of a group photograph additionally identifies a girl wearing a cross as Talula (Lula), but the numbering on the back of the picture seems to be incorrect. The girl wearing the cross instead looks more like her sister Clarissa Young, and the girl to her left looks like Talula: See the portrait by Charles R. Savage in the LDS Church History Library, PH 2173, http://contentdm.lib.byu.edu/u?/Savage2,1371 (accessed 12 April 2009).

32. One of the cross necklaces that Nabbie wears seems to be the same one worn by Talula in the aforementioned photograph. See Utah State Historical Society Classified Photo Collection, no. 11979, http://content.lib.utah.edu/u?/USHS_Class,977 (accessed 12 April 2009). Another photograph of Nabbie wearing a cross necklace can be found at the Utah State Historical Society Classified Photo Collection, no. 11978, http://content.lib.utah.edu/u?/USHS_Class,964 (accessed 12 April 2009). Susa Young Gates also wears a cross charm in a photo dated c.1874. See *On this Day in the Church: An Illustrated Almanac of the Latter-day Saints* (Salt Lake City: Eagle Gave, 2000), 53. Another of Brigham Young's daughters (identified as his "Last Baby") is seen wearing a cross necklace in a drawing published in T. B. H. Stenhouse, *An Englishwoman in Utah: The Story of A Life's Experience in Mormonism* (London, 1880), 168b, http://books.google.com/books?id=N34FAAAAQAAJ& (accessed 9 July 2010).

33. This photo of Georgia (in figure 5.14) appears to have been the basis for an artist's depiction of her on a print showing each member of her Father's polygamous family. See Utah State Historical Society Classified Photo Collection, no. 26916, http://content.lib.utah.edu/u?/

FIGURES 5.11 AND 5.12: *Amelia Folsom Young (left), a plural wife of Brigham Young, and his daughter Talula Young (right), both wore cross jewelry in these portraits.*

FIGURES 5.13 AND 5.14: *Another daughter of Brigham Young, Nabbie Howe Young (left), wearing cross earrings; and Georgia Clawson (right) wearing a large cross necklace.*

FIGURES 5.15 AND 5.16: *Mary Ann Stewart (left) wearing a cross brooch; and Ada Afton Love (right) wearing a cross necklace.*

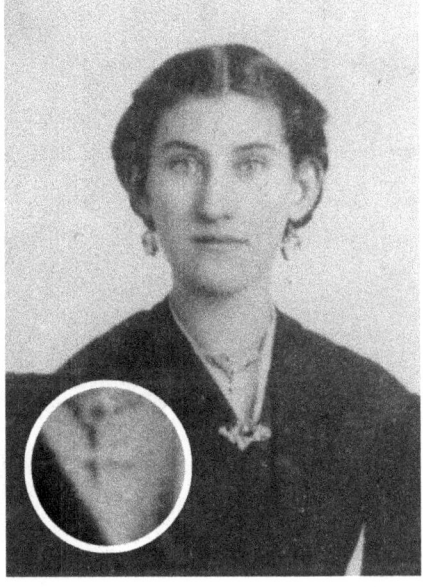

FIGURES 5.17 AND 5.18: *Dora Lowry (left) wearing a cross on a chain, and Carolyn August Ivins (right) wearing a cross necklace.*

FIGURES 5.19 AND 5.20: *John Whittaker Taylor's children (left) with the daughter wearing a cross necklace (1915), as is John Loveless' daughter (right).*

FIGURE 5.21 AND 5.22: *Cross necklace (left) worn by a member of the Walter Killshaw Barton family (c. 1888), and Benjamin Franklin Johnson (right) wearing a watch-chain with a cross (other images show him wearing the same).*

FIGURE 5.23: *A group photo of the Tabernacle Choir (1883), note the cross necklace enlarged in the upper right inset.*

FIGURE 5.24: *The Bishop, superintendents and teachers of the Sixteenth Ward Sunday School (1883), note the cross watch fob enlarged in the upper right inset.*

to Brigham Young, having married two of his daughters, and also served as his personal business manager.

A cross is also found hanging around the neck of Apostle John W. Taylor's daughter (granddaughter of President John Taylor) (c. 1915), while Cedar City's first Primary President Mary Ann Corlett Stewart wore a cross brooch (c. 1870–80). Ada Afton Love, daughter of the prominent churchman, congressman, and director of ZCMI, Stephen H. Love, wore a delicate cross necklace while posing for a picture (c. 1910); as did a daughter (c. 1880–1920) of the LDS John Loveless family—a family that had experienced tremendous persecution at the hands of mob violence in Missouri, and later left for Utah in 1851. Dora Lowry, daughter of Utah Pioneers, whose father (John Lowry Jr.) was a member of the Nauvoo Legion and was the first bishop of the Salt Lake City Second Ward, wore a cross hanging from a chain while having a picture taken (c. 1885–1891). Fourteen year-old Susan Malinda Barton (c.1888) of the Walter Killshaw Barton family was photographed with cross necklaces, and another photo has shown the sister of Apostle Anthony W. Ivins, Carolyn Augusta Ivins, wearing one while sitting on a chair (c. 1865).

Although the cross jewelry was more popular for women, some men wore crosses as tie-tacks and on their watch chains. One example is cross hanging from underneath the coat of a man, posing in a photograph (c. 1883) titled "The Bishop, Superintendents, and Teachers of the Sixteenth Ward Sunday School." Another is found worn by Benjamin F. Johnson on his watch chain.

In short, Mormons in the nineteenth and early twentieth centuries did not consistently shun the cross a taboo symbol. In contrast to modern attitudes and practices, early Mormons made frequent use of the symbol in a variety of contexts.

USHS_Class,983 (accessed 12 April 2009). Another portrait of Hiram B. Clawson and his family members shows a daughter (Georgia?) wearing a similar cross necklace at Ibid., no. 11969, http://content.lib.utah.edu/u?/USHS_Class,979 (accessed 12 April 2009).

FIGURES 5.25 AND 5.26: *Spine (left) of the 1852 European edition of the Doctrine and Covenants decorated with crosses, and Elmeda Stringham Harmon (right) holding a cross.*

CHAPTER SIX

The Ensign Peak Proposal[1]

BY 1910 MOST of the original Utah Mormon pioneers had passed away. Erecting monuments to their honor was the desire of the public and the media for many years,[2] and Ensign Peak[3] was considered to be the ideal location for such.

---

1. Ronald W. Walker wrote a history of Ensign Peak, covering the Church's cross monument proposal controversy, in his excellent article, "A Gauge of the Times: Ensign Peak in the Twentieth Century," *Utah Historical Quarterly* 62, no. 1 (1994): 4-25.

2. The *Box Elder* newspaper, for example, published a statement expressing the importance of building a monument: "The pioneers are gradually slipping away from our midst, and those remaining [in Brigham City] can be counted upon the fingers of one hand. Why would it not be a splendid thing to let the few remaining ones live to see their efforts immortalized... and their hearts made glad in the recognition of unremitting toil so faithfully performed?" "That Pioneer Monument," *Box Elder*, June 22, 1911, http://digital.lib.usu.edu/cdm4/document.php?CISOROOT=/Boxelder&CISOPTR=33147 (accessed 8 September 2008).

3. Ensign Peak is a sacred location for Latter-day Saints, as it was where the spirit of Joseph Smith had reportedly directed Brigham Young (prior to his trek west) to raise an Ensign to the Nations, which would be near where the Saints would finally settle. According to Apostle George Albert Smith, "President Young had a vision of Joseph Smith, who showed him the mountain that we now call Ensign Peak, immediately north of Salt Lake City, and there was an ensign fell upon that peak, and Joseph said, 'Build under the point where the colors fall and you will prosper and have peace.'... When they [the Pioneers] entered it President Young pointed to that peak, and said he, 'I want to go there.'" George A. Smith (1869), *Journal of Discourses*, 13: 85-86. Ever since this time, the peak was considered to be a "natural temple" and was a place for pioneer Saints to receive their endowments before the construction of the Salt Lake City temple was completed. *Encyclopedia of Mormonism*, s.v. "Endowment Houses."

On pioneer day, 24 July 1915, prominent LDS general authority Brigham H. Roberts spoke concerning the proposed landmark. Although a United States flag then adorned the top of the hill, Roberts predicted that a different "ensign" would eventually be raised there:

> The peak, he said, did not derive its name from [the U.S. flag], but from a broader reason, because the leaders foresaw that a broader ensign, the ensign of humanity, was to float from that peak some time.

Roberts proposed that this "broader ensign" would be a cross:

> To the Catholic church belongs credit for being trail blazers. Seventy years before our pioneers came here there were priests on the shores of Great Salt lake with the emblem of Christianity, the cross of Christ, and to that church should be given that credit. The ensign which shall yet float from yonder peak is the ensign of humanity; the ensign of Christ in which every nation shall have part.[4]

A year later, on the fourth of May, 1916, the Church of Jesus Christ of Latter-day Saints petitioned the Salt Lake City Council to erect a pioneer monument on Ensign Peak.

> Your petitioner, in behalf of the Church he represents, requests the privilege of erecting on Ensign peak a suitable cross, the symbol of Christianity, as a memorial to the "Mormon" pioneers who first established here that which the cross implies.
>
> We would like to construct it of cement, re-enforced with steel, of sufficient dimensions that it can be readily seen from every part of the city. Your petitioner believes that it will add to the interest of strangers who are visiting our city, and constitute one more work of art or memorial which will emphasize the fact that, "This Is The Place."
>
> Respect,
> C. W. Nibley,
> Presiding Bishop of the Church of Jesus Christ of Latter-day Saints.[5]

---

4. "All Orators Pay Tribute to Pioneers," *Salt Lake Herald*, July 25, 1915, 5, http://udn.lib.utah.edu/u?/slh14,95109 (accessed 1 November 2010). See also "Masses Pay Tribute, Pioneers Honored," *Salt Lake Telegram*, July 25, 1915, 17, http://udn.lib.utah.edu/u?/tgm6,29471 (accessed 1 November 2010).

5. Charles W. Nibley, "To Erect a Cross on Ensign Peak," *Deseret Evening News* (May 5, 1916), Journal History of the Church of Jesus Christ of Latter-day Saints, vol. 547, 4 May 1916, 3, In *Selected Collections from the Archives of The Church of Jesus Christ of Latter-day Saints* [DVD] (Provo: Brigham University Press, 2002), 2: 33.

The initial reaction of the Salt Lake City Commission was split over the Church's cross proposal. The Commissioner of Public Affairs and Finance, Karl A. Sheid, was emphatically supportive of it, saying that it may "prove [to be] one of the most vital and important documents ever written in the state of Utah," as it had the potential to:

> Do more to remove prejudices and create harmony among fair-minded people... than all the drafting of statutes and ordinances, the preaching of sermons or the publishing of newspapers can ever do in this city and state.

Said Sheid, "Let us Hasten to respond to the liberal and progressive spirit of this petition." With unqualified praise, he continued:

> That the "Mormon" Church, which has so frequently and so unjustly been accused of not being a Christian church at all, should volunteer to place Christianity's most sacred emblem on Ensign peak—that place so hallowed by the memory of pioneer days—is to my mind an event of first importance: one that should be and doubtless will be heralded to the four quarters of the globe, to the ultimate benefit of this commonwealth.... [The cross] is a common heritage. It belongs to all of us.[6]

Emil S. Lund, a member of the lower house of the state legislature, opposed the plan, insisting that a cross monument on public property would be contrary to American ideals and the separation of church and state. Lund denied that the symbol represented the gospel that Mormon pioneers had brought to the state of Utah, and suggested that a cross monument on Ensign Peak, in fact, would mislead the public into thinking that Utah "is a Catholic state."

Lund maintained that it was disingenuous for the LDS Church to project itself as Christian, and argued that such a perception of Mormonism was falsified by "the fundamental principles of the church when it centered [sic] Utah." These fundamental principles included the belief in a God "possessing parts and passions," "a new prophet," "a new bible" (Book of Mormon), and a "new marriage" (polygamy). Considering these beliefs of the early pioneers, Lund sarcastically associated Mormonism

---

6. "Delay Action On Petition," *Deseret Evening News* (May 9, 1916), Journal History vol. 547, 8 May 1916, 3, *Selected Collections*, 2:33.

with Islam, saying, "It is evident that the oriental crescent of the Mohomedan is a better exhibit for the Pioneer as a monument." With sensational rhetoric, he took a jab at Commissioner Scheid, and then attacked Christianity itself:

> Mr. Scheid has drawn upon a vivid inspiration when he predicted that the progressive spirit of the age looks to Idols... for stimulants to ethical and social betterment.... [However] the age of superstition is dying, Christianity has failed, and a new era coming. Based upon material facts and the rights of humanity upon which the cross of Christ has been a burden and obstruction of human freedom in all ages.

Lund concluded his objection, suggesting that a better idea for honoring the Pioneers would be to beautify the location and make it a park.[7]

The Salt Lake City Council decided to delay action on the LDS Church's petition. Meanwhile, commissioner Heber M. Wells sent a private letter of encouragement and counsel to Presiding Bishop Charles W. Nibley, who had originally submitted the petition on the church's behalf. Wells wrote:

> In regard to the cross on the peak[,] don't think I am idle or have forgotten it. I think more will be gained by not appearing too insistent or attempting to railroad favorable action through.

He mentioned Scheid's support of the proposal, but also informed him that others "have expressed themselves as unopposed." There was also support coming from the media and local clergy—an exception being the representatives from the Jewish community in Salt Lake City. Wells noted that "no newspaper has come out against it & no minister except the Rabbi," adding jokingly, "of course it was to be expected [that] a cross anywhere would give him the rabies." Wells assured Bishop Nibley that the proposal will nevertheless be passed by the commission, "I am given to understand that Mr. Shearman will oppose it, but at this writing it is my opinion that the other four will vote 'aye.'" Wells then added:

> For your information... many of our good Mormon brethren have privately expressed to me their opposition... until I suggested that if they

---

7. Emil S. Lund, formal protest delivered to the Board of City Commissioners, 10 May 1916, Charles W. Nibley Papers, LDS Church History Library. This document was provided by the LDS Church History staff.

devised to make an argument against the proposition to please make it to you & then they faded away. One freshman stopped me on the street & said: "What are ye tryin' to do Govener [sic]? Are ye going to put the Catholic sign on the [Peak] or what is it?"[8]

Commissioner Wells' letter turned out to be quite accurate. Just one week previously, Bishop Nibley had his first taste of the anti-Catholic opposition when he received a letter accusing him of "either [being] influenced by the Roman Church officials," or being "ignorant of the moral turpitude of this same powerful influence, which seeks to dominate every institution in the City, State and Nation." The letter-writer argued that the cross is not a symbol of Christianity, but rather is:

> A symbol of catholic domination everywhere.... If you doubt the effort of this Church, note hereafter that one catholic will be a candidate for every office within the gift of the people of Utah.

The letter-writer perceived the Catholic Church to be a religious, political and social threat. For these reasons, he argued that it was the duty of the people of Utah to stand against its influence:

> Bishop Glass [of the Utah Catholic diocese] was sent here to make Utah Catholic, and unless the people of Utah are aroused to that fact he will succeed.

The letter then closes with an accusatory statement aimed at Bishop Nibley: "You are but one means to secure that end. Read the History of this Church if you doubt my word."[9]

Another inflammatory anti-Catholic letter was sent to Bishop Nibley anonymously, claiming to be from one "born and reared in the Catholic church" and who therefore understands "the power and influence it had on our civilization and the degradation it has brought on the Centuries when its dogmas control the masses." The cross "is the sign of death" claimed the anonymous writer, equating the symbol to the "scaffold or the guillotine that made the French Revolution." He then appealed to the

---

8. Heber M. Wells, Letter to Charles W. Nibley, 19 May 1916, Incoming correspondence, Charles W. Nibley Papers. This document was provided by the LDS Church History staff.

9. Charles [illegible], Letter to Charles W. Nibley, 13 May 1916, Incoming correspondence, Charles W. Nibley Papers. This document was provided by the LDS Church History staff.

views of the Protestant iconoclasts, saying, "If John Knox[10] could return and tell you a scotchman what he thinks about this move[,] you would feel hell was a very fine place to cool off in." The letter advised Bishop Nibley to "keep your people free of Rome as long as you can[,] take not its emblems or dogmas[,] or your people will become as the Romans." A better suggestion for the hilltop, claimed the anonymous writer, was envisioned by Alma Pratt (son of Apostle Parley P. Pratt):

> Like all Pratts he was a visionary[,] he told me more than once that he saw in vision from Capital Hill to the top of Ensign Peak was a series of beautiful Parks[,] fountains spraying[,] and beautiful buildings[,] and delightful shades made by a forest of trees[.] At that time I felt he was as crazy as he afterwards became... but in the past six months I have concluded that dreamers and visionaries are sometimes right[,] as the finishing the Capital and grounds will make half of his dream true.

This anonymous writer evidently concurred with Emil S. Lund's suggestion that making Ensign Peak a park would be the best way to honor the pioneers.[11]

Commissioner Heber M. Wells was also correct about the impending protest of local Jewish rabbis. Four days after Bishop Nibley received Wells' letter, Rabbi William Rice and Rabbi Samuel Baskin appeared before the city commission to protest the cross monument proposal on grounds of separation of church and state. The *Salt Lake Tribune* reported that "the two explained that they would as strenuously object to the placing of any religious symbol upon the peak or upon any public ground, a symbol of the Jewish faith as much as any faith." The article continued, noting:

---

10. Mormon Historian James L. Barker wrote, "[Knox] declared that the reformers did not desire to change authority, but to reform religion, suppress idolatry, and 'to cleanse the temple.' After the defeat of the Reformed troops at Sterling by the French troops, Knox declared that their cause must prevail, because it 'is the eternal truth of the eternal God.' Taking their inspiration from Knox's preaching, his hearers destroyed crosses, images, stained glass windows, and monasteries. Knox is quoted as saying, 'Destroy the nests and the crows will not return.'" James L. Barker, "The Protestors of Christendom" (September 1939), *Improvement Era* 32, no. 9, In *LDS Library 2006*.

11. Anonymous, Letter to Charles W. Nibley, 9 May 1916, Incoming correspondence, Charles W. Nibley Papers. This document was provided by the LDS Church History staff.

Both rabbis argued that the cross on Ensign peak would not be representative of all citizens of the city, since the city has no representative religion and all taxpayers of the city are not Christians.

The rabbis warned that the petition, if passed, could potentially reignite religious tension in the state of Utah and "destroy a united spirit of citizenship." After hearing the Rabbi's arguments, commissioner Scheid initially withheld his final view of the cross-monument proposal, but he implied his continued support, saying:

> We would be in an oddly half-gracious position if we granted permission for the erection of the monument on the peak and then undertook to dictate its design.[12]

These objections were not enough to convince the Salt Lake City Council to veto the petition. The proposal was "granted with the understanding, that the present flag pole be left standing, if possible."[13] Despite this final ruling, the protests were far from over. Emil S. Lund and Rabbi Rice continued their fight, taking the matter to the courts.[14]

---

12. "Jews are Opposed to Cross on Peak," *Salt Lake Tribune* (May 23, 1916), JH vol. 547, 22 May 1916, 5, *Selected Collections*, 2: 33. Historian Ronald W. Walker commented on this remark, saying, "Five years earlier the city had thrown off the anti-Mormon partisanship of the American party. Rice and Baskin hinted that if the plans for a public cross went forward the old fires might be rekindled." Ronald W. Walker, "A Gauge the Times: Ensign Peak in the Twentieth Century," *Utah Historical Quarterly*, 15.

13. Salt Lake City Commission, Letter to Charles W. Nibley, 25 May 1916, Incoming correspondence, Charles W. Nibley Papers. This document was provided by the LDS Church History staff. Ronald W. Walker gives additional details: "The desultory discussion ended with a 4-1 vote. Shearman, complaining that the plan had caused enough trouble already, cast the sole negative vote." Ronald W. Walker, "A Gauge of the Times," 15.

14. Lund and Rice "have not dropped their plan of opposition. They threaten that if the Mormon church authorities do not forego their intention they will appeal to the courts to have the legality of the matter passed upon." "Courts May Decide Legality of Cross," *Salt Lake Telegram*, May 28, 1916, http://udn.lib.utah.edu/u?/tgm9,67228 (accessed 10 July 2010). "Suit to restrain the Mormon church from erecting a concrete cross on Ensign peak was filed in the Third district court yesterday by Emil S. Lund. Joseph Smith, president, and C. W. Nibley, presiding bishop, are named in the complaint as having control and management of the church affairs. The information filed with the court is based upon the contention that the action of allowing public property to be used for private religious purposes is contrary to the fundamental right of the common wealth. The plaintiff charges that Bishop Nibley represents the Catholic as well as the Mormon church in the matter of the erection of the cross. He points out that the cross is the recognized symbol of the Catholic church." "Lund Takes Fight on Cross to

A week later, Bishop Nibley received another critical letter from James Zebulon Stewart, a fairly prominent Latter-day Saint who had helped translate the Book of Mormon into Spanish and who had previously served on a Mormon mission in Mexican City under Apostle Moses Thatcher. Although Stewart took pains not to offend Bishop Nibley, he expressed deep concerns about the appropriateness of the symbol of the cross:

> It may be possible that I am somewhat prejudiced against the cross, having traveled for years among cross worshipers... but I am thoroughly convinced that it is the sign of the beast as spoken of in the 13th and 14th chapters of Revelations. I have seen thousands of Catholics wear a cross in their foreheads for for [sic] weeks where it has been placed by the blacked finger of the priest, and they would not wash it off for weeks at a time.[15] The Catholics would rejoice to see such a cross raised on that prominent place, but I have heard many Latter-day Saints express their disapproval of it, and I must say that I would regret very much to see it placed there.[16]

Stewart also expressed concern that a cross monument might be viewed negatively by some local Protestants. Stewart hoped that some more appropriate symbol might be substituted:

> A Bee Hive or something indicating the aspirations and ambitions of our people, give us something, if anything, that the protestant religionists will not look upon with contempt and as a victory for Catholicism.[17]

Court," *Salt Lake Telegram*, June 1, 1916, http://udn.lib.utah.edu/u?/tgm9,68798 (accessed 10 July 2010).

15. Stewart may have been influenced by Apostle Moses Thatcher's anti-Catholic sentiment while serving a Mission in Mexico under his leadership. Moses Thatcher recorded in his missionary journal: "March 2nd [1881]. This morning we see men and women[,] mostly the latter[,] returning from the great cathedral and the fashionable churches with a huge black cross mark on their foreheads.... The priests have listened to the vile confessions and... have 'absolved' them of their iniquities[,] and as a seal of the fact have placed the 'mark of the Beast on their foreheads.'" Moses Thatcher Diary, vol. 3, March 2, 1881, http://contentdm.lib.byu.edu/cdm4/document.php?CISOROOT=/MMD&CISOPTR=30028&REC=5&CISOBOX=cross&CISOSHOW=29915 (accessed 16 November 2008).

16. J[ames] Z[ebulon] Stewart, Letter to Charles W. Nibley, 30 May 1916, Incoming correspondence, Charles W. Nibley Papers. This document was provided by the LDS Church History staff.

17. Ibid.

On May 30th, Apostle Orson F. Whitney joined the protest, arguing before a group of Brigham Young University graduates that the cross should not be used for the pioneer monument because "the cross is really the symbol of the Catholic Church." Whitney instead suggested that:

> The cross proposed for Ensign peak in Salt Lake properly belongs on Mount Timpanogas in memory of Father Escalante, a pioneer Catholic father... [who] was the first white man to visit Utah valley.[18]

Bishop Nibley took offence at his fellow LDS General Authority's public rejection. Whitney noted Nibley's negative reaction in a letter that he sent to Nibley on the following day. "You and your good wife both seemed to be under the impression that I had been 'roasting' you," said Whitney. "This is a mistake. In my remarks at Provo Sunday evening, I made no allusion to you whatever—did not so much as mention your name, as I can prove by many witnesses." Whitney continued:

> I mentioned that it had been proposed by someone to erect a cross on Ensign Peak in honor of the Pioneers and that I thought such an emblem—representing as it does the Roman Catholic Church—might be more appropriately placed on Mt Timpanogas, overlooking Utah Valley, entered by Escalante 140 years ago. "Give us Ensign Peak," I added, "for the Stars and Stripes which the Pioneers brought with them into the desert".... The thought about Timpanogas was original, but in advocating the Stars and Stripes as the appropriate emblem for Ensign Peak, I was merely voicing the general view of the brethren of our Council whom I had heard expressing themselves upon the subject a few days before.

Whitney claimed that he overheard church authorities object to the proposal, and that they thought it would be best to fly an American flag on Ensign Peak instead.[19]

Nibley maintained that his views were in harmony with those Joseph F. Smith Sr., president of the LDS Church, and with the church's First Presidency. The bishop worried that the apostle's public objection to the cross proposal might hurt the image of the church, since it showed a lack

---

18. "Apostle of Mormons Would Honor Catholic," *Salt Lake Telegram* (May 31, 1916), JH vol. 547, 30 May 1916, 3, *Selected Collections*, 2: 33.

19. Orson F. Whitney, Letter to Charles W. Nibley, 31 May 1916, Incoming correspondence, Charles W. Nibley Papers. This document was provided by the LDS Church History staff.

of unity among the leadership. Such public statements could "do you no particular good that I can see, certainly it would not do me any good, nor do I think it would do the Church any good," said Nibley, adding:

> It only shows that there is, if not dissension, at least misunderstanding and perhaps a working at cross purposes between brethren who ought to be united on everything that the Church does.

Nibley explained that he had cleared the proposal with the First Presidency of the church prior to submitting the petition to the Salt Lake City Council:

> J.A. Reeves, General Traffic Manager of the Oregon Short Line, who is not a Catholic at all, but I believe is a member of the Episcopalian Church, suggested to Bishop David A. Smith [son of President Joseph F. Smith Sr. and Nibley's second counselor in the presiding bishopric] and myself that if the time every [sic] came and he had money enough, he would himself erect a cross on the Ensign Peak in honor of the Mormon pioneers who first brought christianity to this section. He added, "Of course it would be more proper, I suppose, for the Mormons to do that." But he said, "I have often thought it ought to be done."
>
> The suggestion appealed to me.... So accordingly as I happened to meet President [Joseph F.] Smith in front of the Bishop's Office I then and there, pointing to the Ensign Peak, made the suggestion to him that I thought it would be a very fine thing to place a cross on that peak of such dimensions that it could be seen from any part of the city; that thousands of people visit here who do not know that we believe in Christ at all. That it should be done as a memorial to the pioneers who first brought christianity and all that the cross symbolizes to this country.... The President seemed to have no objection to it, but I thought was rather pleased with the idea and suggested that I find out who owned the land, etc....
>
> I found out from Commissioner Wells that the city was the owner of the land and I dictated a petition which I took up to the Presidency, and President Smith and President [Charles W.] Penrose looked it over and I asked President Penrose to make such corrections as he would suggest, as his knowledge of grammar and construction of good English is far better than mine. There was little change made in the form of petition as President Penrose said he thought it would do as it was.

Accordingly the petition was sent to the City Commissioners, as you have no doubt seen it in the papers and you know the rest.

To Apostle Whitney's assertion that the symbol of the cross is strictly Catholic, Nibley responded, saying:

> It is true that the Roman Catholic Church have tried to appropriate the symbol of the cross as their particular symbol, but the cross simply brings to my mind... the one who died upon the cross.... [E]very Sabbath day... as I partake of the emblems of his body and blood, I should try to remember something about it. To my mind the cross typifies, or symbolizes[,] Christ or christianity.[20] And not the Roman Catholic Church a particle more than any other Christian church, only that the Roman Catholics have arrogantly, as they do most other things, appropriated this symbol to the glorification of their own church.[21]

Within days of making his public protest against the proposed cross monument before a group of graduate students at BYU, Apostle Whitney received a letter of support complimenting his words. Walter Ackroyd, who sat on the LDS High Council of the Taylor Stake in Alberta, Canada, wrote to say that he "rejoice[d] at [Whitney's] criticism of the cross." Ackroyd mentioned in his letter that he had once wondered why LDS temples did not have crosses on them, and explained his experience researching the matter:

> One day I met Bro. George Osmond [President of the LDS Star Valley Stake] and asked him what the cross meant, and why did not the Latter-day Saints use it as other people did to symbolize the atonement of our Savior. He replied that he did not know, but that one time he heard one of the brethren ask an Apostle[22] that had come

---

20. Incidentally, Bishop Nibley's daughter, Margaret, wears a cross necklace while posing in two group photographs with her sisters. See the *Nibley Family Photograph Collection* at Utah State University Library, Special Collections & Archives, USUSC P0315, 1:04:14, http://library.usu.edu/Specol/photoarchive/p0315/p03150050.html (accessed 10 December 2009); and ibid., http://library.usu.edu/Specol/photoarchive/p0315/p03150048.html (accessed 10 December 2010).

21. Charles W. Nibley, Letter to Orson F. Whitney, 31 May 1916, Outgoing correspondence, Charles W. Nibley Papers. This document was provided by the LDS Church History staff.

22. Who this Apostle was, Ackroyd does not say. It may be that Joseph Fielding Smith Jr. is the apostle he speaks of. Smith joined the Quorum of the Twelve in 1910, and published this very same argument decades later in his book *Answers to Gospel Questions*. It is also possible that the un-named apostle was David O. McKay, who joined the Twelve in 1906; and decades later

from Salt Lake why the Mormon people did not use the symbol of the cross as other people did, and the answer was, "If you had a very near and dear brother that had been unjustly hung on a gibbet, would you always carry the figure of a gibbet with you and have it exhibited in your house?"

With that guidance, Ackroyd said he had done additional research into the history of the symbol discovering that the original cross was the Egyptian *ankh*. According to Ackroyd's research, the *ankh* represented the male and female "organ[s] of generation" and "meant to the populace that the man and the woman in union was the creator of the child, the spirit and body." Ackroyd claimed, "This doctrine exalted man and belittled the personal God who is our Father in Heaven." His further contemplation led to personal revelation on the subject:

> [B]ut [I] was not sure of the true original meaning of the cross that lay behind, that the populace understands, so I asked our Heavenly Father for light. One night as I was reading and thinking on the matter it seemed that a voice spoke to my mind thus: "The cross is Lucifer's symbol and means that there is no pre-existence of spirits."

Ackroyd concluded his letter, saying:

---

asserted that the cross was strictly a symbol of Catholicism. However, both of these apostles seem unlikely candidates. Evidence suggesting that they would have expressed anti-cross views at such an early point in time is lacking; and since George Osmond died in 1913, the window of opportunity would have been fairly small for them: three years for Smith, and seven for McKay. A more likely candidate seems to be Moses Thatcher, who was an apostle from 1876 to 1896, and had expressed his disregard for the cross (both publically and privately) as early as 1881 and 1882. Also, unlike McKay and Smith, Thatcher had a major presence and role in the history of Star Valley Wyoming, where George Osmond had apparently overheard the visiting anonymous apostle's explanation of the cross' absence. Moses Thatcher (with Charles Rich) was appointed to supervise the LDS settlement in Star Valley. Thatcher participated (with Apostle Brigham Young Jr. and Presiding Bishop William Preston) in dedicating the location to the Saints and God (with Young acting as voice). Thatcher was credited for changing its name from "Salt River Valley" to "Star Valley," and had even once said that Star Valley was his preferred place to visit in the summer. See James B. Allen and Glen M. Leonard, *The Story of the Latter-day Saints* (Salt Lake City: Deseret Book, 1992), 392-93; Andrew Jensen, *LDS Biographical Encyclopedia*, 1: 134; and Dean L. May, "Between Two Cultures: The Mormon Settlement of Star Valley, Wyoming," *Journal of Mormon History* 13 (1986-1987): 125-43. It may be that Ackroyd purposefully refrained from naming Thatcher as the source of this statement, since he (Thatcher) was kicked out of the Quorum of the Twelve for apostasy; in consequence of his refusal to sign the political manifesto, his morphine addiction, his attempts to control the quorum, etc. See Edward Leo Lyman, "The Alienation of an Apostle from His Quorum: The Moses Thatcher Case," *Dialogue* 18, no. 2 (Summer 1985): 67-91.

If the accursed symbol is erected on Ensign Peak it is to be hoped that the lightnings of heaven will strike it so that we may still say there is no cross made by the Latter-day Saints.[23]

The next blow to the church's cross-monument proposal came from the unanimous opposition of an LDS congregation in Salt Lake City. On June 16, 1916, Bishop Nibley received a letter from the Salt Lake City Twentieth Ward, which protested:

Dear Brother:

After a full and complete discussion of the Parent Class in the Twentieth ward, it was unanimously decided that we, as a body, do most emphatically protest against the erecting of a cross on Ensign Peak.

But in place of it we recommend that an obelisk be erected bearing the name of Brigham Young and other of the Pioneers, and that from the top of said obelisk float the emblem of our country forever and forever.

Yours very truly,
A. J. Christensen[24]

Although it was clear by now that many Salt Lake City citizens (Mormon and non-Mormon alike) had adopted the rationalizations of past Protestant anti-Catholic iconoclasts, Bishop Nibley and supporters persisted. A church periodical published a statement criticizing those who had objected to the proposal. William A. Hyde, president of the church's stake in Pocatello, Idaho, wrote an article that appeared in the *Liahona*, insisting that Latter-day Saints are indeed Christian, concluding:

Recently the representatives of the "Mormon" Church asked for the privilege of placing upon the side of their highest mountain peak, a mammoth cross of concrete, that could be seen for miles, and that should rest upon the bosom of the mountain as a witness of the fact

---

23. Walter Ackroyd, Letter to Orson F. Whitney, 2 June 1916, Charles W. Nibley Papers. This document was provided by the LDS Church History staff. Ackroyd evidently was unaware of the fact that the Cardston Alberta Temple was currently being constructed in a cruciform design nearly twenty-five miles from his home town (Magrath, Alberta).

24. A. J. Christensen, Letter to Charles W. Nibley, 14 June 1916, Incoming correspondence, Charles W. Nibley Papers. This document was provided by the LDS Church History staff.

that the people who settled those valleys honor His name. That there was opposition to it is one of the surprises, in this Christian age. It would be a noble thing to do, for it would be a visible sign, painted on Nature's canvas, that would hold the sacrifice of the Son of God before the world, that those beholding it would ponder over this fact so apt to be forgotten in this hurried age. Would that the American people could give some sign of their belief that God might see and lead them.[25]

Less than a year later a small wooden cross was erected at another location, nearly six miles away, where Brigham Young was also said to have declared "this is the place"—Emigration Canyon. According to tradition, near this spot, Brigham Young, sick and wearied by the trek, looked across the valley and hillside from Apostle Wilford Woodruff's wagon and proclaimed, "it is enough; this is the place. Drive on."[26] The press release describing the occasion when the cross was erected is given as follows:

> Tuesday morning, July 24 [1917], the hike was made over Little Mountain into Emigration canyon. Here [an LDS group of Boy Scouts] were met by a committee in autos and carried to the mouth of the canyon, to the site of the sign marking the place where President Young, after viewing the valley some minutes in silence said, "It is enough. This is the right place." The party assembled at the place determined upon as being undoubtedly the point at which the now famous remark was made. The large sign board, consisting of an upright with a crossarm, was firmly planted, facing the valley. The inscription reads as follows: "This is the place — Brigham Young, July 24, 1847." Following the erection of the sign, Major Roberts addressed those assembled upon the historical significance of the spot which had just been marked, and expressed the hope that some day a substantial granite monument of suitable design would be erected to replace this simple and unpretentious sign board which marks the spot temporarily.[27]

---

25. William A. Hyde, "Who Are Christian?—A Test," *Liahona*, JH vol. 550, 15 August 1916, 5, *Selected Collections*, 2: 33.
26. John D. Giles, "This Is the Place" (May 1945), *Improvement Era* 58, no. 5, In *LDS Library 2006*.
27. The Church leaders presiding over the event were Apostle B. H. Roberts, Apostle George Albert Smith, Presiding Patriarch Hyrum G. Smith, and George J. Cannon of the Y.M.M.I.A. General board. John D. Giles, "Hike of 1917—Pioneer Trail" (September 1917), Improvement Era 20, no. 11, In *LDS Library 2006*.

Figures 6.1 and 6.2: Temporary cross monument in Emigration Canyon (left) with an artist's reconstruction of the inscription (right).

In figure 6.1 it is obvious that the temporary monument is a cross (and a rather large one at that), and yet the article identifies it merely as "a simple and unpretentious sign board," presumably minimizing the description to avoid additional public backlash.[28]

Having established their authority on the subject by placing a temporary cross in Emigration Canyon, LDS leaders apparently decided

---

28. Three months later (October 1917)—perhaps because he wanted to curb any lingering fears that he had succumbed to Catholic influence—Charles W. Nibley declared over the pulpit that the song "My Rosary" is not appropriate for the Church: "I have seen, too, some of our brethren, leaders of choirs, select a soloist who will come forward-someone with a good voice, who is capable of good singing-who will get up in a 'Mormon' meeting and commence to sing 'My Rosary.' Well now, 'My Rosary' is fine music and a good song for a Catholic meeting, but it is entirely out of place in a 'Mormon' meeting. That song recites how 'I count my beads and kiss my Cross,' and all that sort of thing. Well, I don't do either, I don't believe in doing either, and you don't believe in it. So, a song like that is entirely out of place in a 'Mormon' meeting, as much so, I think, as it would be to sing, 'We thank Thee, O God, for a Prophet, to guide us in these Latter Days,' in a Catholic meeting." Charles W. Nibley, Conference Report (October 7, 1917), 75, In *LDS Library 2006*.

to quietly shelve the controversial granite cross for Ensign Peak. In the summer of 1918, the Salt Lake City's Third District court finally acted on Emil S. Lund's request for an injunction. The complaint was terminated with the stipulation that the defendants (Bishop Charles W. Nibley and President Joseph F. Smith):

> Never again by themselves or by their agents... attempt to further or carry out the project so complained of. The court costs of the action are to be paid by the plaintiffs and each will pay attorney fees.[29]

---

29. "Case of Cross is Dismissed by Stipulation: Court Action Concerning Erection of Concrete Emblem is Terminated," *Salt Lake Herald*, June 21, 1918, 8, http://udn.lib.utah.edu/u?/slh15,45671 (accessed 1 November 2010). In 1934 an obelisk monument, designed by George Cannon Young (local architect and Brigham Young's grandson), was finally erected on Ensign Peak. For more information about this, including additional detail about the controversial cross monument proposal, see Ronald W. Walker, "A Gauge of the Times: Ensign Peak in the Twentieth Century," *Utah Historical Quarterly* 62, no. 1 (1994): 4-25. It seems Gordon B. Hinckley expressed his opinion, that an obelisk design was a better idea than the cross proposal, during a speech he gave at the 1996 dedication ceremony of the Ensign Peak park grounds. According to the *Church News* report of the event, "President Hinckley noted: 'There have been scores of proposals over the years concerning Ensign Peak.' They included, he said, a proposal to build a road to the top and put a building there, and another to erect a concrete cross on the peak. 'There have been a number of proposals to put advertising on the face of the peak with neon lighting. How that would have looked!... I'm glad none of that has ever happened.'... 'Now I'm glad to see that things are as they should be, in my judgment, with reference to the peak.'" R. Scott Lloyd, "Park at Ensign Peak Dedicated," *Church News*, August 3, 1996, http://www.ldschurchnews.com/articles/27875/Park-at-Ensign-Peak-dedicated.html (accessed 12 November 2008).

Chapter Seven

The Emergence of the Mormon Cross Taboo

THE EARLIEST PUBLISHED Mormon statements that question whether the cross should be considered a valid symbol of their faith occur in the late 1870s and early 1880s. Edward Tullidge was among the first Mormons to publish a negative statement about the cross in 1877:

> The Hebrews know nothing of the cross. It is the symbol of heathenism, whence Rome received her signs and her worship. Rome adopted the cross and she has borne it as her mark.[1]

During the Spring 1882 General Conference of the LDS Church, Apostle Moses Thatcher commented on Catholic custom of marking the forehead with a cross on Ash Wednesday, saying,

> Now, while these things... appeared very repugnant, immoral and debasing in their practice and tendency, yet I respected those people in their religious belief, customs and ceremonies.

This "respect" was not one of admiration, but rather of "toleration," comparable to the respect he had for "people of other creeds so long as they

---

1. Tullidge, *The Women of Mormondom*, 79. Two years later, Tullidge left the LDS Church and joined the RLDS Church.

do not infringe upon the rights and liberties of others."[2] Thatcher had revealed his feelings of repugnance for the Catholic tradition more explicitly in his journal the year before:

> March 2nd [1881]. This morning we see men and women[,] mostly the latter[,] returning from the great cathedral and the fashionable churches with a huge black cross mark on their foreheads.... The priests have listened to the vile confessions and... have "absolved" them of their iniquities[,] and as a seal of the fact have placed the "mark of the Beast on their foreheads."[3]

Just as opponents of the proposed Ensign Peak Monument would decades later, Thatcher equated the cross with Catholicism and his opposition to the symbol is thus linked to his general anti-Catholic sensibilities. Nevertheless, anti-Catholic feelings were prevalent in the United States throughout the Nineteenth and early Twentieth Centuries. Why did negativity toward the cross only begin to coalesce among Utah Mormons at the turn of the century?

As was previously mentioned, three major factors contributed to the acceptance of the cross among early Mormons: (1) the use of the cross in folk magic; (2) the use of the cross in Freemasonry; and (3) the perception that certain Pre-Columbian inscriptions were Christian crosses. Of these, the first two began to lose strength among Utah Mormons as the first pioneering generation of Saints passed away. D. Michael Quinn pointed out:

> After the death of LDS leaders who believed in folk magic, some rank-and-file Mormons continued certain magic beliefs and practices for decades. This was in spite of the skepticism (even hostility) which LDS leaders and publications expressed from the 1880s onward.... By the early twentieth century, identifiable magic practices and beliefs were not just declining in the LDS church. They did not exist for the vast majority of Mormons.[4]

---

2. Moses Thatcher (1882), *Journal of Discourses*, 23: 200-201.
3. Moses Thatcher Diary, vol. 3, March 2, 1881, http://contentdm.lib.byu.edu/cdm4/document.php?CISOROOT=/MMD&CISOPTR=30028&REC=5&CISOBOX=cross&CISOSHOW=29915 (accessed 16 November 2008).
4. Quinn, *Early Mormonism and the Magic World View*, 318-319.

Utah Mormons also turned their back on their Masonic past. Although Joseph Smith and the Saints in Nauvoo keenly embraced Freemasonry, fellow Masons in Illinois outside the church were highly critical of the practices of the Nauvoo Lodge. Eventually the Illinois Grand Lodge ordered all Mormon lodges in the state to cease activity, a directive that the Mormons ignored. The Carthage, Illinois, mob that killed Joseph and Hyrum Smith included many non-Mormon Masons—a fact that did not endear Mormons to Freemasonry.[5]

Years later, when the Saints settled in the Salt Lake Valley, non-Mormon settlers organized a new Grand Lodge of Utah. This non-Mormon association established an exclusionary policy disallowing Mormon membership in their fraternities:

> We say to the priests of the Latter-day Church, you cannot enter our lodge rooms—you surrender all to an unholy priesthood. You have heretofore sacrificed the sacred obligations of our beloved Order and we believe you would do the same again. Stand aside; we want none of you. Such a wound as you gave Masonry in Nauvoo is not easily healed, and no Latter-day Saint is, or can become a member of our Order in this jurisdiction.[6]

As the last Utah Mormons who had lived in Nauvoo passed away, the memory of Mormon involvement in Masonry faded. Historian Michael W. Homer observed:

> A new generation of Mormon writers, who had no personal knowledge of Freemasonry, found it easy to [claim]... that there was no connection between the endowment and Masonic rites....
>
> The Nauvoo endowment [that] had been introduced years earlier, had become totally institutionalized, and personal knowledge of Joseph Smith's explanation of the endowment and familiarity with Masonic ceremonies were replaced by reliance on historical accounts of the endowment.[7]

---

5. Homer, *Similarity of Priesthood in Masonry*, 31–33.
6. 1877 Proceedings of the Grand Lodge of Utah (Salt Lake City: Tribune Printing and Publishing Co., 1877), 11-12; as cited in Homer, *Similarity of Priesthood in Masonry*, 66.
7. Homer, *Similarity of Priesthood in Masonry*, 97-98.

As early as the 1880s, Freemasonry and folk-magic were by and large relegated to a forgotten past, and the new generation of Mormons viewed both as incompatible with their faith.

Therefore, of the factors in early Mormonism contributing to acceptance of the cross as a symbol, only one remained: the Pre-Columbian "crosses" which were perceived to help validate the historicity of the Book of Mormon. However, this last factor alone was not strong enough to stand against two new waves of anti-Catholic tension that swept through the LDS Church—the first of these occurring at the turn of the century, and the second approximately forty years later.

Mormon Assimilation

The passing of the pioneer generation was accompanied by changes in Mormon beliefs, practices, and customs far beyond attitudes concerning folk magic and Freemasonry. Over time, the LDS Church and Mormon culture in general shifted away from a phase of "entrenchment" to one of "assimilation" with the surrounding American culture. Sociologist Armand L. Mauss marks this transition precisely at the turn of the twentieth century. Mauss observes that in exchange for religious tolerance and Utah's statehood, LDS leaders discontinued "polygamy, theocracy, collectivist economic experiments, and any other flagrantly un-American institutions." In their new incarnation, "Mormons became models of patriotic, law-abiding citizenship, sometimes seeming to 'out-American' all other Americans."[8] LDS leaders abandoned old themes and softened the rhetoric in their preaching. Mauss observes that the new policies caused:

> A steady decline after the late nineteenth century in such uniquely Mormon themes as Zion and kingdom building, eschatology, missionary work, the apostasy of other churches, the restoration, the corruption of outside governments, and the like.... By contrast there was an increase during the same period in such assimilationist themes as the greatness of American institutions, patriotism, good citizenship, and fellowship with other faiths."[9]

---

8. Armand L. Mauss, *The Angel and the Beehive: The Mormon Struggle with Assimilation*, 22.
9. Ibid., 24-25.

In their new drive to reach out to non-Mormon believers, Latter-day Saints projected themselves as fitting with the Christian mainstream. The 1916 Ensign Peak monument proposal is again illustrative. In employing a universal Christian symbol in such an overt way, LDS leaders hoped to express common ground between Catholics, Protestants, and Mormons. But the negative reaction to the cross proposal also illustrates the countervailing trend: assimilation is regularly accompanied by the fear of losing one's own unique identity.[10]

Conservative Mormons were not the only ones resistant to breaking down the walls separating their faith from the broader Christian community. Just as frequently, non-Mormon Christians were apprehensive of steps taken by Mormons to assimilate. Having defined Mormons as "non-Christian," breaking down the boundaries was a potential threat to mainline Christian identity. In part as boundary maintenance, some Protestants and Catholics therefore regarded Mormon changes to be superficial, insufficient, and even disingenuous.[11] This negativity, in turn,

---

10. Armand Mauss explains this sociological phenomenon: "If, in the quest for acceptance and respectability, a movement allows itself to be pulled too far toward assimilation, it will lose its unique identity altogether. If, on the other hand, in its quest for uniqueness of identity and mission, it allows itself to move too far toward an extreme rejection of the host society, it will lose its very life. Its viability and its separate identity both depend upon a successful and perpetual oscillation within a fairly narrow range along a continuum between two alternative modes of oblivion." Ibid., 5. The lingering fear of previous decades, believing that other denominations were conspiring to de-convert their children further exacerbated this interfaith tension. Episcopal Bishop Tuttle claimed that Latter-day Saint adults "were fanatics, and so beyond the reach of our influence; or else were apostates, and so, grossly deceived once, were unwilling to listen again to any claims of the supernatural. But the plastic minds and wills of the young we could hope to win to better views and could mould in nobler ways." Daniel Sylvester Tuttle, *Reminiscence of a Missionary Bishop* (New York: Thomas Whittaker, 1906), 363; as cited in *Brigham Young University: The First One Hundred Years*, ed. Ernest L. Wilkinson (Provo: Brigham Young University Press, 1975), 1: 552. According to LDS scholar Ernest L. Wilkinson, however, Catholic schools were less concerned about converting Mormons: "The Catholic schools [unlike many Protestant schools] were founded to serve members of the Roman Catholic Church rather than to convert Mormon children, but they, like Mormon and Protestant schools, were open to members of other denominations." Wilkinson, *Brigham Young University*, 554.

11. Thomas G. Alexander, a historian who has written extensively on this transitional period for the Church, observes, "Protestants believed that they had a calling to convert Mormons to 'Christianity' and to undermine the secular power of the church. In October 1900 the Reverend John D. Nutting, a Congregational minister of the Utah Gospel Mission, averred that Mormons were feigning the abandonment of polygamy as a shield to protect themselves from the laws of the land. At a Presbyterian teachers conference, missionaries were encouraged to distribute tracts in order to convert Mormons from their ways, and a group of Methodists called Mormonism

could be read by Latter-day Saints in two ways. For conservatives, it showed that there was never any reason to compromise cherished practices; for progressives, it was an indication of how much further the church needed to go to achieve full acceptance.

Mormon/Catholic Relations

The evolution of the relationship between Mormons and Catholics is likewise important for understanding the appearance of anti-cross sentiment among the former. In 1869, Reverend Patrick Walsh had built the first Catholic chapel in the state of Utah, a few years later the small chapel was replaced by a larger brick church, and finally in 1887 "Catholicism [officially] entered Utah as an organized religion."[12] By the turn of the Twentieth Century, Catholics were only beginning to establish a real presence in the state of Utah.

In some ways, Mormon and Catholic relations outside Utah were more critical. LDS missionary work was very challenging in countries in Europe, such as France, Belgium, and Italy that were predominantly Catholic.[13] And things were sometimes worse in Catholic Latin America. During the Mexican revolution, violence against Mormons in Mexico was serious enough that the entire LDS mission had to be closed down in 1913. Historians Donald Q. Cannon and Richard O. Cowan explain that "the Mexican Saints were left alone to take care of themselves" when the Mormon missionaries departed.

> Just two years after their departure [1915]... the brutal forces of revolutionary conflict and religious prejudice resulted in the murders of [Branch] President Monroy and his cousin, Vincent Morales. As an excuse to persecute these new Mormon converts, Monroy had been falsely accused of being a colonel in a rival revolutionary faction.

The Catholic executioners told them, "Now, as one last chance, we tell you if you will renounce your religion and confess before the Virgin

---

'A Black and Devilish Spot.'" Thomas G. Alexander, *Mormonism in Transition: A History of the Latter-day Saints, 1890-1930* (Chicago: University Illinois Press, 1996), 241-42.

12. William Harris, "Utah," *The Catholic Encyclopedia* 15 (New York: Robert Appleton Company, 1912). http://www.newadvent.org/cathen/15238a.htm (accessed 26 March 2009).

13. Gregory A. Prince and Wm. Robert Wright, *David O. McKay and the Rise of Modern Mormonism* (Salt Lake City: University of Utah Press, 2005), 113.

Mary, we will spare your lives." Upon their refusal to deny the gospel that they had been converted to, Monroy and Morales were shot and murdered.[14]

As a result of such experiences with Catholics abroad, smaller conflicts with Catholics in Utah had a tendency to become amplified. For example, in 1916, Joseph S. Glass, Bishop of the Utah diocese of the Catholic Church, wrote a letter to the *Salt Lake Tribune* publicly criticizing Latter-day Saints for dancing on Good Friday:

> As a newcomer to our city, I trust that I shall be pardoned for expressing my surprise, my utter astonishment, at the many dances taking place tonight—Good Friday night! Is Salt Lake City so largely a city of unbelievers that the death of Christ upon the cross is nothing to us as a commonwealth?
>
> Are there not enough Christians in Salt Lake City to command some kind of general respect for the holiest day of the year?
>
> In the name of the Christians of this city, non-Catholic and Catholic,
>
> I beg to enter a solemn protest of this against the wanton desecration of this day.
>
> Very faithfully yours,
> (signed) Joseph S. Glass[15]

Bishop Glass's protest insulted Mormons who traditionally did not celebrate the holiday. It also apparently irked non-Mormons in Utah who found it presumptuous for the Catholic Bishop to impose his own religious convictions upon others.

When Charles W. Nibley, the presiding bishop of the LDS Church, presented the proposal for the cross monument atop Enign Peak just two weeks later, Bishop Glass's letter was fresh in the minds of many Utah citizens. The Catholic bishop's remarks seemed to validate Mormon fears that the "Catholic threat"—which they perceived in the experience doing missionary work abroad—soon exist in the state of Utah. One opponent to the cross monument explicitly stated:

---

14. Donald Q. Cannon and Richard O. Cowan, *Unto Every Nation: Gospel Light Reaches Every Land* (Salt Lake City: Deseret Book, 2003), 245-46.
15. "Bishop Protests Against Dancing on Good Friday," *Salt Lake Tribune* (April 22, 1916), JH vol. 546, 21 April 1916, 6, *Selected Collections*, 2: 33.

Bishop Glass a few weeks ago roasted the people who danced on Good Friday. He did not condemn dancing for its indecencies[,] but because the dancing was on Good Friday. Next year I suppose he will force the Mormon Church to establish lent.[16]

Another letter protesting the monument may have also been reactionary to Glass's remarks, when it was asserted that "Bishop Glass was sent here to make Utah Catholic";[17] and James Z. Stewart, although he did not mention Glass, was clearly angst over Catholic approval of the monument, when told Charles W. Nibley in a letter, "Catholics would rejoice to see such a cross raised on that prominent place."[18]

---

16. Anonymous, Letter to Charles W. Nibley, 9 May 1916.
17. Charles [illegible], Letter to Charles W. Nibley, 13 May 1916.
18. James Z. Stewart, Letter to Charles W. Nibley, 31 May, 1916. Tensions between Mormons and Catholics persisted after the Ensign Peak controversy. Apostle Hyrum M. Smith (son of President Joseph F. Smith) publically attacked Catholicism over the pulpit at the following General Conference (October 1916), claiming that it "is a great liability in any nation. It wields a power for evil... [Catholicism] does not promote civilization, it binds them in the thralldom of superstition." "Second Day's Session General Conference," *Deseret Evening News* (October 7, 1916), JH vol. 552, 7 Oct. 1916, 6, *Selected Collections*, 2:33. Offended by these and other remarks, Bishop Glass wrote a letter President Joseph F. Smith: "Now as the head of the Catholic Church in this Diosese, I desire to ask you, the President of the above mentioned Church of the Latter-Day Saints—do the sentiments expressed by Hyrum M. Smith represent the feelings of the Latter-Day Saints toward the Catholic Church? and does the attack of Hyrum M. Smith upon the Catholic Church meet with the approval of the First Presidency and Council of the Apostles." Joseph S. Glass, Letter to Joseph F. Smith (Oct. 7, 1916) *Joseph F. Smith Incoming Correspondence*, box 23 folder 5, *Selected Collections*, 1:28. Rather than answer these questions himself, President Smith instead handed the letter to his son Hyrum to answer. Apostle Hyrum M. Smith replied to Bishop Glass, "It would have been more consistent, in my judgment, had you submitted your questions to me rather than to the President of the Church, since I alone am responsible for the remarks to which you make reference.... You would hardly expect me to address a communication to the Pope asking if the expressions of Cardinal Gibbons, Bishop Vaughan, or other Catholic clergymen, attacking the 'Mormon' people and their belief, were the expressions of the Pope, the College of Cardinals or the Catholic Church at large. And yet it would be just as consistent." Apostle Smith then proceeded to quote several anti-Mormon statements from the aforementioned Catholic clergymen, and ended his letter, saying, "Let me ask you, are these expressions approved by you, and are they the views of the Catholic Church respecting Mormonism and the Mormon people?" Hyrum M. Smith, Letter to Joseph S. Glass (October 11, 1916) *Joseph F. Smith Incoming Correspondence*, box 23 folder 5, *Selected Collections*, 1:28. Hyrum's negative comments against Protestants in his General Conference talk were not well received either. See "Dr. Sutteliffe Replies to Apostle [sic] Statement 'Christianity is a Failure,'" *The Idaho Falls Post* (October 16, 1916), JH vol. 552, 16 Oct. 1916, 6, *Selected Collections*, 2:33.

CHAPTER EIGHT

Opposition to the Cross Institutionalized

ALTHOUGH THE CONTROVERSY over the proposed Ensign Peak monument highlighted a growing aversion to the symbol of the cross among Mormons, the fact that the LDS Church itself took a pro-cross stance shows that the aversion had not yet become official protocol. For over three more decades, Latter-day Saints from the leadership on down, continued to be divided over the appropriateness of the cross. While some rejected the symbol, others continued to embrace it.

B. H. Roberts was one of the LDS General Authorities who favored placing a cross monument for Ensign Peak. Additionally, Roberts frequently argued that Pre-Columbian crosses were evidence in favor of the Book of Mormon's historical claims.[1] When he died in 1933, former missionaries who had served under his leadership joined with the Roberts family to mark his grave site with a headstone inscribed with a large Latin cross (see figure 8.1).[2] Up to that late date, then, it was easily con-

---

1. B. H. Roberts, "A New Witness for God," *The Contributor* 9, no. 11 (September 1888). Roberts also publically identified the "cross of Christ" as "the emblem of Christianity." See "All Orators Pay Tribute to Pioneers," *Salt Lake Herald*, July 25, 1915, 5, http://udn.lib.utah.edu/u?/slh14,95109 (accessed 1 November 2010).
2. "B.H. Roberts' Grave in Centerville... is adorned with a massive marble cross purchased by the missionaries who served under his direction in the Eastern States Mission." Hugo Olaiz, "Letter to the Editor," *Dialogue* 35, no. 2 (Summer 2002): vii.

FIGURE 8.1: *The headstone of LDS General Authority, B. H. Roberts, erected in 1933, was inscribed with a prominent Latin cross.*

ceivable that a devout Mormon leader and his family would view the cross as a symbol inclusive of their own faith.

A similar attitude toward the cross can be discerned the following decade in a spiritual experience recounted by Spencer W. Kimball (who later became the twelfth president of the LDS Church). In 1943, Kimball received the call from church leaders to join the Quorum of the Twelve Apostles. With great feelings of inadequacy, Kimball turned to God in prayer. As he wrote shortly after the experience:

> No peace had yet come, though I had prayed for it almost unceasingly these six days and nights. I had no plan or destination. I only knew I must get out in the open, apart, away... I dressed quietly and without disturbing the family, I slipped out of the house. I turned toward the hills. I had no objective. I wanted only to be alone.

Kimball then describes the tearful hike he made up the hillside:

> I climbed on and on. Never had I prayed before as I now prayed. What I wanted and felt I must have was an assurance that I was acceptable to the Lord. I told Him that I neither wanted nor was worthy of a vision or appearance of angels or any special manifestation. I wanted only the calm peaceful assurance that my offering was accepted. Never before had I been tortured as I was now being tortured. And the assurance did not come.

Finally, Kimball saw a sign that gave him assurance that God was with him:

> As I rounded a promontory I saw immediately above me the peak of the mountain and on the peak a huge cross with its arms silhouetted against the blue sky beyond. It was just an ordinary cross made of two large heavy limbs of a tree, but in my frame of mind, and coming on it so unexpectedly, it seemed a sacred omen.[3]

This experience made such an impact on the future prophet, that he revisited the place two years later in 1945. As Kimball recorded in his journal:

> I began to re-live my unusual experiences.... I followed my footsteps of that early morning.... Finally at the top of my sacred mountain I found my cross of July '43 was broken. I found a cross beam and carried it up the hill (remembering the Savior as he carried his cross up Calvary) and fixed it the best I could.[4]

These and similar examples show that, as of middle of the Twentieth Century, LDS Church leaders had not yet internalized the aversion to the cross. Crosses were still regarded as valid symbols of faith among Mormons. In fact, the official LDS Church position regarding the cross did not become formalized until the presidency of David O. McKay (1951–70).

---

3. Edward L. Kimball and Andrew E. Kimball, *Spencer W. Kimball: Twelfth President of the Church of Jesus Christ of Latter-day Saints* (Salt Lake City: Bookcraft, 1977), 192-94 [original spelling and punctuation retained].

4. Ibid., 221-22.

Formalization of the Taboo

McKay was one of the growing number of Mormons in the early Twentieth Century with anti-Catholic feelings who likewise equated the symbol of the cross wholly with Catholicism. As he confided in his journal in 1957, "Latter-day Saint girls [as well as others] should not purchase and wear them." Crosses are "purely Catholic," he said.[5] McKay was already a member of the Quorum of the Twelve when the church petitioned the Salt Lake City Council to erect a cross monument on Ensign Peak, and it is possible he was numbered among the anonymous "brethren of our council" that Orson F. Whitney said objected to the proposed monument's design.[6] Although McKay's opinions on the cross and Catholicism in 1916 are unknown, his feelings concerning the latter clearly had turned negative by the 1920s. McKay's biographers Gregory Prince and Wm. Robert Wright note that:

> While McKay's exposure to Roman Catholicism had been minimal in Utah, his appointment as president of the European Mission sent him into countries where it was the dominant church and where most Mormons were converts from Catholicism.... In 1923 he visited Liege, Belgium, and wrote in his diary: "A Catholic Church celebration was held last night [Saturday]—People drinking and carousing until 6:30 this morning. O what a Godless farce that organization is!"[7]

From McKay's first-hand experience in Europe, the future church president observed that Protestant countries brought "thousands of nineteenth-century converts, including [McKay's] own grandparents." Conversely, "proselytizing efforts to predominantly Roman Catholic countries had been limited... and had generally been unsuccessful."[8]

Mormon relations with the Catholic Church in Utah were additionally challenging in 1930, when Catholic Bishop Duane Hunt began a radio show intended to reaffirm the faith of Utah's Catholic minority. But because the radio station (KSL) was owned by the LDS Church,

---

5. David O. McKay Diaries, April 29, 1957. Transcription provided by Gregory A. Prince. MS 668, Manuscripts Division, J. Willard Marriott Library, University of Utah.
6. Said Whitney, "I was merely voicing the general view of the brethren of our council whom I had heard expressing themselves upon the subject a few days before." CW Nibley Papers, Orson F. Whitney to Charles W. Nibley (31 May 1916), 3.
7. Prince and Wright, *David O. McKay*, 113.
8. Ibid.

Mormons misunderstood the intent of the addresses, and assumed that Hunt was trying to convert Latter-day Saints.[9]

The situation was further exacerbated in 1948, when J. Reuben Clark Jr. of the LDS First Presidency began a radio series of his own on KSL, inviting Bishop Hunt to participate. Hunt accepted the invitation, and both men reaffirmed their faith during the broadcasts. But, as Prince and Wright explain, Clark "misinterpreted Hunt's addresses on the primacy of the Pope and the Holy See in Rome as an assault on Mormonism." Clark countered Hunt's remarks with an aggressive attack on Catholicism in his next radio program, and even published his radio transcripts the following year.[10]

The dispute between Hunt and Clark did not directly involve David O. McKay. However, it is obvious whose side he was on. Shortly after the aforementioned conflict, McKay wrote in his diary that Catholics seemed determined "to convert as many Mormons here in the West as they possibly can. There is no doubt but that there is an organized campaign on in this respect."[11]

Relations with Bishop Hunt and other Utah Catholics were further challenged later that year when Hunt's assistant Leo J. Steck published a pamphlet lamenting the poor living conditions of many of Utah's Catholics.[12] Although the pamphlet said nothing about proselytizing in the state of Utah, or anything about Mormonism at all, it was entitled "A Foreign Mission Close to Home." The term "mission" had radically different connotations for Mormons and Catholics, as Prince and Wright explain:

> In the Catholic vernacular, and certainly in the context of the pamphlet, *mission* meant a rudimentary, underfunded parish. In the LDS vernacular, however, *mission* meant only proselytizing. A Mormon who saw the pamphlet without reading its contents could thus easily have concluded that it was the first foray of a new initiative to lure Latter-day Saints away from their own faith into Roman Catholicism. One such Mormon was David O. McKay. Speaking to local church leaders

---

9. Ibid.
10. Ibid., 114. The book Clark published was entitled *On the Way to Immortality and Eternal Life* (Salt Lake City: Deseret Book Company, 1950).
11. Ibid., 115.
12. Ibid.

in his hometown of Huntsville, "I presented to them the avowed activity of the CATHOLIC CHURCH here in Utah, and called their attention to a leaflet that designates Utah as 'a foreign Mission close to home.'"[13]

McKay and the First Presidency directed Apostle Mark E. Peterson to organize a series of meetings with local church leaders, during which time Peterson accused the Catholic Church of attacking Latter-day Saints. Bishop Hunt explained to McKay that the Mormons were misinterpreting Steck's pamphlet. Further, Hunt promised that the Catholic Church had discontinued the pamphlet's distribution after realizing the confusion, but McKay proved hard to convince.[14] Eventually Hunt and McKay were able to patch up their relationship, but the Mormon leader was unwilling to give up his negative views of the Catholic Church.

McKay's underlying attitude was revealed in comments made during a 1953 visit to California. Pointing at a Catholic church, he declared, "There are two great anti-Christs in the world: Communism and that church."[15]

McKay's anti-Catholic bias, coupled with his equation of the cross with Catholicism contributed directly to the formalization of LDS Church on the cross in 1957. McKay wrote in his journal:

> Bishop Joseph L. Wirthlin called me by telephone and asked me the Church's position on the following question: He stated that he had been asked today if it would be proper for L.D.S. girls to purchase crosses to wear. It is Bishop Wirthlin's understanding that there is a company downtown which is pushing the selling of these crosses to girls.

---

13. Ibid., 115-116.
14. Ibid., 116-118.
15. Ibid., 120. That same year David O. McKay again paired Catholicism and Communism together as two of the Church's great enemies "As long as we are one, and we have the Lord with us, nothing else need worry us or give us concern. No matter how many enemies attack us, no matter how subversive the influence of Catholics, Communism or other isms, we are all right as long as we are united in supporting one another." DOMD, September 8, 1953. Less than a year later, McKay again asserted, "It is more apparent than ever, becoming more apparent each day, that two great organized forces, the purpose of which is to undermine the high principles of the Restored Gospel, are operating. One is Communism, which is moving aggressively over the face of the earth, fundamentally prompted by disbelief in the existence of God, a rejection of the life of Jesus Christ as the Savior of the world, and is against the Church. The other is the Catholic Church, which is showing more clearly than ever before that they are determined to counteract the influence of the Church in this western country." DOMD, June 3, 1954.

> I told Bishop Wirthlin that this is purely Catholic and Latter-day Saint girls should not purchase and wear them. I stated further that this was a Catholic form of worship. They use images, crosses, etc. Our worship should be in our hearts.
>
> Bishop Wirthlin said that this had been his opinion, but he felt that he should check with me before making a statement.[16]

Thus began the formal church policy banning use of the cross among Mormons.

---

16. DOMD, April 29, 1957. Transcription provided by Gregory A. Prince. Also cited and partially quoted in Gregory A. Prince and Wm. Robert Wright, *David O. McKay*, 121. Early October 1957, Ezra Taft Benson—who was simultaneously serving as LDS Apostle and US Secretary of Agriculture—asked President David O. McKay if he (Benson) should accept a "government appointment" to meet with the Pope. Presumably, the papacy was looking for advice on how to rebuild war-torn Europe. After discussing the matter with his counselors in the First Presidency, McKay replied to Benson, saying, "[W]e are all united in the feeling that if you can in honor, and without embarrassment, avoid that conference it would be well for you to do it.... We have in mind particularly the effect upon our own people.... And the dignity that you would have to give to such a conference.... [Catholics] have everything to gain and nothing to lose, and we have everything to lose and nothing to gain.... We all feel that it would be pretty embarrassing to you, and we are helping you out of what might prove to be a conference that will reflect upon our Church." Ezra Taft Benson agreed: "Well, I think it could be embarrassing both to me and to the Church.... I shall do my best, and I think I can work it out [i.e. decline the appointment]." DOMD, October 1-2, 1957.

CHAPTER NINE

The Taboo Reinforced

LDS GENERAL AUTHORITIES have reinforced the cross taboo ever since its institutionalization. Among the most prominent and influential to do so were Apostles J. Reuben Clark, Mark E. Petersen, and Seventy (and later Apostle) Bruce R. McConkie. All three of these church leaders, incidentally, were (at some time in their lives) members of the Salt Lake City Twentieth Ward—the congregation that had unanimously protested the 1916 Ensign Peak cross monument proposal. In addition to these three church authorities, Joseph Fielding Smith Jr. (McConkie's father in-law) and Gordon B. Hinckley (who, as the executive secretary of the Church Radio Committee, assisted J. Reuben Clark Jr. during his aforementioned radio series[1]) reaffirmed that the symbol of the cross was incompatible with the Mormon faith.

J. Reuben Clark found justification for condemning the use of the cross in arguments dating from the division in Medieval Christianity over the propriety of "icons" or religious images. Although ultimately ruled heretical, Iconoclasts believed that religious images were idols that

---

1. J. Reuben Clark wrote, "I thank all who have helped in these broadcasts... Elder Gordon B. Hinckley of the Church Radio Committee, for his valued kindness and suggestions." J. Reuben Clark, *On the Way to Immortality and Eternal Life*, 212.

should be destroyed. Clark questioned the arguments of their orthodox opponents:

> In the iconoclastic conflict (A. D. 808), Theodore, appearing before Leo V, declared that: "The Old Testament prohibitions of images... are abolished by the incarnation: if the law of Moses were to be regarded, how is it that we worship the cross, which the law speaks of as accursed?"

Clark denounced Theodore's rationalization, saying, "Here again one heresy is invoked to justify another. There is no scripture justifying the worship of the cross."[2]

Mark E. Peterson likewise denied that the cross was a symbol of Christianity: "The world at large has the idea that the symbol of Christianity is the cross, but it's no such thing." According to Peterson, the cross was nothing more than:

> The cruelest form of torture and execution that the Romans could devise; that is what the cross is for. Christ did not give us the cross as the symbol of his great Atonement."[3]

Following the same logic, Joseph Fielding Smith perceived the symbol to be utterly abhorrent:

> To bow down before a cross or to look upon it as an emblem to be revered because of the fact that our Savior died upon a cross is repugnant and contrary to the true worship of our Redeemer.

Smith struggled to see any meaning in the cross beyond what it depicted (i.e. an instrument of torture and death):

> We may be definitely sure that if our Lord had been killed with a dagger or with a sword, it would have been very strange if religious people

---

2. J. Reuben Clark Jr., *On the Way to Immortality and Eternal Life*, 297. Clark was not only opposed to the use and veneration of the cross, but also the use of paintings, statues, and other religious images. Ibid, 293-309.

3. Mark E. Petersen, "The Covenant People of God" (1980), *Speeches*, http://speeches.byu.edu/reader/reader.php?id=6773 (accessed 31 March 2009). Petersen made the same claim in a book he authored a year before, saying, "Most people use the sign of the cross and declare it to be the true symbol of Christianity. But it is not so. The cross is but a symbol of the brutal form of execution used by the Romans." *The Forerunners* (Salt Lake City: Bookcraft, 1979), 92.

this day would have graced such a weapon by wearing and adoring it because it was by such a means that our Lord was put to death.[4]

As a member of the Quorum of the Twelve, Gordon B. Hinckley first publicly expressed his rationalization—which has become the standard response of twenty-first century Mormonism—as early as May 1975:

> I do not wish to give offense to any of my Christian brethren who use the cross.... But for us, the cross is the symbol of the dying Christ, while our message is a declaration of the living Christ....The lives of our people must become the only meaningful expression of our faith and... symbol of our worship.[5]

Bruce R. McConkie was less tactful and more sensational than Hinckley in his influential book *Mormon Doctrine*. McConkie not only

---

4. Joseph Fielding Smith, *Answers to Gospel Questions* (Salt Lake City: Deseret Books, 1963), 4: 17-18.

5. Gordon B. Hinckley, "The Symbol of Christ," *Ensign*, May 1975, 92. Gordon B. Hinckley (who later served as Church president 1995-2008) repeated and republished this argument several times since. See "The Symbol of Christ," *Liahona*, March 1989; Ibid., *New Era*, April 1990; "The Symbol of Our Faith," *Ensign*, April 2005; Ibid, *Liahona*, April 2005. This rationale (identifying the cross with the "dying Christ") did not originate with Hinckley. In a BYU speech delivered in 1963, James Lee Wilde reported, "A short time ago a mission president of the Church of Jesus Christ of Latter-day Saints was asked the question, 'Why don't Mormons put the cross on their churches?' The mission president replied, 'As Mormons we believe in a living, not a dead Christ.' The most vital message of the Church of Jesus Christ of Latter-day Saints is that Jesus Christ does live and that he speaks to us today. One important manifestation of a living Christ's power is his ability to generate a spiritual rebirth in the lives of his children." James Lee Wilde, "A Living Christ," Heber J. Grant Oratorical Contest, *BYU Speeches of the Year* (November 19, 1963), 2. Elder Robert E. Wells of the First Quorum of the Seventy also taught, "To us, the cross is a symbol of His passion, His agony. Our preference is to remember his resurrection. We seek to honor the living Christ who was brought forth in glory from the tomb on the third day." *The Utah Evangel* 33 (May 1986): 8; as cited in Daniel C. Peterson and Stephen D. Ricks, *Offenders for a Word* (Provo: FARMS, 1992), 131-132. Apostle M. Russell Ballard likewise writes, "We rejoice in the knowledge of a living Christ, and we reverently acknowledge the miracles He continues to work today in the lives of those who have faith in Him. That is why we choose to place less emphasis on a symbol that can be construed to represent primarily His death." M. Russell Ballard, *Our Search for Happiness: An Invitation to Understand the Church of Jesus Christ of Latter-day Saints* (Salt Lake City: Deseret Book, 1993), 13. Prominent BYU professor of religion, Daniel H. Ludlow, similarly taught, "Members of the Church of Jesus Christ of Latter-day Saints, however, emphasize the resurrected and living Jesus Christ: the symbol of the cross or crucifix, which depicts the dead or dying Christ, is therefore not part of our worship." Daniel H. Ludlow, *A Companion to Your Study of the New Testament: The Four Gospels* (Salt Lake City: Deseret Book, 1982), 56. This explanation is now part of Church curriculum, published in book *True to the Faith* (Church of Jesus Christ of Latter-day Saints, 2004), 45-46.

asserted that the cross was a pagan symbol introduced to Christianity via the Roman Emperor Constantine, but he also declared its sign to be the "mark of the beast."[6] Under the entry "Catholicism" McConkie's book said "See Church of the Devil". Under the latter heading, McConkie bluntly stated as doctrine that:

> The Roman Catholic Church specifically—singled out, set apart, described, and designated as being "most abominable above all other churches."[7]

Ironically, Bruce R. McConkie's *Mormon Doctrine* was so extreme in its polemics against Catholicism, it persuaded some LDS leaders to reconsider their own overtly anti-Catholic views. David O. McKay's own anti-Catholic views were similar to McConkie's, but the church president had been careful not to express them publicly. By contrast, McConkie's views were not tactfully guarded in the slightest, which put McKay in an embarrassing situation. After *Mormon Doctrine* was published, an LDS bishop asked McKay:

> Is this the attitude of the Church that the Catholic Church is the "Great and Abominable Church," as expressed in the latest book of Bruce McConkie's?

McKay responded by reprimanding McConkie. The church president ordered that the publication of *Mormon Doctrine* be discontinued, and established a policy insisting that all future books written by General

---

6. "In apostate days the degenerate Christian Church developed the practice of using symbolic crosses in the architecture of their buildings and as jewelry attached to the robes of their priests. Frequently this morbid mania for dwelling on the personal death struggle of our Lord has caused these apostate peoples to put sculptured representations of Christ on their crosses, thus forming so-called crucifixes. All this is inharmonious with the quiet spirit of worship and reverence that should attend a true Christian's remembrance of our Lord's sufferings and death." Bruce R. McConkie, *Mormon Doctrine* (Salt Lake City: Book Craft Company, 1958), 160. McConkie condemns the sign of the cross elsewhere in his book: "As part of their worship, members and priests of that great church which is not the Lord's Church make the sign of the cross. In doing so they draw a cross in the air with the right hand beginning at their forehead. Their purpose is to show devoutness in worship or to consecrate and bless persons or objects. This religious formality is without scriptural or divine warrant. Indeed many see in it at least a partial fulfillment of John's vision in which he saw that the great apostate beast would cause 'all, both small and great, rich and poor, free and bond, to receive a mark in their right hand, or in their foreheads: And that no man might buy or sell, save he that had the mark, or the name of the beast, or the number of his name.' (Rev. 13.)" Ibid., 642.

7. Gregory and Wright, *David O. McKay*, 122. See McConkie, *Mormon Doctrine* (1958), 129.

FIGURE 9.1: *The headstone of US Navy Captain Lavell Bigelow, a Mormon veteran of World War II and the Korean War.*

Authorities must first be approved by the First Presidency.[8] This event became a major turning point for the LDS Church. Since McKay's re-evaluation, Mormon leaders have largely succeeded in ridding themselves of their former anti-Catholic bias.

Nevertheless, the cross taboo—originally an extension of those anti-Catholic sentiments—still remains. From McKay's time, the church reaffirmed the perceived inappropriateness of the symbol in its teaching curriculum, grouping "the use of the cross" among the numerous "non-apostolic additions to Christianity."[9]

In 1980, the LDS Church successfully applied to the Veteran's Administration for a Mormon-specific gravestone marker. Previously, the graves of Mormon veterans would have been marked with a standard Christian cross; now they had the option of marking them with an image of the Angel Moroni. As the LDS *Church News* reported:

---

8. Ibid.

9. T. Edger Lyon, *Apostasy to Restoration: Course of Study for the Melchizedek Priesthood Quorums of The Church of Jesus Christ of Latter-day Saints* (Salt Lake City: Deseret Book Co., 1960), 233.

Other churches and religious organizations have had designations for years; Catholics, the cross; Hebrews, the star of David; Buddhists, the wheel of righteousness, etc.... Mormon families have not had a choice when their servicemen died.... The new Mormon emblem [angel Moroni seal] and its approval by the V.A. changes that.[10]

---

10. "Gravestone Emblem Approved," *Church News*, May 31, 1980, 13. A couple apologists have denied that the LDS Church has an aversion toward the symbol, citing as evidence the fact that Mormon military chaplains wear cross badges. Indeed, LDS chaplains do wear these badges, but this is because there is only a limited number available: a crescent for Islam, wheel for Buddhism, Star of David (with stone tablets) for Judaism, and a cross for Christianity. See "Chaplain Badges," *USA Military Medals*, http://www.usamilitarymedals.com/chaplain-badges-c-2071_2470_2506.html (accessed 24 October 2008). LDS Church Authorities today likely feel as they did about gravestone markers prior to 1980—that they "have not had a choice." One should expect that if a different symbol was made available for LDS chaplains (such as the angel Moroni seal), then the Church would instruct their chaplains to use the new badge instead. But in order for this to happen, paperwork must again be filed and passed, and bad publicity (which almost certainly would follow) endured. For an example showing the kind of criticisms that the Church received after getting their new angel Moroni marker in 1980, see "Gravestone Emblem Approved/Mormons Reject the Cross, and Accept Moroni Instead," (Westlake Village, CA: Ministry to Mormons, 198-); in Harold B. Lee Library Special Collections American Collection.

Chapter Ten

Comparative Perceptions of the Cross

ALTHOUGH THE overwhelming majority of Latter Day Saints today are members of the Utah-based Church of Jesus Christ of Latter-day Saints, there are several hundred distinct denominations that view the Book of Mormon as scripture and trace their origin to the movement founded by Joseph Smith Jr. As a comparative study, the attitudes of two of these groups will be examined: the Strangite Church and the Community of Christ (formerly known as the Reorganized Church of Jesus Christ of Latter Day Saints).

Strangites and the Cross

In the decade following Joseph Smith's death, James Strang emerged as the most successful challenger to Brigham Young's leadership. Although Strang was a relatively recent convert, many early Saints found his claims to Smith's prophetic mantle appealing. Strang possessed a letter he said was written by the late prophet just before his death, appointing Strang as the next president of the Church.[1] Strang also asserted

---

1. The letter reads, "And now behold my servant James J. Strang... to him shall the gathering of the people be for he shall plant a stake of Zion in Wisconsin and I will establish it, and there shall my people have peace and rest, and shall not be moved.... And I will have a house built unto me there of stone, and there will I show myself to my people by many mighty works, and the name of the city shall be called Voree, which is being interpreted, garden of peace, for there shall my

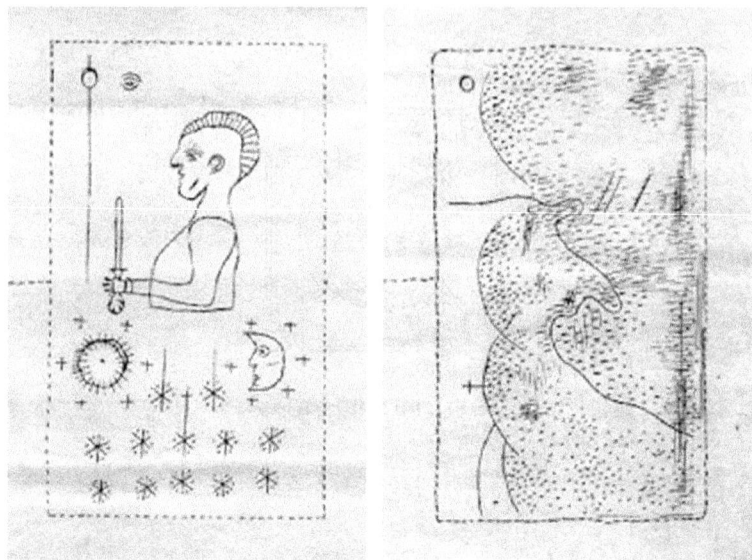

FIGURES 10.1 AND 10.2: *Facsimiles of Strang's plates containing two prominent crosses. In the first diagram (left), the middle star below the man is marked with what Strang called a "cross pillar," while the hill of promise (depicted sideways at right) has a cross atop it.*

that an angel appeared to him (ordaining him to the office) at the very moment Joseph Smith died.[2] And, just as Smith had claimed concerning the Book of Mormon, Strang announced that he had found ancient records engraved upon metal plates that he subsequently translated by the power of God using the *urim* and *thummum*.[3]

Although these plates were eventually lost,[4] we have a good idea of what they looked like since Strang published a facsimile of the plates

---

people have peace and rest and wax fat and pleasant in the presence of their enemies.... Voree shall be the gathering of my people, and there shall the oppressed flee for safety and none shall hurt or molest them.... So spake the Almighty God of heaven. The duty is made plain and if thou lackest wisdom ask of God in whose hands I trust thee and he shall give thee unsparingly[,] for if evil befall me thou shalt lead the flock to pleasant pastures." Joseph Smith (18 June 1844), letter to James J. Strang; transcription of the letter provided in Speek, "God has Made Us a Kingdom," 357-60. The authenticity of this letter has been heavily disputed.

2. Speek, "God has Made Us a Kingdom," 22.
3. Ibid., 24-26.
4. "The Voree plates have disappeared. Chas. J. Strang writes concerning: 'I do not know where the plates are. I never saw them.' Wingfield Watson writes: 'The three Voree plates are in the hands of some one of Mr. Strang's family, whose address I do not now know.'" Henry E. Legler, *A Moses of the Mormons: Strang's City of Refuge and Island Kingdom* (1897), 174, http://books.

that included two illustrations. The first of these (see figure 10.1) depicts a crowned man with scepter in hand, an all-seeing eye, sun and moon, and several stars. James Strang described the central star as having "cross pillar above and resting upon [it]."[5] The second illustration (figure 10.2) apparently depicts the "hill of promise," which is marked by a cross where Strang and his followers excavated the plates.

A number of early Mormon leaders were convinced by these signs and many relocated to Strang's headquarters in Voree, Wisconsin. By 1846, Strang's organization was second only to Brigham Young's in size. John C. Bennett, former mayor of Nauvoo and former member of Smith's First Presidency was among Strang's most prominent and most controversial converts. Upon reaching Voree, Bennett helped Strang organize a quasi-Masonic auxiliary know as the *Order of Illuminati* (also known as the "Halcyon Order"). Initiation into the order required members to swear oaths by placing their hands on a cross inside a Bible.[6] According to Bennett, Joseph Smith had received the revelation concerning the Illuminati ritual in 1841. Bennett further claimed that a cross-carrying angel originally gave this ritual the Roman Emperor Constantine:

> Constantine the Great, after his defeat at Magentius, received from heaven an express command to institute the 'Order of the Illuminati' for the defense of the Christian religion. This command was brought by an angel who held in his hand a cross of gold.[7]

This same angel—with cross in hand—was depicted on a cloth panel displayed in the church tabernacle during Strang's coronation as "king of Zion."[8]

From these examples, it is clear that early Strangites had a very favorable view of the cross. The fact that their quasi-Masonic ritual specifically employed the cross harmonizes well with the previously stated

---

google.com/books?id=u33hAAAAMAAJ&printsec=frontcover&source=gbs_ge_summary_r&cad=0#v=onepage&q&f=false (accessed 2 July 2010).

5. *Zion's Reveille*, 4 February 1847.

6. Vickie Cleverley Speek, *"God Has Made Us a Kingdom": James Strang and the Midwest Mormons* (Salt Lake City: Signature Books, 2006), 116, 120. Roger Van Noord, *Assassination of a Michigan King: The Life of James Jesse Strang* (Ann Arbor: University of Michigan Press, 1997), 101.

7. Milo Milton Quaife, *The Kingdom of Saint James: A Narrative of the Mormons* (New Haven: Yale University Press, 1930), 50.

8. Noord, *Assassination of a Michigan King*, 101.

proposition that Freemasonry was a contributing factor to the early Mormon acceptance of the symbol.

After Strang's own martyrdom in 1856, his followers were scattered and most ultimately affiliated with Joseph Smith's son, Joseph Smith III. A small remnant remained faithful to Strang's teachings. Their church, known today as the "Church of Jesus Christ of Latter Day Saints (Strangite)" is once again headquartered in Voree (now a part of Burlington, Wisconsin). None of their current church buildings are decorated with crosses. While the church has no specific prohibition on the use of the symbol, members today generally associate the cross with Protestant and Catholic Christianity, which they believe is in a state of apostasy.[9]

The Cross and the RLDS/Community of Christ

In the 1840s and 1850s, the Strangite Church was the second largest denomination within Mormonism. From the 1860s onward, that distinction has been held by the Reorganized Church of Jesus Christ of Latter Day Saints (RLDS), which in 2001 was renamed the "Community of Christ." Although the Community of Christ shares its origins with the LDS Church and the Strangite Church, its understanding of the cross and use of the cross as a sacred symbol has evolved along a very different path.

Joseph Smith Jr.'s sole legal wife,[10] Emma Hale Smith, was one of the earliest members of the church and her influence on the movement is difficult to overstate. She was present at the Hill Cumorah when Joseph said that he gained possession of the golden plates; indeed, according to Joseph's account, the angel who gave him the plates required that the "right person" be brought and the right person turned out to be Emma. When Joseph began to dictate the Book of Mormon, Emma was one

---

9. E-mail correspondence, 21 June 2012, between Strangite High Priest David August and historian John C. Hamer.

10. Although Joseph Smith Jr. introduced the practice of "plural" or "celestial marriage" into Mormonism and ultimately "married" approximately twenty-seven women in addition to Emma, his practice of polygamy differed significantly from later Mormon polygamy. All of Smith's plural marriages were conducted in secret, most were unknown even to Emma; they involved little, if any, intermingling of property, and Smith only cohabited with his plural wives coincidentally, e.g., if they were already living in his home as maids. By contrast, James Strang and Brigham Young both ultimately acknowledged their plural marriages and lived in openly polygamous households.

FIGURE 10.3: *Emma's quilt (left) and the cross-and-star details (right).*

of the first scribes. Revelation singled Emma out as "an elect lady" and called her to prepare the church's first hymnal. And a later revelation ordered her to accept her husband's practice of polygamy or face "destruction." At the time of Joseph's death, Emma was pregnant with their last child and left to raise their four other young children alone.

Emma's attitude toward the cross may be revealed in a Smith family quilt (see figure 10.3). Tradition holds that Emma herself made the quilt from the clothing her husband and brother-in-law Hyrum were wearing during their martyrdom. The stitching takes the form of Greek crosses surrounded by five-pointed stars. As has previously been observed, the same juxtaposition of these symbols—the cross and the five-pointed star—exists in the windows of the Nauvoo Temple.[11]

Despite entreaties that they join the trek west, Emma and her children continued to live in Nauvoo after the departure of Brigham Young and his followers in 1847. Leaders of the competing Mormon factions, including Brigham Young, James Strang, Lyman Wight, Alpheus Cutler, and William Smith, expressed varying beliefs that Emma's son Joseph Smith III would one day succeed his father as prophet. However, Emma and her children remained aloof from the different groups until 1860, when Joseph Smith III reported receiving a divine calling. That year, he and Emma attended a conference of Midwestern Latter Day Saints who

---

11. See pages 49–52 of this book regarding the cross pentagrams on the Nauvoo Temple.

"reorganized" their church and ordained Joseph III as their prophet and president.[12]

This group, which became known as the RLDS Church, initially retained the same basic attitudes toward the cross that had been present in Joseph Smith Jr.'s lifetime. As has been argued, connections with folk-magic and Freemasonry, alongside the perception that Pre-Columbian crosses validated the Book of Mormon, were factors contributing to a positive perception of the cross, while anti-Catholic sentiment and the association of the cross with Catholicism remained dormant as negative factors in the background.

The Reorganization brought together Saints who had followed a number of different leaders since 1844. The bulk of the followers of James Strang, Lyman Wight, William Smith, Alpheus Cutler, and other leaders whose organizations had stagnated or collapsed were eventually gathered into Joseph Smith III's new group. This naturally brought diverse doctrinal opinions into the RLDS Church, including differing attitudes concerning the cross. For example, the positive experiences with the cross in James Strang's organization probably meant that former Strangites were a factor further supporting a positive attitude toward the cross in the RLDS Church.[13]

On the other hand, converts from the Utah church (after the late 1870s) may have had the opposite effect on RLDS culture. Disaffected followers of Brigham Young were key targets of RLDS missionaries. According to historian Roger D. Launius:

> [T]he Reorganized Church [during the nineteenth century] was seeking largely to reclaim old Mormons.... In mid-1863 Joseph Smith sent the church's first missionary team to work among the Mormons of the Great Basin, and within six months they had built a mission of over 300 members. By 1880 that number had grown to 820, and in the

---

12. There is occasionally some confusion about Emma's affiliation with the RLDS Church. Because the RLDS Church considered itself to be the sole legitimate heir to the early church, early members were not rebaptized upon affiliating with the Reorganization. Thus from the RLDS perspective, Emma and Joseph III did not need to "join" the RLDS Church; they were already members who merely "affiliated" with the Reorganization.

13. Scholar Vickie Speek observes, "Ultimately, Latter Day Saints who left the Strangite church, both before and after the death of James J. Strang, made significant contributions to the membership and the leadership of the Reorganization." Speek, *"God Has Made Us a Kingdom,"* 141. See also Quaife, *Kingdom of Saint James*, 113, 114.

1890s membership in Utah had risen to over 1,000. At the same time, the Reorganized Church moved into California and enjoyed remarkable success among the followers of Brigham Young who had settled in the Golden State. Within ten years after the opening of the Pacific slope mission the Reorganization had developed a following of almost 1,000 members.[14]

These Mormons transferred their membership to the RLDS Church just as LDS bias against the cross was emerging. This connection may have been a vehicle for cross-pollinating that taboo between the churches.

As with their LDS cousins in Utah, RLDS interest in folk magic faded with the passing of the first generations of Saints. And, just as in the West, RLDS writers continued to use perceived Pre-Columbian crosses in Book of Mormon apologetics. For example, as early as 1866, an article in the RLDS *Latter Day Saints' Herald* editorialized on discoveries of crosses in Mesoamerica, concluding that the presence of the symbol revealed the existence of Christianity among the ancient inhabitants:

> Places of worship are said to be numerous, and upon the reverse of a statuette of a man is carved the emblem of Christianity—the cross.

Henry A. Stebbins[15], an RLDS elder, wrote an article for the same periodical in 1872, in which he likewise asserted that the discovery of Pre-Columbian crosses verified claims that ancient Americans "had a true knowledge of the Savior; of his crucifixion, and of his gospel." Stebbins explicitly took issue with skeptics who refused to acknowledge that Pre-Columbian crosses were connected with Christianity, and who instead regarded "all such suppositions as those of the Catholic missionaries." Stebbins anticipated a time "when the perfect knowledge concerning the efficacy of the cross of Christ shall again fill the land."[16]

---

14. Roger D. Launius, *Joseph Smith III: Pragmatic Prophet* (University of Illinois Press, 1995), 292-93.
15. Stebbins was then serving as president of the north Illinois and south Wisconsin district.
16. Elder H.[enry] A. Stebbins, "Antiquarian Researches – No. 5." *Saints' Herald* 19, no. 22 (15 November 1872), 63; http://books.google.com/books?id=wlgoAAAAYAAJ&pg=PA673 (accessed 2 July 2010). A few years later (1876) Stebbins' criticized "Christian or skeptic" authors who denied "that the symbol of the cross was ever essentially the sign of Christ, all rejecting such a theory as impossible. *They* think that its being found in America is conclusive proof against its having had, in any country, any special relationship to him." On the contrary, the Stebbins contends that the cross in pre-Columbian remains is a "great and remarkable confirmation of the

FIGURE 10.4: *The RLDS First Presidency in the 1950s, F. Henry Edwards (left), Israel A. Smith (center), and W. Wallace Smith (right) posing in front of a replica of the "Tablet of the Cross" — the most famous Pre-Columbian cross (see Figure 4.1).*

For the remaining two early factors—Freemasonry and anti-Catholic bias—the RLDS experience differed from the LDS experience. In the isolation of Utah, Mormons became estranged from Masonry, which became identified with Utah's non-Mormon and anti-Mormon community. Reorganized Saints continued to live in the predominantly non-Mormon Midwest. From the day of his ordination, Joseph Smith III vocally rejected divisive doctrines, including polygamy and theocracy. Under his leadership, the RLDS Church adopted "Peace" as its motto and worked to live in harmony with their neighbors. Reorganized Saints never devel-

---

truth of the Book of Mormon, when it states that the former inhabitants of this continent had a full knowledge of the previous existence and expected coming of the Lord Jesus Christ, and of his atonement and of his crucifixion on the cross." Since this knowledge was always foretold, it is therefore understandable "why his cross became a sacred symbol from the morn of time." H.[enry] A. S.[tebins], "Antiquity of the Cross as a Religious Symbol, and of the Doctrine of Vicarious Atonement," *Saints' Herald* 23, no. 4 (15 February 1876), 102-104, http://books.google.com/books?id=IVE0AAAAYAAJ&pg=PA102 (accessed 2 July 2010).

oped the same antagonism for Masonry. Indeed, Joseph Smith III's son and successor, Frederick M. Smith, was an active Mason.[17]

As we have seen, anti-Catholic animus was widespread in the United States in the nineteenth and early twentieth centuries, among Protestants and Latter Day Saints (both LDS and RLDS). Nevertheless, isolation in Utah and the LDS Church's focus on overseas proselyting missions allowed LDS attitudes to develop uniquely. By contrast, located as they in predominantly Protestant areas, RLDS attitudes towards Catholicism more closely tracked those of their Protestant neighbors.

Early RLDS Uses of the Cross

Despite some lingering associations of the symbol of the cross with Catholicism, many Reorganized Saints in the late-nineteenth and early-twentieth centuries clearly viewed the cross more broadly. Beyond the crosses on Emma's quilt, RLDS members saw crosses in visions, wore crosses as jewelry, built cruciform churches, and decorated churches with crosses.

For example, in 1869, Isaac N. White (who later became an RLDS Apostle) wrote a letter to Joseph Smith III, concerning vision "from the Lord." White reported that he had seen several men forming a long line "nearly across the heavens." The vision also contained "a figure in the form of a cross, which had writing on, but I could not read it on account of its distance."[18] In 1875, Mary Ruben, an RLDS member from Rock Island, Illinois, predicted that the day would come when Jesus' cross would appear, and "we will feel to hide our blushing face, and melt our eyes to tears."[19] In 1890, the RLDS Church's youth magazine described a monument where a cross stood "in bold relief upon a crag of rocks." While the monument was not RLDS, the author identified the cross as the

---

17. See William R. Denslow, *10,000 Famous Freemasons* (Richmond VA: Macoy Publishing, 1957), http://www.phoenixmasonry.org/10,000_famous_freemasons/Volume_4_Q_to_Z.htm (accessed 11 April 2012).

18. "Correspondences," *Saints' Herald* 17, no. 2 (15 January 1870), 56, http://www.google.com/books?id=9FcoAAAAYAAJ&pg=PA56 (accessed 2 July 2010).

19. Mary Ruben, "Sacrifice," *Saints' Herald* 22, no. 20 (15 October 1875), 615, http://books.google.com/books?id=4nHUAAAAMAAJ&pg=PA615 (accessed 2 July 2010).

FIGURE 10.5: *Dora Burton wearing a cross necklace.*

"emblem of life eternal," betraying an overall positive attitude toward the symbol.[20]

Similar to LDS practice of the time, crosses were worn as jewelry by RLDS members. For example, Dora Burton, daughter of patriarch/evangelist Joseph F. Burton,[21] can be seen in a photograph from the RLDS *Journal of History* wearing a large cross necklace.[22]

Crosses on buildings purchased from other Christian denominations were of little concern. For example, a 1904 photograph of an RLDS chapel in St Louis, purchased from the Presbyterians, show the stone cross on the church's apex.[23] A cross also adorned the top of the

---

20. "Editor's Corner." Autumn Leaves 3, no. 8 (August 1890), 388, http://books.google.com/books?id=8G8vAAAAMAAJ&pg=PA388 (accessed 2 July 2010). Image of landscape was published on 391.

21. *Journal of History* (RLDS) 3:126, http://books.google.com/books?id=LN8WAQAAIAAJ&pg=PA126 (accessed 2 July 2010). RLDS *Doctrine and Covenants* 127:5d mentions Joseph F. Burton.

22. *Journal of History* 6 (Lamoni, Iowa: Reorganized Church of Jesus Christ of Latter Day Saints, 1913), 334, http://books.google.com/books?id=xOMWAQAAIAAJ&pg=PA334 (accessed 2 July 2010). For genealogical data on Dora Burton, see http://www.familysearch.org/eng/search/IGI/individual_record.asp?recid=100286590350&lds=1&region=11&regionfriendly=North+America&frompage=99 (accessed 2 July 2010) and http://wc.rootsweb.ancestry.com/cgi-bin/igm.cgi?op=GET&db=brons&id=I1398 (accessed 2 July 2010).

23. This chapel (since destroyed) was constructed in 1880 located in Kansas City Missouri on the corner Glasgow Avenue and Dickson Street, and purchased by the church sometime between 1901 and 1904. "Presbyterianism in St. Louis," *Encyclopedia of the History of Missouri: a Compendium of History and Biography for Ready reference*, vol. 5 (July 1901), 217, http://books.

FIGURE 10.6: *The RLDS Central Church in Kansas City, Missouri.*

large Central Church of Kansas City, Missouri. The RLDS Church purchased this chapel in 1908 from a Methodist Episcopal congregation.[24]

A story published in 1905 in the RLDS publication *Autumn Leaves*, described several details about another RLDS chapel. Although its location is stricken, identified merely as "the church in J—," it is fortunate that the story is more elaborate in describing religious symbolism seen from the inside:

> The Naves are surmounted by small gables, each containing a circle sash. The sash on the south is glazed with a design showing in a dark blue field the figures of the sun, moon, and stars and a cross and crown representing the three glories; the celestial, the terrestrial, and the telestial glory, according to the writings of the apostle Paul to the Corinthians. The sash on the north is glazed with a design showing the cup and the bread of the sacrament, surrounded by a fruit-bearing vine.[25]

Based on that description, it can be surmised that "J—" stood for "Jackson County" and the building in question was the Stone Church in Independence, Jackson County, Missouri. This large edifice, constructed by the RLDS Church between 1888 and 1892, celebrated the return of the Saints to Jackson County. (The early Saints had been driven from the county by mob violence in 1833.) When RLDS headquarters moved

---

google.com/books?id=_2wUAAAAYAAJ&pg=PA217 (accessed 2 July 2010); *Album of Ministers and Workers* (Independence, Mo: Ensign Publishing House, 1904), http://books.google.com/books?id=4mQtAAAAYAAJ& (accessed 2 July 2010).

24. A photograph of the Central Church in Kansas City, Missouri, was published in *Autumn Leaves* 24, no. 6 (June 1911), 248.

25. H. B. Taddicken, "Fred Martin—A True Story," *Autumn Leaves* 18, no. (July 1905), 58-60, http://books.google.com/books?id=f3QvAAAAMAAJ&pg=PA460 (accessed 2 July 2010). An article in 1890 instructed readers how to construct a cross as a holiday decoration. "Two very pretty designs for festive decorations are a star and a cross.... A good cross is about as difficult to make as any of the festive designs, but I will endeavor to outline one, so that with a little patience, and some knowledge of the use of the saw and hammer, you may construct a very respectable cross. The frame-work does not require a display of fine wood or workmanship.... Now, for an illustration, suppose we take four laths and nail them together in the form of a flat cross; that is, have two laths perpendicular and two horizontal, leaving space between them of say two inches. Take another frame the same size and shape, and then fasten small blocks or squares of wood between the two frames at the top, bottom and arms. You will next want a base. This can be made out of two boxes, one being a little larger than the other. Nail the small box to the upper side of the larger one, leaving an equal space on each side. To the center of the small box fasten the frame, and the cross is ready to be decorated." "Round Table," *Autumn Leaves* 3, no. 1 (January 1890), 55, http://books.google.com/books?id=8G8vAAAAMAAJ&pg=PA55 (accessed 2 July 2010).

FIGURE 10.7: *Stained glass with the image of a crown and a cross from the Stone Church in Independence, Missouri, preserved in the church's basement.*

FIGURE 10.8: *Stone Church stained glass window with a cross.*

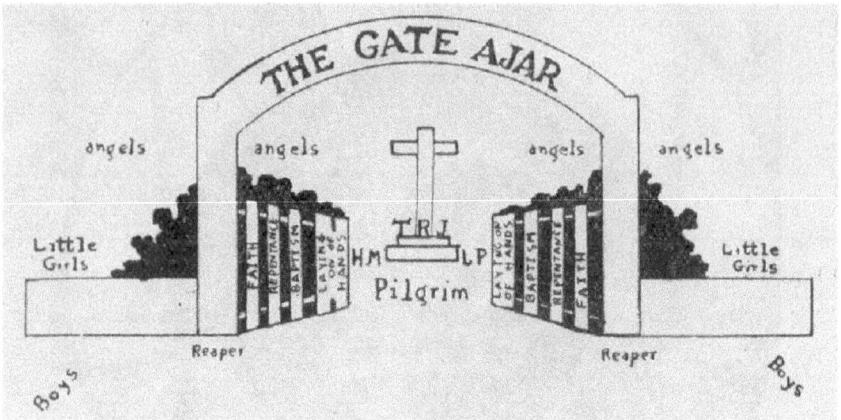

FIGURE 10.9: *Advertisement for an RLDS Easter pageant staged in 1926.*

to Independence in the early twentieth century, the Stone Church took on special prominence and informally became known as "the pulpit of the presidency."

The original stained-glass window from the Stone Church with the image of a cross and crown has been preserved and is on display the building's lower level (see figures 10.7–10.8). The cross and crown image is an allusion to the motto[26] popularized by William Penn, "No cross, No crown." Penn himself interpreted the phrase to mean that "Christ's

---

26. "[S]oon [Jesus] will come 'the second time without sin unto salvation,' never again to leave his church, but to receive those who followed Him in His cross, to be everlasting partakers with Him in His crown." Marien B. Graybell, "Another 'Word of Promise,'" *Saints' Herald* 4, no. 4 (15 August 1863), 56, http://books.google.com/books?id=hVYoAAAAYAAJ&pg=RA2-PA56#v=onepage&q&f=false (accessed 2 July 2010). "I am determined to fight on in this good fight of the faith until I exchange the cross for a crown." Geo. E. Ross, "Correspondence," *Saints' Herald* 17, no. 11 (1 June 1870), 340, http://books.google.com/books?id=9FcoAAAAYAAJ&pg=PA340 (accessed 2 July 2010). "Yet there are those like Simeon of old, who are not only waiting, but patiently laboring for Israel's consolation; for the Latter Day cause shineth bright unto them, and they expect not a crown without bearing the cross." James Caffall, *Saints' Herald* 21, no. 8 (1 May 1874), 263, http://books.google.com/books?id=TXHUAAAAMAAJ&pg=PA263 (accessed 2 July 2010). Brighamites likewise made use of this motto: "A desire often darts across the mind to retire from the midst of the cares and busy scenes of life, to some secluded spot; but in a moment I reflect—'No cross, no crown,' and go a-head." W. W. Phelps, "Extracts of Letters From Nauvoo," *Latter-day Saints Millennial Star* 6, no. 10 (1 November 1845), 154, http://books.google.com/books?id=KCEEAAAAQAAJ&pg=RA2-PA154 (accessed 2 July 2010). "Their all was laid upon the altar to gain that glory which the Lord had given my mother a slight glimpse of, in answer to her humble heart-broken prayer. 'Where there's no cross, there's no crown.'" Helen

Cross is Christ's Way to Christ's Crown," and "they that cannot endure the Cross, must never have the Crown. To reign, it is necessary first to suffer."[27] According to an 1880 account, this motto was also inscribed on the walls of the Kirtland Temple. Dedicated in 1837, this was the only temple completed in the lifetime of Joseph Smith Jr. Although "No cross, No crown" was already on the temple walls when the RLDS Church took legal possession of the building, it is not known when the phrase was first inscribed there.[28]

In 1926, RLDS members staged a church-wide Easter pageant, including a youth performance based on the "No Cross, No Crown" theme. For the play, two large props took center stage: a wooden cross and a gate leading up to it. The pageant's script describes a pilgrim weighed down by a "sin-sick soul," "wandering hopelessly" on the path of mortal life. He comes to the white gate, behind which stands the cross, and exclaims, "Ah, what a beautiful place! How wonderful! So pure and white! What can it be?" Despite this initial spark of interest, however, the pilgrim disregards his optimistic thoughts as "useless," since his "garments are sin-stained."[29]

The play further unfolds and the personified characters of Mercy, Justice, Hope, Truth, Prayer, Love, and Resurrection each persuade the pilgrim to enter the gate and approach the cross of Christ. Upon entering, a smaller cross blocks his way and the pilgrim learns that there is still something else he must do. Love tells him:

> They who enter through the gate must be willing to take up their cross and follow Christ. This cross is yours. Each Pilgrim finds it in his pathway. He who shoulders it can enter in. He who scorns it must turn backward.

Mar Kimball Whitney, "Scenes and Incidents in Nauvoo," *Woman's Exponent* 11 (1881-82), http://www.signaturebookslibrary.org/journals/helen.htm (2 July 2010).

27. William Penn, "No Cross, No Crown," *The Selected Works of William Penn* (London, 1825), 1:333, 354.

28. Frederic G. Mather, "Early Days of Mormonism," *Lippincott's Magazine* (1880) 26:152, http://olivercowdery.com/smithhome/1880Math.htm (accessed 28 April 2010). Mather states the motto "still remained" upon the walls implying that his impression was that the motto had been there for quite some time.

29. Elise M. Barraclough, "The Gate Ajar," *Autumn Leaves* 39, no. 3 (March 1926), 95-96.

FIGURE 10.10: *Cross monument at Mount Rubidoux, California.*

The pilgrim then lifts the cross, continues his journey, and Love assures him:

> When the reapers shall gather you home and Justice metes out her reward you shall not be ashamed and can exchange your cross for the crown you have won.

Finally, the pilgrim meets his destination and is crowned with the "new name" "Saint," written on a white band in gold letters.[30]

Elbert A. Smith, a descendant of Joseph Smith Jr. who served in the RLDS First Presidency before becoming Presiding Patriarch/Evangelist, held an especially positive view of the cross. In a 1921 sermon, he asserted that the lack of crosses on church spires was a testimony "that there was an apostasy" in Christianity, arguing that "otherwise on top of that spire there would be a cross of gold."[31] After visiting and photographing a cross monument at Mount Rubidoux, California, in 1928, he was inspired to write a reverential poem entitled "The Cross":

> The cross stands with feet in the earth;
> But leaning its head on the skies;
> Its two great arms are a symbol,

---

30. Ibid., 96-101.
31. Elbert A. Smith, *Square Blocks, and Other Sermons and Articles* (Independence, Missouri: Herald Publishing House, 1921), 430, http://www.archive.org/details/squareblocksotheoosmit (accessed 5 July 2010).

Compelling the gaze of all eyes.
The cross speaks to us of his wounds;
Invites us to drink of his cup.
The way of the cross is rocky—
But the way of the cross is up.
The cross makes us humble of heart;
For here must each man bend the Knee—
Yet be a man still, for Christ says:
"Arise, now, my son, follow me!"[32]

RLDS Counter Examples

Although the preceding examples reflect a generally positive attitude toward the cross in the RLDS tradition, other RLDS members simultaneously maintained the opposite view, engaging in the same anti-Catholic polemics as some contemporary Protestants and LDS members. For example, RLDS member Richard Bullard insinuated a negative perception of the cross in 1892, while describing a vision he had in London, England. Bullard reported seeing:

> Suspended in the air a cross, composed of a vapor or cloud of a grey stone color, and the voice... said to me, "The Catholic cross." While I was looking at this cross, there appeared underneath it the outlines of a large building with a dome.

According to Bullard, the building in his vision was consumed by fire and fell to the ground, causing him to exclaim:

> Praise the Lord; the whore of all the earth is fallen, is fallen. BABYLON THE GREAT, THE MOTHER OF HARLOTS AND ABOMINATION OF THE EARTH, is fallen, is fallen![33]

Other Reorganized Saints also had negative associations with the cross and the Catholic Church. In 1910, RLDS missionary Walter J. Haworth, authored a book entitled *The Fall of Babylon and the Triumph of the Kingdom of God*, in the which he asserted:

---

32. Both the photo and poem were published together in 1941, while Elbert Smith was serving as the Presiding Patriarch of the church. *Saints' Herald* 88, no. 5 (1 February 1941), cover page.
33. Richard Bullard, "A Dream or Night Vision," *Autumn Leaves* 5, no. 2 (February 1892), http://books.google.com/books?id=znAvAAAAMAAJ&pg=PA80 (accessed 5 July 2010).

> As the most terrible warning contained in God's word is recorded against those who receive this mark [of the beast], we should find out what it is and then carefully avoid it. What is the term "beast" a symbol? We agree that the Papacy is prophetically designated.

Haworth continued his anti-Catholic diatribe, claiming:

> The effort of the Popes has ever been to maintain the usurper's hypocritical pretensions. It is therefore likely that the mark of the papal "beast" will be the use of some sign calculated to inspire tender sentiment in the minds of Christian people, and thus impose upon them.... The sign of the cross has been put to such a use.... It is used as the mark of papal authority in all the changed sacraments of that church.... Furthermore, it was the distinguishing banner of anti-christ long before Jesus came to earth.[34]

More influential in his anti-cross attitudes was Roy A. Cheville, longtime professor of religion at the RLDS Church's Graceland University in Lamoni, Iowa. Cheville was ordained Presiding Patriarch/Evangelish of the RLDS Church in 1958. Nineteen years later, at a ground breaking ceremony for a chapel on the university campus to be named in his honor, Cheville declared:

> And one more thing. No crosses in this chapel! If you put a cross on this chapel, take my name down. I worship a living Christ and not a dead Jesus.[35]

Cheville later attempted to clarify his position, arguing:

> I only said don't fill it with a lot of crucifixes.... I don't want it to be some sad dying-on-the-cross place.[36]

At best, this attempted clarification muddled Cheville's position. The term "crucifix" is generally reserved for depictions of Jesus hanging on the cross, as opposed to the bare cross. Crucifixes were essentially unheard of in RLDS chapels. If Cheville had actually only meant to prohibit the

---

34. Walter J. Haworth, *The Fall of Babylon and the Triumph of the Kingdom of God* (Rozelle, New South Wales: Standard Publishing House, 1910), 203, http://www.archive.org/details/fallofbabylontrioohaworich (accessed 5 July 2010).

35. William D. Russell, email to author, June 22, 2010. Russell stood next to Roy Cheville as he delivered these remarks.

36. David Goehner, "A Century of Inspiration at Graceland," *Saints' Herald* 142 (October 1995), 416.

COMPARATIVE PERCEPTIONS OF THE CROSS

FIGURE 10.11: *An RLDS church in Bryant, Texas.*

FIGURE 10.12: *An RLDS church in Seattle, Washington.*

FIGURE 10.13: *An RLDS church Berkeley, California.*

FIGURE 10.14: *A cross inside the RLDS chapel in Berkeley, California.*

crucifix, his initial declaration was superfluous. There was little to no chance of anyone making the Cheville Chapel a "sad dying-on-the-cross place." Indeed, his original rhetoric of worshiping "a living Christ and not a dead Jesus" is a fairly standard anti-cross polemic. As we have seen, this argument, as formulated by Gordon B. Hinckley, is the most popular defense of the cross taboo among Utah Mormons to this day. Whatever Cheville's intent, Graceland University students and faculty have refrained from displaying a cross on the chapel that bears his name.

Official RLDS/Community of Christ Policies

Decades before Cheville's controversial remarks, an article in the RLDS *Saints' Herald* periodical, published in 1949, spoke out against the attitude of members who wished to "eliminate all signs of the visible cross from our church buildings, publications, and ornaments on the ground," merely because they believed "that such displays are 'too much like' some of the more liturgical religious institutions around us" i.e., Ro-

FIGURE 10.15: *A large cross on the exterior of the Community of Christ Temple in Independence, Missouri.*

man Catholicism. Arguing that such a position "is unfair to our people," the author instead advised:

> We need the beauty of the symbol of the cross in our environment, just as we need to sing the gospel hymns often to bring us to our real purpose by making us feel the lift of God's love. Many of our attractive Latter Day Saint chancels emphasize a simple cross, sometimes over a central altar. The effect of such an arrangement seems to help us center our attention where it belongs and to make the most of the experience of worship.... [A] Latter Day Saint with a tiny cross in his lapel is not going to be any worse for the wearing of it. Indeed, the experience of

some of us seems to indicate—all other things being equal—that he might be considerably better.[37]

As this quote indicates, crosses decorated the interior of many RLDS chapels by 1949.

By the late 1950s prominent crosses began to appear on the *exterior* of new church facilities (see figures 10.11–10.13). The tradition has continued with great enthusiasm into the twenty-first century. Most notably, a large cross decorates the exterior of the Community of Christ temple at church headquarters in Independence (see figure 10.15). In the decades since Cheville argued that the cross represented "a dead Jesus," more and more members of his church have come to accept it as an inclusive symbol of their living Christian faith. Indeed, the overwhelming majority of members of the Community of Christ today have banished any lingering taboo the church may have once held.

The LDS Church and the Community of Christ have a common origin and both denominations inherited the same positive and negative factors influencing attitudes about the cross. Just as most mainline American Protestant churches have largely evolved past the primary negative factor of anti-Catholic bias, the vast majority of LDS and Community of Christ members have put anti-Catholicism behind them. However, while the anti-cross attitude born of that bias was institutionalized by LDS leaders in the 1950s and 60s, RLDS leaders in the same decades worked to promote acceptance of the cross. As a result, the two largest denominations of the Latter Day Saint movement today have achieved positions on the cross that are diametrically opposed.

---

37. Warren H. Chelline, "A Latter Day Saint Looks at the Cross," *Saints' Herald* 96 (1949), 380.

Chapter Eleven

Conclusion

THE MORMON CROSS TABOO had the same basis as the nineteenth century Protestant rejection of the symbol: a desire to disassociate themselves from the Catholic Church. Contrary to the assumptions of many historians today, however, the Mormon aversion to the cross was more a late development that occurred around the turn of the twentieth century, and by this time, Protestants had already widely accepted the symbol.

It is true that early Mormons echoed many of the same anti-Catholic polemics that concurrently circulated throughout Protestant America. Nevertheless, early Mormons initially avoided condemning the cross, and did so for three fundamental reasons: (1) The early Mormon involvement in folk magic and (2) Freemasonry both encouraged the use of the cross; and (3) the pre-Columbian cross validated the authenticity of the Book of Mormon.

The influence of the first two factors lost their strength as later generations turned away from past involvement in folk magic and Freemasonry. The third factor alone was insufficient for Latter-day Saints to preserve the general acceptance of the cross. This became true particularly as two waves of anti-Catholicism hit Utah, the first at the turn of the twentieth century and the second at mid-century. Attitudes toward the cross polarized in Utah at the grass-roots level, manifesting rather loudly in 1916 when many vocal Saints protested their leader's petition to erect a cross monument on Ensign Peak. A generation later, President David O. McKay officially institutionalized the taboo into the Church of Jesus Christ of Latter-day Saints, defining the cross as inappropriate for members, claiming that it was a purely "Catholic form of worship."

The lateness of this evolution was largely forgotten. Church authorities and apologists have since persisted in echoing early nineteenth century Protestant anti-Catholic polemics[1] to justify their aversion. These

---

1. Most (if not all) of the arguments Mormons used to justify their opposition to the cross (i.e. the symbol being pagan, Catholic, an idol, an instrument of torture, a symbol of death, the Mark of the Beast, or too much in vogue) were previously promoted by Protestants: "[T]he figure of the cross may not be used as a badge of the religion and profession of the Protestants.... [T]he papists regard the cross as the altar whereon our Lord was offered.... [T]hat which was execrable to our Lord, the sign of it should not be honourable to us. But so was the cross of our Lord; it made his death accursed; nor was it a pure instrument of meer [sic] martyrdom unto him." Cotton Mather, *Magnalia Christi Americana: Or, The Ecclesiastical History of New England* vol. 2 (Hartford, 1853), 501, http://books.google.com/books?id=fiQx6HZKVBkC&pg=PA501&dq= (accessed 30 March 2009). "For many ages, the Cross has been specially identified with the Church of Rome. Some of the ablest commentators have supposed it to be the '*mark of the beast,*' so frequently mentioned in Revelation. It is indeed the public and private badge of Anti-Christ. It is carried before the Pope wherever he goes.... From the earliest beginnings of the Papal power, the apostasy has existed under the form of religion and with the very emblem of the crucifixion. It is not without reason, therefore, that the external mark of Popery has been thought to be the '*mark of the beast.*'" Bishop M'Ilvaine, "One Faith," or, *Bishop Doane vs. Bishop M'Ilvaine, on Oxford Theology* (Burlington: J. L. Powell 1843), 71, http://books.google.com/books?id=Uq9LAAAAMAAJ&pg=PA71&dq= (March 30, 2009). "[The death of Christ] cannot possibly be represented by an image; and the very attempt to represent the sufferings of Christ in such a way shows that the person who does so, has false and degrading notions of the death of Christ—such as, in fact, show that he is no Christian.... [T]he cross is one of the great bloody idols of the church of Rome; and has occasioned, I suppose, a greater waste of human life than any one idol known in the heathen world." William M'Gavin, *The Protestant: Essays on the Principal Points of Controversy Between the Church of Rome and the Reformed* vol. 1 (Hartford, 1833), 496, http://books.google.com/books?id=DQARAAAAIAAJ&pg=PA496&dq= (accessed 30 March 2009). Anti-cross sentiment was not a phenomenon restricted to American Protestantism. Protestants throughout Europe also held contempt for the symbol: "[The cross] is painful, and even revolting, to see it employed to serve the purposes of vanity, frivolity, and worldly fashion. The representation of a gallows or a guillotine would form a very ghastly ornament. To me, the cross in that character seems more unbecoming still—not to speak of its startling impiety.... The cross on which our Saviour hung represented the curse of God.... The cross therefore represented sin, wrath, suffering, and death then. It cannot represent anything else now, and therefore it signifies the triumph of Satan rather than the triumph of Christ. Christ's triumph was accomplished at His resurrection, and the triumph of all His believing people in him.... And his believing people live in Him. Their subject of interest therefore is life, not death.... Why should I, a living resurrection member of God's family, go back to the cross for comfort and inspiration? It speaks to me only of my

arguments—coupled with the assumption that the rejection of the cross has always existed in Mormon culture—helped to perpetuate the aversion into the twenty-first century.

However, from the same early roots in early Mormonism, other traditions within the Latter Day Saint movement have followed strikingly different paths. In the RLDS tradition, the cross taboo was never institutionalized, nor did it ever dominate their culture. Instead, the church increasingly embraced the symbol, which is now freely used by the Community of Christ today.

Negative attitudes toward the cross in the LDS Church have softened since the second half of the 20th century, so much so that it would be surprising (if not shocking) to hear today's Church authorities disparage the symbol as the "mark of the Beast," "symbol of the Devil," or "image of the Great and Abominable Church." However, does this shift indicate a trajectory leading to the taboo's ultimate extinction? As old habits die hard, resistance to change is even greater when certain practices are institutionalized, rationalized, and declared true by Church authorities. It may indeed be that Church leaders will eventually decide that there is no real doctrinal or revelatory basis for the taboo, and hence feel inclined to

---

shame and ruin." S. A. Walker, *The Remembrancer*, ed. Reverend William Lush (London, 1873), 78, http://books.google.com/books?id=MjsEAAAAQAAJ&pg=RA2-PA78&dq= (accessed 30 March 2009). "It is one of the most appalling signs of the age ripening for judgment, the common prevalence of things which tell of a mass of mere profession where the power of godliness is denied. We see the cross at every corner. It is worn around almost every neck, or hanging to the watch. The mental degradation which the use of this symbol implies in so many cases, ought to make true believers weep. Not only is it now dangled about the necks of those who are the gayest of the gay in this world's vanities; but… it is worn by the most abandoned outcasts. Do those among the well-meaning and high-principled or among true Christians, who follow the fashion, ever seriously consider and ask the question, 'What does the practice mean?' Do they know, that before our Lord's crucifixion the cross was a Pagan symbol? Do they remember that the identical cross upon which the Son of God was nailed, was like the gibbet in our jails, made to serve for every murderer and malefactor that was condemned to death? Do they, after sober consideration of the subject, think it seemly to wear a model of the instrument of torture, by which wicked men tortured and killed the very Son of God? All history which we are acquainted shows us that only the most savage tribes deck their bodies with the emblems of torture, and the trophies of their victims—the very memorials of their dying pangs. Let us remember what became of the golden calf. 'And Moses ground it to powder, and made the children of Israel drink it.' The cross, once the favoured symbols in the Pagan temple, has become, in the hands of the Papacy, and in those of modern ritualism, even 'the mark of the beast.'" John Hampden, "The Cross as an Ornament," *The Voice Upon the Mountains* vol. 2 (1 May 1869), 57, http://books.google.com/books?id=qwgFAAAAQAAJ&pg=PA57&lpg=PA57&dq= (accessed 30 March 2009).

weigh the costs against its benefits. Until this happen, interfaith tension over this issue will likely persist and interfere with the Church's efforts to be accepted into the Christian denominational family. Many new converts will also remain disheartened by the taboo, and feel compelled to hide jewelry, discard decorations, and pack away cherished heirlooms that were once used to expressed their faith in and love for Jesus Christ.

APPENDIX

Early Christians and the Cross

SOME MORMONS HAVE justified their aversion to the cross by pointing to the practices of early Christians. For example, Roger Keller has said has written that Mormons, "like the earliest Christians, are reluctant to display the cross because they view the 'good news' of the gospel as Christ's resurrection more than his crucifixion."[1] Unfortunately, this argument is misleading on several levels.

It is true that most scholars concur that Christian artistic uses of the symbol, in reference to the passion event, cannot be found prior to the time of Constantine.[2] One scholar has pointed out that the universality of the symbol in general—from Quetzcoatl's four cardinal points of the winds to the Hammer of Thor— "makes more poignant the striking lack of crosses in early Christian remains."[3] Nevertheless, it is wrong to conclude from the absence of material depictions that early Christians

---

1. *Encyclopedia of Mormonism*, s.v. "Cross."
2. Ibid.
3. Snyder, *Ante Pacem*, 27. Those who reject this conclusion may cite as counter-examples the 1938 excavation discovery of a cross engraved on a wall of an unearthed house in Herculaneum, or the Palatine drawing found in 1856 that depicts a donkey being crucified with graffiti that mockingly reads, "Alexamenos, worship god." Although these findings may postdate the rise of Christianity and antedate the reign of Constantine, there is much to dispute about these evidences. Since the discovery of the cross at Herculaneum, "Further consideration," says Everett Ferguson, "has given a more utilitarian purpose: the imprint in the plaster was left by wooden brackets for a wall cabinet or perhaps a shelf or mantle with a supporting upright piece." Everett Ferguson, *Backgrounds of Early Christianity* (Grand Rapids: Eerdmans Publishing Co., 2003), 590. Graydon Snyder agrees, "[T]his so-called cross could have been anything attached to the wall by two cross pieces." Graydon F. Snyder, *Ante Pacem* (Macon, GA: Mercer University Press, 1991), 27. But even if the "new consideration" is wrong—and that the imprint indeed marked where a Latin-style-cross was once displayed—there is little reason to conclude that the cross was hung by a Christian, and not a pagan. As previously noted, the cross has been used throughout antiquity by nearly every known culture. In Minucius Felix's *Octavius*, for example, pagans were rebuked for materially depicting crosses, saying, "You, indeed, who consecrate gods of wood, adore wooden crosses perhaps as parts of your gods.... Your victorious trophies not only imitate the appearance of a simple cross, but also that of a man affixed to it." Minucius Felix, "The Octavius" ch. 29, ANF vol. 4, In *Complete Christian Collection* [CD-ROM] (Packard Technologies, 1999). The Palatine cross should not count as a Christian material depiction of the cross either, simply because the image was not drawn by a Christian—but rather, an *opponent* of Christianity. Snyder, *Ante Pacem*, 28.

did not hold the symbol as sacred. In fact, reverence for the cross is pervasive in early Christian literature with its focus on the ideals of asceticism and martyrdom. Reverence for the cross is reflected in a number of ante-Nicean traditions, such as Peter's refusal to be crucified the same way as Jesus: "[F]or I am not worthy to be crucified like my Lord," declares Peter.[4]

The apparent contradiction between reverence for the symbol and the lack of material depictions can be explained by three concerns of early Christians: (1) Christians often needed to worship surreptitiously in order to avoid persecution; (2) the cross was an image of capital punishment to Jews and Gentiles, and therefore was not an effective tool for evangelizing; (3) some Christians believed that it was a sin to materially depict an image, especially images that had sacred significance.

Many Christians worshiped surreptitiously to avoid drawing the attention of their enemies. Tertullian (c. 160–230) speaks to Christians who are afraid to assemble "in large numbers to the Church. You are afraid that we may awaken their anxieties," he says.[5]

> But you [Christians] say, 'How will we assemble together [if we do not pay tribute to avoid persecution]?' To be sure, just as the apostles also did—who were protected by faith, not by money.... Finally, if you cannot assemble by day, you have the night—the light of Christ luminous against its darkness.... Be content with a church of threes. It is better that you sometimes should not see the crowds [of other Christians], than to subject yourselves.[6]

This inconspicuous and sometimes nocturnal worship did not always ease persecutions, however, and instead had a tendency to exacerbate the suspicion of their enemies. The pagan Roman philosopher of the second century, Caecilius, leveled charges against Christians for "the very obscurity which shrouds this perverted religion." He asks, "Why else should they go to such pains to hide and conceal whatever it is they

---

4. "Apocrypha of the New Testament: Acts of the Holy Apostles Peter and Paul," *ANF vol 8, In Complete Christian Collection*. *The Acts of Peter*, chapter 38, however, explains that Peter was crucified upside down to represent the birth of man in his fallen state. See Bart D. Ehrman, *Lost Scriptures: Books that Did Not Make It into the New Testament* (New York: Oxford University Press, 2003), 153.

5. Turtullian, "De Fuga In Persecutione" ch. 3, *ANF* vol. 4, In *Complete Christian Collection*.

6. Ibid., ch. 14.

worship? One is always happy for honorable actions to be made public; crimes are kept secret." Caecilius continues to ask accusatory questions: "Why do they have no altars, no temples, no publicly-known images? Why do they always assemble in stealth?"[7] Caecilius apparently failed to understand that Christians worshiped surreptitiously in order to avoid persecution. There were "no publicly-known images" like the cross because many Christians did not wish to be identified.

The New Testament reveals another factor that contributed to the absence of the cross. Paul observes, "Christ crucified [is a] stumbling block to Jews and foolishness to Gentiles."[8] The mere idea that Jesus was crucified was an embarrassment that attracted a substantial amount of mockery from critics.[9] Writing to "Those [Christians] who are ashamed of the cross of Christ," Bishop Methodius (c. 260–312) of Olympus proclaims that "God Himself esteems [the cross] to be beautiful, even though it be contemned and despised by all else.... [B]y this figure He hath willed to deliver the soul from corrupt affections." Therefore, he says, "we ought to receive it, and not to speak evil of it."[10] The oft repeated counsel and rebukes against ashamed or embarrassed Christians, as well as the celebration and glorifying of the cross by religious leaders, underscores just how common this concern was.

There was also concern among Christians for artwork in general. Like their Jewish contemporaries,[11] early Christians had varying ideas over the second commandment's prohibition of material images. Origen (c. 185–255) remarks about God's command to Israel against engraved images, saying:

---

7. "Minucius Felix: Octavius" ch. 10, ed. Bart D. Ehrman, *After The New Testament: A Reader In Early Christianity* (New York: Oxford University Press, 1999), 56.

8. 1 Cor. 1:23 NRSV.

9. The Palatine Cross graffiti mockingly displays a depiction of a person (presumably, a Christian) worshipping a man (with an ass' head) hanging on a cross. The *Octavius* of Minucius Felix records several sensational accusations that were being leveled against Christians in the second and third century: "I hear, for example, that they [Christians] do reverence the head of the most degraded of beasts, an ass: I cannot imagine what absurdity has persuaded them to consecrate it, but it is indeed a cult born of such morals and well suited for them." "Minucius Felix: Octavius" ch. 10, ed. Ehrman, *After The New Testament*, 56.

10. Methodius, "Three Fragments from the Homily on the Cross and Passion of the Christ" 2, *ANF* vol. 6, In *Complete Christian Collection*.

11. See Carmel Konikoff, *The Second Commandment and its Interpretation in the Art of Ancient Israel* (Genève: Imprimerie du Journal de Genève, 1973).

Neither painter nor image-maker existed in the nation of Israel, for the Law expelled all such persons from it. In that way, there was no pretext for the construction of images. For image-making is an art that attracts the attention of foolish men. It drags the eyes of the soul down from God to earth. Accordingly, there was among them a Law to the following effect: 'Do not transgress the Law and make to yourselves a carved image, or any likeness of male or female.'[12]

Elsewhere Origen proclaims, "[Pagans], in imagining that the hand of lowly artisans can frame representations of divinity, are uneducated, servile, and ignorant."[13] Hippolytus of Rome (c. 170–236) also stressed the importance of God's second commandment, by criticizing the gnostic-Christian disciples of Carpocrates for making "counterfeit images of Christ."[14]

By evidence of the Christian catacombs, we know that some Christians created and displayed controversial images despite the taboo.[15] A letter from Epiphanius (Bishop of Salamis, Cyprus) also confirms this deviant behavior, as well as his negative iconoclastic reaction to it. According to the letter (dated 394), Epiphanius discovered in a Christian church a veil depicting Jesus or a disciple on it; and upon seeing the veil he immediately tore it down and replaced it with a plain one.[16] This occa-

---

12. Origen, *ANF* 4.510; as quoted in David W. Bercot, *A Dictionary of Early Christian Beliefs* (Massachusetts: Hendrickson Publishers, 1998), 352.
13. Origen, *ANF* 4.579; as quoted in Bercot, *A Dictionary*, 352-53.
14. Hippolytus, *ANF* 5.114; as quoted in Bercot, *A Dictionary of Early Christian Beliefs*, 352. Arnobius (c.305) contends that depicting images is a fruitless endeavor. "It has been sufficiently shown," says Amobius, "how vain it is to form images." Amobius, *ANF* 6.518; as quoted in Bercot, *A Dictionary*, 354.
15. Some Gnostics purposefully broke the Old Testament's commandments because they believed the God of the Old Testament was inferior and contrary to the true God. Religious historian Bart D. Ehrman explains, "The true God was above the inferior God of the Jews. And so, according to the Cainites, anyone who opposed the God of the Jews by breaking his law—as done, for example, by Cain, the first fratricide, and the men of Sodom and Gomorrah—was actually standing for the truth." Bart D. Ehrman, foreword to *The Lost Gospel: The Quest for the Gospel of Judas Iscariot*, by Herbert Krisney (DC: National Geographic, 2006), xvi.
16. Says Epiphanius, "Moreover, I have heard that certain persons have this grievance against me: When I accompanied you to the holy place called Bethel, there to join you in celebrating the Collect, after the use of the Church, I came to a villa called Anablatha and, as I was passing, saw a lamp burning there. Asking what place it was, and learning it to be a church, I went in to pray, and found there a curtain hanging on the doors of the said church, dyed and embroidered. It bore an image either of Christ or of one of the saints; I do not rightly remember whose the image was. Seeing this, and being loath that an image of a man should be hung up in Christ's

sion shows that, even after Constantine's reign, there remained disagreements among some Christians over how to properly interpret God's second commandment.

The most distinguished teacher of Alexandria, Clement (c. 150–215), expressed his conservative view of the second commandment, insisting that works of art by their nature "cannot be sacred and divine."[17] Clement explains, "The senseless earth is dishonored by the makers of images, who change it by their art from its proper nature, and induce men to worship it." According to Clement, "the image is only dead matter shaped by the craftsman's hand." For this reason Christians "have no sensible image of sensible matter, but an image that is perceived by the mind alone—God, who alone is truly God."[18]

Clement makes one exception to the second commandment, however, allowing for what he thought to be "necessary" images:

> But there are circumstances in which this strictness may [be] relaxed.... [I]f it is necessary for us, while engaged in public business, or discharging other avocations in the country, and often away from our wives, to seal anything for the sake of safety, He (the Word) allows us a signet [ring] for this purpose only. Other finger-rings are to be cast off.

Rather than depict a person or divinity artistically, continues Clement, you should simply observe a person fishing, and then "remember the apostle, and the children drawn out of the water. For we are not to delineate the faces of idols, we who are prohibited to cleave to them."[19]

---

church contrary to the teaching of the Scriptures, I tore it asunder and advised the custodians of the place to use it as a winding sheet for some poor person. They, however, murmured, and said that if I made up my mind to tear it, it was only fair that I should give them another curtain in its place. As soon as I heard this, I promised that I would give one, and said that I would send it at once. Since then there has been some little delay, due to the fact that I have been seeking a curtain of the best quality to give to them instead of the former one, and thought it right to send to Cyprus for one. I have now sent the best that I could find, and I beg that you will order the presbyter of the place to take the curtain which I have sent from the hands of the Reader, and that you will afterwards give directions that curtains of the other sort—opposed as they are to our religion—shall not be hung up in any church of Christ. A man of your uprightness should be careful to remove an occasion of offence unworthy alike of the Church of Christ and of those Christians who are committed to your charge." Jerome, "The Letters of St. Jerome" 51: 9, *Nicene and Post Nicene Fathers*, vol. 6, In *Complete Christian Collection*.

17. Clement, *ANF* 2.530; as quoted in Bercot, *A Dictionary of Early Christian Beliefs*, 352.
18. Clement, "Exhortation to the Heathen" ch. 4. *ANF* vol. 2, In *Complete Christian Collection*.
19. Clement, "The Instructor" 3: 11, *ANF* vol. 2, In *Complete Christian Collection*.

It is noteworthy that Clement does not list the image of the cross as a suitable seal, perhaps revealing an extra sensitivity towards depicting the cross openly.[20] What is especially significant in this quote, however, is Clement's remark about seeing a fisherman, and "remembering" the apostle (Jesus?), rather than depicting it. This quote may shed light on what Clement meant (in the previous quote) by insisting that God must be perceived "by the mind alone."

Rather than depict sacred and spiritual realities materially, many Christians instead observed their natural occurrence, even searching for their manifestations in the world around them. Christians observed the cross in particular, as revealed in a quote from Minucius Felix (c. late second–early third century CE). He states that although they do not outwardly use the physical image of the cross ("we [Christians] neither worship nor wish for [the cross]"), they brought it to mind when they saw its resemblance in other things:

> We assuredly see the sign of a cross, naturally, in the ship when it is carried along with swelling sails, when it glides forward with expanded oars; and when the military yoke is lifted up, it is the sign of a cross; and when a man adores God with a pure mind, with hands outstretched. Thus the sign of the cross either is sustained by a natural reason, or your own religion is formed with respect to it.[21]

Consistent with the views of Clement, Minucius explains that Christians observed the manifestation of the cross, rather than create the outward image of it. The images they viewed were natural manifestations of spiritual realities, perceived by the mind.

This practice of observing or searching for the cross was a common practice for early Christians. Justin Martyr (c. 110–165) discovered that a ship's sail, a plough, the banners and trophies of the government, and the human form (body and face) each manifest "no other form than that

---

20. It is also quite possible that Clement is suggesting the use of "crypto-crosses" when he lists the ship and anchor. Says art historian Robin Margaret Jensen, "Scholars will need to reconsider whether there is, in fact, a complete absence of crucifixion in early Christianity. Possible indirect references to the passion include such signs and symbols as simple crosses, 'crypto-crosses' (anchors, ships' mast, trees, plows, axes), and tau-crosses." Robin Margaret Jensen, *Understanding Early Christian Art* (New York: Routledge, 2000), 137.

21. Minucius Felix, "The Octavius" ch. 29, *ANF* vol. 4, In *Complete Christian Collection*.

of the cross."²² Tertullian speaks of the cross being manifested in the human posture, and by "Every piece of timber which is fixed in the ground in an erect position."²³ Jerome (c. 340–420) mentions perceiving the manifestation of the cross in a swimming man, a flying bird, and a man praying with extended arms.²⁴

Christians similarly looked for the cross in the Old Testament.²⁵ Tertullian observes how Moses, "at the time when Joshua was battling against Amalek, pray[ed] sitting with hands expanded." The sacred symbol was also found in the brazen serpent that Moses lifted up for the Israelites to look to and be healed. "[H]e was exhibiting the Lord's cross," said Tertullian.²⁶

The Epistle of Barnabas likewise finds a manifestation of the crucifixion in the number of men Abraham circumcised in his household:

> For [the Scripture] saith, "And Abraham circumcised ten, and eight, and three hundred men of his household." What, then, was the knowledge given to him in this? Learn the eighteen first, and then the three hundred. The ten and the eight are thus denoted—Ten by I, and Eight by H. You have [the initials of the name of] Jesus. And because the cross was to express the grace [of our redemption] by the letter T, he says also, "Three Hundred." He signifies, therefore, Jesus by two letters, and the cross by one. He knows this, who has put within us the engrafted gift of His doctrine. No one has been admitted by me to a more excellent piece of knowledge than this, but I know that ye are worthy.²⁷

The Greek letter *tau* (T or +) has the numeric value of three hundred. This letter took on sacred significance, not only because it was in the shape of a cross, but also because the same character in Hebrew, *tav*,

---

22. Justin Martyr, "First Apology of Justin" ch. 55, ANF vol. 1, In *Complete Christian Collection*.
23. Tertullian, "AD Nationes" 1: 12, ANF vol. 3, In *Complete Christian Collection*.
24. Adam Clarke, "Matthew 27:35," *Adam Clarke's Commentary on the Bible*, http://www.godrules.net/library/clarke/clarkemat27.htm (accessed 28 October 2008).
25. Hippolytus and Clement see the image and message of the cross in the Greco-Roman myth, when the Ulyssies is tied to the mast of the ship (Cross of Christ), that he may not give way to the voice of the sirens. Hippolytus, "The Refutation of all Heresies" 7: 1, ANF vol. 5; and Clement, "Exhortation to the Heathen" ch 12, ANF vol. 2, In *Complete Christian Collection*.
26. Tertullian, "Answers to the Jews" ch 10, ANF vol. 3, In *Complete Christian Collection*.
27. Barnabus, "Epistle of Barnabas" ch. 9, ANF vol. 1, In *Complete Christian Collection*.

was the last letter of the Hebrew alphabet.[28] The *tau* and *tav* therefore became associated with the name of God, just as the last letter of the Greek alphabet did—*omega*. Clement of Alexandria reported that some Christians similarly perceived the cross in the proportions of Noah's ark, saying, "Now there are some who say that three hundred cubits are the symbol of the Lord's sign."[29]

By actively searching for the cross, this exercise allowed Christians to embrace the symbol without breaking the second commandment or drawing the attention of their enemies. Christians also got around these obstacles by tracing the "Lord's sign" (T or +) upon their foreheads. Tertullian records:

> We feel pained should any wine or bread, even though our own, be cast upon the ground. At every forward step and movement, at every going in and out, when we put on our clothes and shoes, when we bathe, when we sit at table, when we light the lamps, on couch, on seat, in all the ordinary actions of daily life, we trace upon the forehead the sign.[30]

The Christian act of tracing the sign reenacted obedience to God's command described in Ezekiel 9:4. Tertullian explains this elsewhere:

> He [Christ] signed them with that very seal of which Ezekiel spake: "The Lord said unto me, Go through the gate, through the midst of Jerusalem, and set the mark Tau upon the foreheads of the men." Now the Greek letter Tau and our own letter T is the very form of the cross, which He predicted would be the sign on our foreheads in the true Catholic Jerusalem… Now, inasmuch as all these things are also found amongst you, and the sign upon the forehead, and the sacraments of the church, and the offerings of the pure sacrifice, you ought now to

---

28. "St. Jerome and many others have thought that the letter tau was that which was ordered to be placed on the foreheads of those mourners; and Jerome says, that this Hebrew letter t tau was formerly written like a cross. So then the people were to be signed with the sign of the cross! It is certain that on the ancient Samaritan coins, which are yet extant, the letter t tau is in the form +." Adam Clarke, "Ezekiel 9:4," *Adam Clarke's Commentary*, http://www.godrules.net/library/clarke/clarkeeze9.htm (accessed 28 October 2008).
29. Clement of Alexandria, "The Stromata" 6: 11, *ANF* vol. 2, In *Complete Christian Collection*.
30. Tertullian, "The Chaplet, or De Corona" ch. 3, *ANF* vol. 3, In *Complete Christian Collection*

burst forth, and declare that the Spirit of the Creator prophesied of your Christ.[31]

Tracing the cross (*tau*) upon their forehead was not in conflict with the second commandment either, since doing so did not manipulate dead matter. The private action also helped Christians to avoid the attention of critics, since the symbol was traced invisibly. By tracing the sign, rather than drawing it visibly Christians were able to worship surreptitiously, comply with the second commandment, and still embrace the visual symbol of the cross.

In conclusion, the absence of the image of the cross in Christian artwork was due to three fundamental reasons: (1) Christians desired to worship surreptitiously; (2) the image was a stumbling block to Jews and Gentiles, and therefore not an effective emblem for evangelizing; and (3) Christians had reservations about depicting the cross materially, fearing that doing so would violate the second commandment.

None of these factors are relevant to Mormons today. Mormons are not mocked for their belief that Jesus was crucified; they do not avoid logos or symbols for fear that they would blow their own cover; and they seem to have no aversion to using overt symbols (we can be certain that early Christians would have objected to placing a gold statue of an angel on their meetinghouses). The Mormon taboo is quite different from the early Christian taboo; moreover, the assumption often made by Mormon scholars and apologists—that the absence of the cross in early Christian artwork proves that they (like Latter-day Saints) viewed the symbol as abhorrent—is false.

---

31. Tertullian, "The Five Books Against Macion" 3: 22, *ANF* vol. 3, In *Complete Christian Collection*; see also Tertullian, "An Answer to the Jews" ch. 11, *ANF* vol. 3.

Bibliography

Agrippa, Heinrich Cornelius. *Occult Philosophy* (London, 1655), book 4, http://www.esotericarchives.com/agrippa/agrippa4.htm (accessed April 12, 2009).

Alexander, Thomas G. *Mormonism in Transition: A History of the Latter-day Saints, 1890-1930*. Chicago: University Illinois Press, 1996.

Allen, James B., and Glen M. Leonard, *The Story of the Latter-day Saints*. Salt Lake City: Deseret Book, 1992.

Anderson, Christian Nephi. "Are We Americans?" *Improvement Era* (October 1900) 3, no. 12. LDS Library, 2006. CD-ROM.

Anderson, Lavina Fielding, ed. *Lucy's Book: A Critical Edition of Lucy Mack Smith's Family Memoir* (Salt Lake City: Signature Books, 2001).

Asay, Carlos E. "'Look to God and Live.'" *Ensign*. November 1978, 52-54.

Ashment, Edward H. "The LDS Temple Ceremony: Historical Origins and Religious Value," *Dialogue: A Journal of Mormon Thought* 27, no. 3 (Fall 1994): 289-298.

Ballard, M. Russell. *Our Search for Happiness: An Invitation to Understand The Church of Jesus Christ of Latter-day Saints*. Salt Lake City: Deseret Book, 1993.

Barker, James L. "The Protestors of Christendom." *Improvement Era* 32, no. 9, September 1939. In *LDS Library 2006*. CD-ROM. LDS Media, 2006.

Barkun, Michael. *Crucible of the Millennium: The Burned-Over District of New York in the 1840s*. New York: Syracuse University Press, 1986.

Barrett, Francis. *The Magus* (London, 1801), http://onlinebooks.library.upenn.edu/webbin/book/lookupid?key=olbp11588 (accessed April 12, 2009).

Baskin, Robert. *Reminiscences of Early Utah*. Salt Lake City, Tribune-Reporter Printer Co., c.1914. http://www.archive.org/details/reminiscencesofeoobaskrich (accessed November 10, 2008).

Baurrl, Abbe. *Memoirs, Illustrating the History of Jacobinism: A Translation from the French of The Abbe Barruel* vol. 2. New York, 1799. http://books.google.com/books?id=v-wvAAAAMAAJ (accessed November 16, 2008).

Bellville, Peter K. "A Year Without a Summer." *Ensign*, January 1983, 65.

Bennett, John Cook. *The History of the Saints: or, An exposé of Joe Smith and Mormonism*. Boston, 1842, http://books.google.com/books?id=WGUoAAAAYAAJ (accessed 18 May 2010).

Bercot, David W. *A Dictionary of Early Christian Beliefs*. Massachusetts: Hendrickson Publishers, 1998.

Bernard, David, ed. *Light on Masonry*. Utica: William Williams, 1829. http://books.google.com/books?id=QlIZAAAAYAAJ (accessed November 7, 2008).

Book of Recorded Marks and Brands. Salt Lake City: Deseret News, 1874. http://images.archives.utah.gov/cdm4/document.php?CISOROOT=/540&CISOPTR=2597&REC=4 (accessed November 10, 2008).

Brigham Young University Digital Collections. http://www.lib.byu.edu/online.html

Bringhurst, Newell G., and John C. Hamer, ed. *Scattering of the Saints: Schism within Mormonism*. Independence: John Whitmer Books, 2007.

Brooke, John L. *The Refiner's Fire: The Making of Mormon Cosmology, 1644-1844*. Cambridge: Cambridge University Press, 1996.

Bryant, Seth L. "Latter-Day Anguish and the Epic of greater Mormonism." Master's thesis, University of Florida, December 2008.

Bullock, Steven C. "A Pure and Sublime System: The Appeal of Post-Revolutionary Freemasonry," *Journal of the Early Republic* 9 (Fall 1989): 359-73.

Bushman, Richard L. "A Joseph Smith for the Twenty-First Century." *Brigham Young University Studies* 40, no. 2 (2001): 155-71.

———. *Joseph Smith and the Beginnings of Mormonism*. Chicago: University of Illinois Press, 1984.

———. "Joseph Smith and the Translation of the Book of Mormon," *Mormon Stories Podcast* 049. Interview by John Dehlin, 2007. http://mormonstories.org/ (accessed August 21, 2008).

———. "Joseph Smith's Many Histories," The Worlds of Joseph Smith: An International Academic Conference at the Library of Congress, May 6, 2005. http://www.lds.org/library/display/0,4945,510-1-3067-1,00.html (accessed January, 20 2009).

———. *Joseph Smith: Rough Stone Rolling*. New York: Alfred A. Knopf, 2006.

Butler, Jon. *Awash in a Sea of Faith: Christianizing the American People*. Cambridge: Harvard University Press, 1992.

———. "Magic, Astrology, and the Early American Religious Heritage, 1600-1760," *American Historical Review* 84, no. 2 (April 1979): 317-346.

Cannon, Donald Q., and Richard O. Cowan, *Unto Every Nation: Gospel Light Reaches Every Land*. Salt Lake City: Deseret Book, 2003.

Carnack, Noel A. "Images of Christ in Latter-day Saint Visual Culture." *Brigham Young University Studies* 39, no. 3 (2000): 18-76.

Carnes, Mark C. *Secret Ritual and Manhood in Victorian America*. New Haven: Yale University Press, 1989.

Cerza, Alphonse, and Louis L. Williams, eds. *Masonic Symbols in American Decorative Arts*. Lexington: Scottish Rite Masonic Museum and Library, 1976.

Charles W. Nibley Papers, LDS Church History Library. Several documents from this collection were provided by the LDS Church History staff.

Clark Jr, J. Reuben. *On the Way to Immortality and Eternal Life*. Salt Lake City: Deseret Book, 1950.

Clarke, Adam. *Adam Clarke's Commentary on the Bible*. http://www.godrules.net/library/clarke/clarke.htm (accessed October 28, 2008).

Coltrin, Zebedee. "Diary Excerpts of Zebedee Coltrin." In *New Mormon Studies: A Comprehensive Library*. CD-ROM. Smith Research Associates, 1998.

Complete Christian Collection. CD-ROM. Packard Technologies, 1999.

Cook, Lyndon W., and Andrew F. Ehat, eds. *The Words of Joseph Smith: The Contemporary Accounts of the Nauvoo Discourses of the Prophet Joseph*. Salt Lake City: Deseret Book, 1996. In *LDS Library 2006*. CD-ROM. LDS Media, 2006.

Cross, Mary Bywater. *Quilts & Women of the Mormon Migrations: Treasures of Transition*. Nashville: Routlege Hill Press, 1996.

Davies, Douglas J. "Gethsemane and Calvary in LDS Soteriology." *Dialogue: A Journal of Mormon Thought* 34, no. 3-4 (2001): 19-30.

———. *An Introduction to Mormonism*. Cambridge, UK: Cambridge University Press, 2003.

Debus, Allen G. "Scientific Truth and Occult Tradition: The Medical World of Ebenezer Sibley (1751-1799)," *Medical History* 26 (1982): 259-78.

Reed C. Durham, Jr., "Is there No Help for the Widow's Son?" Presidential Address at the Mormon History Association Convention (April 20, 1974), http://www.cephasministry.com/mormon_is_there_no_help.html (accessed 20 May 2010).

Dwyer, Robert J. "Pioneer Bishop: Lawrence Scanlan, 1843-1915," *Utah Historical Quarterly* 20 (1952): 135-58.

Ehrman, Bart D. Ehrman, ed. *After The New Testament: A Reader In Early Christianity*. New York: Oxford University Press, 1999.

———. Foreward to *The Lost Gospel: The Quest for the Gospel of Judas Iscariot*, by Herbert Krisney. DC: National Geographic, 2006.

———. *Lost Scriptures: Books that Did Not Make It into the New Testament*. New York: Oxford University Press, 2003.

Esbeck, Carl H. "Dissent and Disestablishment: The Church-State Settlement in the Early American Republic." *Brigham Young University Law Review* 4 (2004): 1385-1592.

Ferguson, Everett. *Backgrounds of Early Christianity*. Grand Rapids: Eerdmans Publishing Co., 2003.

The Freemasons' Quarterly Magazine and Review. London, 1843. http://books.google.com/books?id=mq8EAAAAQAAJ&q=&pgis=1 (accessed April 2, 2009).

Frosberg Jr., Clyde R. *Equal Rights: The Book of Mormon, Masonry, Gender, and American Culture*. New York: Columbia University Press, 2004.

Fulling, Edmund H. "American Witch Hazel: History, Nomenclature and Modern Utilization," *Economic Botany* 7, no. 4 (October-December 1953): 359-381.

Giles, John D. "Hike of 1917—Pioneer Trail." *Improvement Era* 20, no. 11, September 1917. In *LDS Library 2006*. CD-ROM. LDS Media, 2006.

———. "This Is the Place." *Improvement Era* 58, no. 5, May 1945. In *LDS Library 2006*. CD-ROM. LDS Media, 2006.

Givens, Terryl L. *People of Paradox: A History of Mormon Culture*. New York: Oxford University Press, 2007.

Grow, Matthew. "The Whore of Babylon and the Abomination of Abominations: Nineteenth-Century Catholic and Mormon Mutual Perceptions and Religious Identity," *Church History: Studies in Christianity and Culture* 73, no. 1 (March 2004): 139-67.

Grunder, Rick. *Mormon Parallels: A Bibliographic Source*. CD-ROM. La Fayette, New York: Rick Grunder Books, 2008.

Hamilton, C. Mark. *Nineteenth-Century Mormon Architecture & City Planning*. New York: Oxford University Press, 1995.

Hampden, John. "The Cross as an Ornament," *The Voice Upon the Mountains* vol. 2. May 1, 1869. http://books.google.com/books?id=qwgFAAAAQAAJ&pg=PA57&lpg=PA57&dq= (accessed March 30, 2009).

Hand, Wayland D. "Magic and the Supernatural in Utah Folklore," *Dialogue* 16 (Winter 1983): 51-64.

Harris, William. "Utah," *The Catholic Encyclopedia* 15. New York: Robert Appleton Company, 1912. http://www.newadvent.org/cathen/15238a.htm (accessed March 26, 2009).

Haworth, Walter J. *The Fall of Babylon and the Triumph of the Kingdom of God*. Rozelle, New South Wales: Standard Publishing House, 1910, http://www.archive.org/details/fallofbabylontrioohaworich (accessed 5 July 2010).

Hill, Donna. *Joseph Smith: The First Mormon*. Salt Lake City: Signature Books, 1999.

Hill, Marvin S. "A Note on Joseph Smith's First Vision and Its Import in the Shaping of Early Mormonism," *Dialogue: A Journal of Mormon Thought*, 12, no. 1 (Spring 1979): 90-99.

———. "Money Digging Folklore and the Beginnings of Mormonism: And Interpretive Suggestion," *BYU Studies* 24 (Fall 1984): 473-488.

Hinckley, Gordon B. "The Symbol of Our Faith." *Ensign*, April 2005, 2-6.

———. "The Symbol of Christ." *Ensign*, May 1975, 92-94.

The History of the Reorganized Church of Jesus Christ of Latter Day Saints (Independence: Herald House, 1976), 8 vols.

History of The Church of Jesus Christ of Latter-day Saints (Salt Lake City: Deseret Book, 1974), 7 vols.

"A History of the Divining Rod; With the Adventures of an Old Rodsman," *The United States Democratic Review* 26, no. 141 (March 1850): 218-226. http://cdl.library.cornell.edu/cgi-bin/moa/moa-cgi?notisid=AGD1642-0026-66 (accessed March 27, 2009).

Homer, Michael W. "'Similarity of Priesthood in Masonry': The Relationship Between Freemasonry and Mormonism." *Dialogue: A Journal of Mormon Thought* 27, no. 3 (Fall 1994): 1-113.

Howe, Eber D. *Mormonism Unvailed*. Painesville Ohio: Telegraph Press, 1834, http://solomonspalding.com/docs/1834howf.htm#pg221 (accessed 1 July 2010).

Hullinger, Robert N. *Joseph Smith's Response to Skepticism*. Salt Lake City: Signature Books, 1992.

Hyde, William A. "Who Are Christian?—A Test," *Liahona*. In *Journal History of The Church of Jesus Christ of Latter-day Saints*, vol. 550, August 15, 1916, 5. *Selected Collections from the Archives of The Church of Jesus Christ of Latter-day Saints*. DVD-ROM 2:33. Provo: Brigham Young University Press, 2002.

Internet Archive: American Libraries. http://www.archive.org/details/americana

Jensen, Andrew. *Conference Report*. October 1923. In *LDS Library 2006*. CD-ROM. LDS Media, 2006.

———. *Encyclopedic History of the Church of Jesus Christ of Latter-day Saints*. Salt Lake City: Deseret Book, 1941.

———. *LDS Biographical Encyclopedia: A Compilation of Biographical Sketches of Prominent Men and Women in the Church of Jesus Christ of Latter-day Saints*. 4 vols. Salt Lake City: Andrew Jenson History Co., 1901-1936.

Jensen, Robin Margaret. *Understanding Early Christian Art*. New York: Routledge, 2000.

Jessee, Dean C., ed. *The Papers of Joseph Smith: Autobiographical and Historical Writings*. 2 vols. Salt Lake City: Deseret Book, 1989-92.

Jillson, Clark. *Green Leaves from Whitingham, Vermont: A History of the Town*. Worchester, 1894, http://books.google.com/books?id=G7ATAAAAYAAJ&pg= (accessed 18 May 2010).

Johnson, Benjamin F. *My Life's Review: Autobiography of Benjamin Franklin Johnson*. Provo: Grandin Book, 1997.

———. Benjamin F. Jonson to George F. Gibbs, 1903. In *New Mormon Studies: A Comprehensive Library*. CD-ROM. Smith Research Associates, 1998.

The Joseph Smith Papers: Revelations and Translations, Manuscript Revelation Books—Facsimile Edition. Church Historian's Press, 2009.

Journal of Discourses. 26 vols. 1854-1886. Reprint, Salt Lake City: 1964.

Kenny, Scott G., ed. "Willford Woodruff's Journal." Midvale, Utah: Signature Books, 1983. In *New Mormon Studies: A Comprehensive Library*. CD-ROM. Smith Research Associates, 1998.

Kimball, Andrew E., and Edward L. Kimball. *Spencer W. Kimball: Twelfth President of the Church of Jesus Christ of Latter-day Saints*. Salt Lake City: Bookcraft, 1977.

Konikoff, Carmel. *The Second Commandment and its Interpretation in the Art of Ancient Israel*. Genève: Imprimerie du Journal de Genève, 1973.

Largey, Dennis L., ed. *Book of Mormon Reference Companion*. Salt Lake City: Deseret Book Company, 2003.

Launius, Roger D. *Joseph Smith III: Pragmatic Prophet*. University of Illinois Press, 1995.

The LDS Endowment. http://www.ldsendowment.org/

LDS.org Gospel Library. http://lds.org/ldsorg/v/index.jsp?vgnextoid=2b6f3c7ff44f2 010VgnVCM1000001f5e340aRCRD&locale=0

LDS Library 2006. CD-ROM. LDS Media, 2006.

Legler, Henry E. *A Moses of the Mormons: Strang's City of Refuge and Island Kingdom*. 1897. http://books.google.com/books?id=u33hAAAAMAAJ&printsec=frontcover&source=gbs_ge_summary_r&cad=0#v=onepage&q&f=false (accessed 2 July 2010).

Ludlow, Daniel H. *A Companion to Your Study of the New Testament: The Four Gospels*. Salt Lake City: Deseret Book, 1982.

———, ed. *Encyclopedia of Mormonism*. 4 vols. New York: Macmillan, 1992.

Lyman, Edward Leo. "The Alienation of an Apostle from His Quorum: The Moses Thatcher Case," *Dialogue: A Journal of Mormon Thought* 18, no. 2 (Summer 1985): 67-91.

Lyon, T. Edger. *Apostasy to Restoration: Course of Study for the Melchizedek Priesthood Quorums of The Church of Jesus Christ of Latter-day Saints*. Salt Lake City: Deseret Book Co., 1960.
Marquardt, H. Michael, and Wesley P. Walters, *Inventing Mormonism: Tradition and the Historical Record*. Salt Lake City: Smith Research Associates, 1994.
Mace, Wandel. *Autobiography of Wandle Mace*. In *New Mormon Studies: A Comprehensive Library*. CD-ROM. Smith Research Associates, 1998.
Mackey, Albert G. *Encyclopedia of Freemasonry and Its Kindred Sciences* vol. 2. New York: The Masonic History Company, 1921.
Mackey, Albert G. *Encyclopedia of Freemasonry and Its Kindred* Sciences. Philadelphia: Moss & Company, 1879. http://books.google.com/books?id=fAgIAAAAQAAJ (accessed November 7, 2008).
Macoy, Robert, ed. *Universal Masonic Library* vol 7. New York, 1855. http://books.google.com/books?id=IgBKAAAAMAAJ&pg=RA1 (accessed April 2, 2009).
Mather, Cotton. *Magnalia Christi Americana: Or, The Ecclesiastical History of New England* vol. 2. Hartford, 1853. http://books.google.com/books?id=fiQx6HZKVBkC (accessed March 30, 2009).
Mauss, Armand L. *The Angel and the Beehive: The Mormon Struggle with Assimilation*. Chicago: University of Illinois Press, 1994.
May, Dean L. "Between Two Cultures: The Mormon Settlement of Star Valley, Wyoming," *Journal of Mormon History* 13 (1986-1987): 125-43.
McConkie, Bruce R. *Mormon Doctrine*. Salt Lake City: Book Craft Company, 1958.
Messages of the First Presidency of The Church of Jesus Christ of Latter-day Saints 2 (1965-75): 316.
M'Gavin, William. *The Protestant: Essays on the Principal Points of Controversy Between the Church of Rome and the Reformed* vol. 1. Hartford, 1833. http://books.google.com/books?id=DQARAAAAIAAJ (accessed March 30, 2009).
Millet, Robert. *What Happened to the Cross? Distinctive LDS Teachings*. Salt Lake City: Deseret Book, 2007.
Missionary Handbook. Salk Lake City: The Church of Jesus Christ of Latter-day Saints, 2006.
———. Salk Lake City: The Church of Jesus Christ of Latter-day Saints, 1973.
Mountain West Digital Library. http://www.mwdl.org/
New Mormon Studies: A Comprehensive Library. CD-ROM. Smith Research Associates, 1998.
Nibley, Charles W. *Conference Report*. October 1917. In *LDS Library 2006*. CD-ROM. LDS Media, 2006.
Nielson, Carol Holindrake. *The Salt Lake City Album Quilt, 1857: Stories of the Relief Society Women and Their Quilt*. Salt Lake City: University of Utah Press, 2004.
Noord, Roger Van. *Assassination of a Michigan King: The Life of James Jesse* Strang. Ann Arbor: University of Michigan Press, 1997.
Olaiz, Hugo. "Letter to the Editor," *Dialogue: A Journal of Mormon Thought* 35, no. 2 (Summer 2002): vii.

Old Testament Gospel Doctrine Manual. Salt Lake City: The Church of Jesus Christ of Latter-day Saints, 2001.

Oliver, George. "The Masonic Manual," *Universal Masonic Library.* ed. Robert Macoy. New York, 1855. http://books.google.com/books?id=gflJAAAAMAAJ (accessed March 25, 2009).

"One Faith," or, *Bishop Doane vs. Bishop M'Ilvaine, on Oxford Theology.* Burlington: J. L. Powell, 1843. http://books.google.com/books?id=Uq9LAAAAMAAJ&pg= (March 30, 2009).

Ordo ab Chao: The Original and Complete Rituals, 4th-33rd Degrees of the first Supreme Council, 33rd Degree at Charleston, South Carolina. Kessinger Publishing, 1995.

Owens, Lance S. "Joseph Smith and Kabbalah: The Occult Connection," *Dialogue: A Journal of Mormon Thought* 27, no. 3 (Fall 1994): 117-194.

Penn, William. "No Cross, No Crown," *The Selected Works of William Penn.* London, 1825.

Peterson, Daniel C., and Stephen D. Ricks. *Offenders for a Word: How Anti-Mormons Play Word Games to Attack the Latter-day Saints.* Provo: Foundation of Ancient Research and Mormon Studies, 1992.

Peterson, Mark E. "The Covenant People of God," *Speeches.* Fireside talk, Brigham Young University, September 28, 1980. http://speeches.byu.edu/reader/reader.php?id=6773 (accessed March 31, 2009).

———. *The Forerunners.* Salt Lake City: Bookcraft, 1979.

Pratt, John P. "The Restoration of Priesthood Keys on Easter 1836, Part 1: Dating the First Easter." *Ensign,* June 1985, 59-68.

Pratt, Orson. *The Seer.* 1853-54. Reprint, Salt Lake City: Eborn Books, 2000.

Pratt, Parley P. *Autobiography of Parley P. Pratt.* Salt Lake City, Deseret Book, 1985.

Prince, Gregory A., and Wm. Robert Wright. *David O. McKay and the Rise of Modern Mormonism.* Salt Lake City: University of Utah Press, 2005.

Quaife, Milo Milton. *The Kingdom of Saint James: A Narrative of the Mormons.* New Haven: Yale University Press, 1930.

Quinn, D. Michael. *Early Mormonism and the Magic World View.* Salt Lake City: Signature Books, 1998.

———. *The Mormon Hierarchy: Origins of Power.* Salt Lake City: Signature Books, 1994.

Reed, Michael G. "The Development of the LDS Church's Attitude Toward the Cross." Master's thesis, California State University of Sacramento, Spring 2009.

Rees, Robert A. "Mormons and the Cross," Sunstone Symposium-West, Claremont Graduate University, CA, March 15, 2008.

Remini, Robert V. *Joseph Smith.* New York: Viking Penguin, 2002.

Roberts, B. H., ed. *A Comprehensive History of the Church of Jesus Christ of Latter-day Saints.* 6 vols. Provo: Brigham Young University, 1965. In *LDS Library 2006.* CD-ROM. LDS Media, 2006.

———, ed. *History of the Church of Jesus Christ of Latter-day Saints.* 7 vols. 1902-1932. Reprint, Salt Lake City: Deseret Book, 1994.

———. *Studies of the Book of Mormon.* Salt Lake City: Signature Books, 1992.

Robinson, Stephen E. "Nephi's 'Great and Abominable Church,'" *Journal of Book of Mormon Studies* 7, no. 1 (1998): 32-39.

Rossetti, Gabriel P. *Disquisitions on the Antipapel Spirit Which Produced the Reformation* vol. 2. Translated by Caroline Ward. London, 1834. http://books.google.com/books?id=gdcAAAAAcAAJ&pg= (accessed March 30, 2009).

Rust, Val D. *Radical Origins: Early Mormon Converts and Their Colonial Ancestors.* Chicago: University of Illinois Press, 2004.

Schlesinger, Arthur M. "Biography of a Nation of Joiners," *American Historical Review* 50, no. 1 (October 1944): 1-25.

Scot, Reginald. *Discovery of Witchcraft* (London, 1584), http://www.esotericarchives.com/solomon/scot16.htm (accessed April 12, 2009).

Selected Collections from the Archives of The Church of Jesus Christ of Latter-day Saints. 2 vols. DVD-ROMs. Provo: Brigham Young University Press, 2002.

Shipps, Jan. *Mormonism: The Story of a New Religious Tradition.* Chicago: University of Illinois Press, 1987.

Sibl[e]y, Ebenezer. *New and Complete Illustration of the Occult Sciences* (London, c.1795), http://www.esotericarchives.com/solomon/sibly4.htm (accessed April 12, 2009).

Sjodahl, Janne M. *Introduction to the Study of the Book of Mormon.* 1927. Reprint, Kessinger, 2003. http://books.google.com/books?id=GxBLdgrLCkEC (accessed November 10, 2009).

Skeen, C. Edward. "'The Year without a Summer': A Historical View." *Journal of the Early Republic* 1, no. 1 (Spring 1981): 51-67.

Smith, Elbert A. *Square Blocks, and Other Sermons and Articles.* Independence, Missouri: Herald Publishing House, 1921, http://www.archive.org/details/squareblocksotheoosmit (accessed 5 July 2010).

Smith, Ethan. *A Key to the Figurative Language Found in the Sacred Scriptures.* New Hampshire: C. Norris & Co., 1814. http://olivercowdery.com/texts/ethn1814.htm (accessed October 30, 2008).

Smith, George D. *An Intimate Chronicle: The Journals of William Clayton.* Salt Lake City: Signature Books, 1995.

Smith, Joseph Fielding. *Answers to Gospel Questions.* 5 vols. Salt Lake City: Deseret Books, 1957-66.

Smith, Ryan K. "The Cross: Church Symbol and Contest in Nineteenth-Century America," *Church History: Studies in Christianity and Culture* 70, no. 4 (2001): 705-734.

———. *Gothic Arches, Latin Crosses: Anti-Catholicism and American Church Designs in the Nineteenth Century.* Chapel Hill: University of North Carolina Press, 2006.

Smooth, Ephraim. "To Richard Carlile Dorchester Goal," *The Republican* 12. London, 1825. http://books.google.com/books?id=Cx8rAAAAYAAJ&pg= (accessed March 25, 2009).

Snyder, Graydon F. *Ante Pacem.* Macon, GA: Mercer University Press, 1991.

Stenhouse, T. B. H. *An Englishwoman in Utah: The Story of A Life's Experience in Mormonism*. London, 1880. http://books.google.com/books?id=N34FAAAAQAAJ& (accessed 9 July 2010).

Stothers, Richard B. "The Great Tambora Eruption in 1815 and its Aftermath." *Science—American Association for the Advancement of Science* 223, no. 4654 (June 15, 1984): 1191-98.

Stuy, Brian H., ed. *Collected Discourses: Delivered by President Wilford Woodruff, His Two Counselors, The Twelve Apostles, and Others*. 5 vols. B.H.S. Publishing, 1991; 1999.

Taylor, John Taylor. *An Examination into and an Elucidation of the Great Principle of the Mediation and the Atonement of Our Lord and Savior Jesus Christ*. Salt Lake City: Deseret News Co., 1882. http://books.google.com/books?id=eERCAAAAIAAJ (accessed November 10, 2008).

Thatcher, Moses. "Moses Thatcher Diary" vol. 3,1881. *Mormon Missionary Diaries*. http://contentdm.lib.byu.edu/cdm4/document.php?CISOROOT=/MMD&CISOPTR=30028&REC=5&CISOBOX=cross&CISOSHOW=29915 (accessed November 16, 2008).

Town, Salem. *A System of Speculative Masonry*. New York, 1818.

Tresidder, Jack. *Dictionary of Symbols*. San Francisco: Chronicle Books, 1997.

Tullidge, Edward W. *Women of Mormondom*. New York: Tullidge & Crandall, 1877. http://www.archive.org/details/womenofmormondoo0tullrich (accessed April 7, 2009).

Umbach, Greg. "Learning to Shop in Zion: The Consumer Revolution in Great Basin Mormon Culture, 1847-1910." *Journal of Social History* 38, no. 1 (Fall 2004): 29-61.

University of Utah Digital Collections. http://webpac.lib.utah.edu/digital/browseLetter.php

Utah Digital Newspapers. http://digitalnewspapers.org/

Utah State History Online Photos. http://history.utah.gov/research_and_collections/photos/index.html

Utah State University Digital Initiatives. http://digital.lib.usu.edu/

Viladesau, Richard. *The Beauty of the Cross: The Passion of Christ in Theology and in the Arts—From the Catacombs to the Eve of the Renaissance*. Oxford: Oxford University Press, 2005.

Vogel, Dan, ed. *Early Mormon Documents*. 5 vols. Salt Lake City: Signature Books, 1996-2003.

———. *Indian Origins and the Book of Mormon*. Salt Lake City: Signature Books, 1986. http://www.signaturebookslibrary.org/indian/indian4.htm (accessed October 10, 2008).

———. *Religious Seekers and the Advent of Mormonism*. Salt Lake City: Signature Books, 1988. http://www.signaturebookslibrary.org/seekers/Introduction.htm (accessed February 4, 2009).

Wagoner, Richard Van. *Sidney Rigdon: A Portrait of Religious Excess*. Salt Lake City: Signature Books, 1994.

Walker, James. "Enemies of the Cross," Internet Christian Library. http://www.iclnet.org/pub/resources/text/apl/jw/jw-071.txt (accessed December 29, 2008).

Walker, Ronald W. "Edward Tullidge: Historian of the Mormon Commonwealth," *Journal of Mormon History* 3 (1976): 55-72.

———. "A Gauge of the Times: Ensign Peak in the Twentieth Century," *Utah Historical Quarterly* 62, no. 1 (1994): 4-25.

———. "The Persisting Idea of American Treasure Hunting," *Brigham Young University Studies* 24, no. 3 (Fall 1984): 429-59.

Walker, S. A. *The Remembrancer*, ed. Reverend William Lush. London, 1873. http://books.google.com/books?id=MjsEAAAAQAAJ (accessed March 30, 2009).

Waterman, Bryan, ed. *The Prophet Puzzle: Interpretive Essays on Joseph Smith*. Salt Lake City: Signature Books, 1999.

Weber State University Digital Collections. http://librarydigitalcollections.weber.edu/

Welch, John W., ed. *Opening the Heavens: Accounts of Divine Manifestations 1820-1844*. Salt Lake City: Brigham Young University Press, 2005.

Wilkinson, Ernest L., ed. *Brigham Young University: The First One Hundred Years*. 4 vols. Provo: Brigham Young University Press, 1975-1976.

Index

Ackroyd, Walter, 96-98.
Angell, Truman, 72, 76.
Anti-Catholicism, 2, 27-36, 90, 91, 119-120; Protestant anti-Catholicism, 2, 27-29, 33, 91, 93, 98, 103, 146; LDS Anti-Catholicism, 29-36, 90-93, 98, 103, 103, 104, 108, 109, 113-116, 120-121, 144-146; RLDS Anti-Catholicism, 131, 139-140, 144.
Ballo, Sarah Ann, 76.
Barton, Susan Malinda, 84.
Barton, Walter Killsha, 82, 84.
Baskin, Rabbi Samuel, 91-92.
Beebe, Calvin, 68.
Bennett, John C., 41 fn 14, 125.
Book of Mormon, 8 fn 1, 9 fn 2, 20, 21, 29, 30, 32, 39 fn 10, 62, 64-66, 69, 70, 88, 93, 105, 110, 123, 124, 126, 128, 129, 130 fn 16, 145.
Brigham Young University, 94.
Burton, Dora, 132.
Burton, Joseph F., 132.
Cannon, George J., 99 fn 27.
Carter, Simeon, 68.
Catholicism, 26, 27-36, 39, 87, 88, 90-91, 93, 94, 96, 106, 119-120, 126, 146; Bishop Duane Hunt, 113-11; Bishop Joseph S. Glass, 90, 108-109; Patrick Walsh, 107. See also Anti-Catholicism.
Cheville, Roy A., 140-142, 144.
Christianity, Early, 1, 9 fn 4, 21, 51 fn 40, 69, 120, 149-157.
Church of Jesus Christ of Latter-day Saints, see LDS Church.
Church of Jesus Christ of Latter Day Saints (Strangite), see Strangites.
Church/State, separation of in the United States 12, 11; Ensign peak cross monument proposal conflicts with the separation of 91, 92; Joseph Smith and "theodemocracy," 22.
Clark, J Reuben, 114, 117-118.
Clawson, Georgia, 79, 80.
Clawson, Hiram B., 79.
Coltrin, Zebedee, 44, 53 fn 43.
Community of Christ, see RLDS.
Constantine, Emperor, 120, 125, 149, 153.
Corrill, John, 68.
Cowdery, Oliver, 21, 30, 31, 44, 59-60.
Cross, removed by LDS, 5 fn 9 and fn 10; Removed by Protestant, 28-29, 35-36.
Cross, jewelry, among LDS, 79-85; among RLDS, 132; David O. McKay's opposition to, 115-116.
Cross, symbol, LDS acceptance of, 67-85, 87, 95-96, 98-99, 100, 110-112; LDS Rejection of, 2-3, 90-91, 93-94, 97-98, 102-103, 105, 108-109, 117-122, 149, 157; RLDS acceptance of, 132-139, 141-144, 147; RLDS rejection of, 139-140, 142, 144; Strangite acceptance of, 123-126, 128; Strangite rejection of, 126; Protestant rejection of 2, 27-28, 33, 35-36, 68, 91, 93, 98, 146.
Cross, Material Symbolism vs. Literary Symbolism, 4, 5, 149-57.
Cutler, Alpheus, 24, 127, 128.
Doctrine and Covenants, 59-60, 85.
Ensign Peak, 86-101, 103, 106, 109 fn 18, 110, 113, 117, 146.
First Great Awakening, 12, 13.
Floral Arrangements, 75-78.
Freemasonry, 9 fn 4, 14, 15, 22-23, 36, 37, 46-58, 60, 69-72, 103-105, 125-126, 128, 130-131, 145.
Glass, Bishop Joseph S. (Catholic), 90, 108-109.

169

Graceland University (Lamoni, Iowa), 140, 142.
Graves and Tomb Stones, 75, 110-111, 121-122.
Hawkins, Ann Sewell, 76.
Hill of Promise (Strangite), 125.
Hinckley, Gordon B., 2, 101 fn 29, 117, 119, 142.
Hunt, Bishop Duane (Catholic), 113-115.
Islam, 89, 122 fn 10.
Ivins, Anthony W., 82, 84.
Ivins, August, 81, 84.
Ivins, Carolyn Augusta, 82, 84.
Jewish community, 89, 91-92.
Johnson, Benjamin Franklin, 22 fn 54, 33, 82, 84.
Kimball, Heber C., 22 fn 54, 48.
Kimball, Spencer W., 111-112.
Knight, Newel, 68.
LDS Church, Are Mormons Christian?, 1, 88, 98, 106, 148; assimilation of, 25-26, 105-107, 148; patriotism, 8, 26, 87, 94, 105; acceptance of cross symbol, 67-85, 87, 95-96, 98-99, 100, 110-112; rejection of cross symbol, 2-3, 90-91, 93-94, 97-98, 102-103, 105, 108-109, 117-122, 149, 157; use of cross jewelry, 79-85. See also Temples, LDS.
Love, Ada Afton, 81, 84.
Loveles, John, 82, 84.
Lowry, Dora, 81, 84.
Lund, Emil S., 88-90, 91, 92, 101.
Mackey, Albert G., 49 fn 39, 51, 57.
Magic, 14, 17, 36, 38-47, 55, 58-60, 76.
Marsh, Thomas B., 68.
McConkie, Bruce R., 117, 119-120.
McKay, David O., 3, 96 fn 22, 112-116, 120-121, 146.
Miller, George, 48, 52 fn 42.
Morgan, William, 47 fn 27, 51 fn 40.
Morley, Isaac, 68.
Mormonism, American context of, 10-13, 62, 63-64.
Morris, Robert, 49.
Mount Rubidoux, California, 138.
Nibley, Charles W., 87-96, 98-101, 108-109.
Order of Illuminati (Strangite "Halcyon Order"), 125-126.
Order of the Eastern Star, 49.
Osmond, George, 96.
Partridge, Edward, 68.
Penn, William, 136.
Penrose, Charles W., 35, 95.
Peterson, Mark E., 115, 118.
Phelps, William W., 64, 68, 136 fn 26.
Polygamy, 23-25, 31, 33, 39, 76, 79, 88, 105, 106 fn 11, 126 fn 10, 127, 130.
Pratt, Orson, 32.
Pratt, Parley P., 22 fn 54, 32, 33, 68, 91.
Pre-Columbian Natives, 36, 59 fn 56, 61-66, 69, 70, 103, 105, 110, 128-130, 145.
Price, Lydia Rebecca Baker, 76.
Protestants, 3, 12-13, 14, 17, 26, 29-34, 37, 106, 109 fn 18, 113, 126, 131, 139, 144, 145; Protestant anti-Catholicism, 2, 27-29, 33, 91, 93, 98, 103, 146; Protestant cross taboo, 2, 27-28, 33, 35-36, 68, 91, 93, 98, 146.
Quilts, 75-76; Emma Smith's quilt, 127.
Rice, Rabbi William, 91-92.
Rigdon, Sidney, 24, 47, 48, 68.
RLDS/Community of Christ 6, 7; RLDS Anti-Catholicism, 131, 139-140, 144; RLDS Rejection of the Cross, 139-140, 142, 144; Acceptance of the Cross, 132-139, 141-144, 147; Architecture, 132-137, 143-144.
Roberts, Brigham H., 65, 87, 99, 110-111.
Rod of Aaron, 53-60.
Salt Lake City Commission, 88, 92.
Salt Lake City Council, 87, 89, 92, 95, 113.
Scheid, Karl A., 88, 89, 92.
Second Great Awakening, 9-18.
Sibley, Ebenezer, 46.
Smith, Asael, 13, 14 fn 24.

Smith, Elbert E., 138, 139.
Smith, Emma, 126-127, 125 fn 12, 131.
Smith, George Albert, 22, 72, 86 fn 3, 99 fn 27.
Smith, Hyrum G., 99 fn 27.
Smith, Hyrum M., 109 fn 18.
Smith, Hyrum, 15, 47, 68, 104, 127.
Smith, Israel A., 130.
Smith, Joseph F., Sr., 92 fn 14, 94, 95, 101, 109 fn 18.
Smith, Joseph Fielding, 96 fn 22, 117, 118.
Smith, Joseph III, 6, 24, 126-128, 130-131.
Smith, Joseph, 2 fn 4, 6, 8-10, 13, 15, 16, 18-24, 27, 30, 31, 38, 39, 44-50, 52-58, 60-62, 64, 67, 68, 76, 86 fn 3, 104, 123-126, 128, 137, 138.
Smith, Joseph, Sr., 14, 15, 41, 45 fn 18, 47 fn 30.
Smith, Lucy, 14, 15, 18 fn 37, 38-39, 46-47, 48 fn 30, 61.
Smith, Sophia, 16, 48 fn 30.
Smith, William, 15, 24, 64, 127, 128.
Smith, William, 24, 128.
Snow, Eliza R, 31, 76.
Standing, Joseph, 76.
Stewart, James Zebulon, 93, 109.
Stewart, Mary Ann, 81, 84.
Strangites, 6, 7, 24, 64; Strangites and the Cross, 123-128.
Taylor, John W., 82, 84,
Taylor, John, 31-32, 36 fn 30, 61 fn 2, 65, 77-78, 84.
Taylor, Obed, 75.
Temples, LDS, 22, 60, 67-68, 71, 96; LDS Temple Ceremony (endowment/initiatories), 3 fn 6, 22-23, 31 fn 16, 48, 49-53, 57 fn 52, 72, 86 fn 3, 104; Kirtland Temple, 137; Nauvoo Temple, 60, 127; Salt Lake Temple, 86; Manti Temple, 71; Laie Hawaii Temple, 75; Cardston, Alberta Temple, 75, 98 fn 23; RLDS/Community of Christ Temple, 143-144; Pre-Columbian temples 63, 66.
Thatcher, Moses, 33 fn24, 93, 97 fn 22, 102-103.
Treasure Seeking, 38-46, 47 fn 27, 58, 59 fn 56, 76.
Universalism, 14.
Voree Plates (Strangite), 124-125.
Walsh, Reverend Patrick (Catholic), 107.
Wells, Daniel H., 76.
Wells, Heber M., 88, 89, 90, 91, 95.
Whitmer, David, 24, 68.
Whitmer, David, 24, 68.
Whitmer, John, 68.
Whitney, Newell K., 48.
Whitney, Orson F., 94-96, 98.
Wight, Lyman, 24, 68, 127, 128.
Wirthlin, Joseph L., 115-116.
Woodruff, Wilford, 63-64, 99.
Young, Amelia Folsom, 34 fn 26, 79-80.
Young, Brigham, 5 fn 10, 6, 24, 31, 32, 34, 35 fn 27, 48, 52 fn 42, 69, 86 fn 3, 98, 99, 123, 125, 126 fn 10, 127; Brigham Young's family, 34 fn 26, 76, 79-80, 84, 101 fn 29.
Young, Charlottee Talula, 34 fn 26, 79, 80.
Young, Clara Decker, 79.
Young, Harriet Amelia Folsom, 34 fn 26, 79, 80.
Young, Joseph, 76.
Young, Nabbie Howe, 34 fn 26, 79, 80.

About the Author

MICHAEL G. REED has a BA in Humanities/Religious Studies, a MA in Liberal Arts from California State University of Sacramento, and is currently pursuing a PhD in Christian History at the Graduate Theological Union, Berkeley. His work on Mormons and the cross began as a Master's Thesis, which received media attention from both the *Salt Lake Tribune* and *Deseret News'* "Mormon Times." Having presented his research at several Mormon studies conferences and symposia across the country, Michael Reed is pleased to finally have his Master's Thesis now revised and expanded for the publication of this book. His other research interests include North American Christianity of the Jacksonian era, folk-magic, and Freemasonry.

www.ingramcontent.com/pod-product-compliance
Lightning Source LLC
Chambersburg PA
CBHW070756100426
42742CB00012B/2150